CYPRIAN THE BISHOP

This is the first up-to-date, accessible study dedicated to the rule of Cyprian as the Bishop of Carthage in the 250s AD.

Using the tools of cultural anthropology, *Cyprian the Bishop* examines the interplay between the shift in the social structures of Christian churches in third-century Roman Africa, the development of their ritual practices, and the efficacy assigned to them in changing a person's standing – not only within a community – but before God.

During the Decian persecution, Bishop Cyprian attempted to steer the middle ground between compromise and traditionalism; he redefined the performance of the sacraments – particularly penance and reconciliation – and showed that their efficacy depended upon the unity of the church.

Cyprian succeeded where his rivals failed by defining the boundary between the empire and the church. By concentrating on social structures, J. Patout Burns Jr. reveals the logic of Cyprian's plan, the basis for its success in his time, and the reason why it failed in later centuries when the church was integrated into imperial society. This book will be of great interest to classicists, ancient historians and sociologists as well as theologians.

J. Patout Burns Jr. is Edward A. Malloy Professor of Catholic Studies at Vanderbilt Divinity School. He is the author of *The Development of Augustine's Doctrine of Operative Grace*, and the editor of *Theological Anthropology*.

CYPRIAN
THE BISHOP

J. Patout Burns Jr.

London and New York

First published 2002
by Routledge
11 New Fetter Lane, London EC4P 4EE

Simultaneously published in the USA and Canada
by Routledge
29 West 35th Street, New York, NY 10001

Routledge is an imprint of the Taylor & Francis Group

© 2002 J. Patout Burns Jr.

Typeset in Garamond by Taylor & Francis Books Ltd
Printed and bound in Great Britain by Biddles Ltd, Guildford and
King's Lynn

British Library Cataloguing in Publication Data
A catalogue record for this book is available from the British Library

Library of Congress Cataloging in Publication Data
Burns, J. Patout.
Cyprian the Bishop / J. Patout Burns, Jr.
(Routledge early church monographs)
Includes bibliographical references and index.
1. Cyprian, Saint, Bishop of Carthage. 2. Church–Unity–History of
doctrines–Early church, ca. 30-600. I. Title. II. Series
BRI720 c8 B87 2002
270.1'092–dc21
[B]
2001049229

ISBN 0–415–23849–8 (hbk)

ISBN 0–415–23850–1 (pbk)

CONTENTS

PREFACE

This study began in a faculty seminar in the Department of Religion at the University of Florida in which Dennis Owen and Sheldon Isenberg explained the value of Mary Douglas' scheme for correlating the social structure of a community and its assumptions about its position in the cosmos and the efficacy of its practices. The foundational essay, "Cultural Bias,"[1] and the book, *Natural Symbols*,[2] suddenly appeared to offer tools for understanding the theological positions which Cyprian, the bishop of Carthage in the middle of the third century, had developed to help his community cope with the defections they experienced during the persecution of Decius and the divisions within the church which followed it. Cyprian presented a scripturally based and tightly argued theory of sacramental efficacy which was rejected by the Roman church, championed by the African Donatists, and then so reinterpreted by Augustine that it had little further influence. How could such a coherent and cogent system have been simply abandoned in favor of one whose sole supports were custom and political influence? Cyprian's system was not so much refuted as shoved aside and ignored. The answer to understanding its success and then its failure might lie, then, in the social rather than the intellectual context. It might have failed because the social structures supporting it changed with the toleration and support of Christianity by the Roman Empire. Fortunately, the collection of Cyprian's letters provide significant information about his church community and its members, as well as his dealings with both his fellow bishops and opponents. These documents provide clues for understanding what his people and his colleagues, as well as their opponents, were doing and thinking. Douglas' schema for comparing communities was first applied to the opposing positions taken by the African and the Roman bishops in the baptismal controversy. When the results proved satisfactory, the present broader study of the understanding of the unity of the church and the efficacy of its rituals of purification was undertaken.

The objective of this study is not to provide a biography of Cyprian or historical study of his church. Even within the limits of the English language, the supply of such studies is not seriously lacking. Archbishop Benson's 1897 book is dated but still useful in many ways.[3] Michael Sage's study presents the advances during the three-quarters of a century separating his own work from that of Benson.[4] The introductions to each of the four volumes of G.W. Clarke's translation of Cyprian's letters supply an excellent summary of the bishop's life and ministry; the commentary on the individual letters provides an exhaustive review of the current state of knowledge and a judicious advance on many points.[5] The present study will attempt to revise Graeme Clarke's historical work on the letters and Maurice Bévenot's editorial advances on the versions of Cyprian's *On the Unity of the Catholic Church*[6] in very limited ways, such as arguing for a different dating of one of the letters in the baptismal controversy and proposing a double rather than a single rewriting of *On Unity* by Cyprian himself. Michael Fahey's study of Cyprian's use of scripture, amended by Clarke, proved particularly helpful in developing the patterns of citation which are the basis for the present proposals for this new chronology.[7] Otherwise, this study is unashamedly dependent upon and derivative from the excellent historical work done on Cyprian during the last century.

The goal of this study is to elucidate the correlation between Cyprian's theology and his practice as a bishop. The foundational contributions of the North African theologians – Tertullian, Cyprian and Augustine – to the development of Latin Christian thought were nearly all immediately related to problems of Christian life in the church. Such theology can best be interpreted, appreciated and even appropriated by understanding it within the context of its original development. For the problems with which Cyprian dealt – the unity and rituals of the church – the social context was more important than the intellectual: the structures by which his church community was organized and its ways of distinguishing itself from the imperial society. Thus chapters 3 and 4, for example, will argue that the positions which Cyprian took on the reconciliation of the lapsed can best be understood as means of reorganizing the community in the face of the crisis of the Decian persecution which nearly destroyed it. Chapters 5 and 8 will show that the process of selecting, installing and removing bishops was foundational to the theory of the unity of the local and universall church. Chapter 6 explores what Cyprian took to be the practical consequences of accepting schismatic baptism and chapter 7 investigates the limits of enforceable standards of purity for the church and its clergy in particular.

By understanding a theology within its developmental cultural context, the adjustments necessary to adapt and appropriate it in a different social world might be specified. Though each had to appeal to Cyprian, neither the Donatists nor the Catholics in Africa could adopt his theory of the purity or holiness of the church exactly as he presented it to his people and colleagues. The church's relationship to imperial society had been changed radically by the Constantinian toleration and the Theodosian establishment of Christianity. In parallel, the conception of the purity of the church and the rituals which protected its boundary with the empire had to be reworked. The Donatists made assertions about the transmission of contagion within the unity of the church and episcopate which Cyprian neither made nor acted upon. Augustine, in contrast, appealed to a significance of intention within the functioning of the earthly church which Cyprian explicitly rejected in his focus on performance. By specifying the connection between Cyprian's thought and his social context, the study signals modifications which could be anticipated when the social circumstances changed.

The study will begin with a review of the events and an analysis of the social structure of the Christian church in Carthage on the eve of the Decian persecution. Subsequent chapters will focus on the rituals of penance and baptism, the purity of the church, and the unity of the local and universal church. The influence of Mary Douglas is ubiquitous but not explicitly noted.

An earlier version of the study of the rebaptism controversy here covered in chapters 1 and 5 was published in the first volume of *Journal of Early Christian Studies*.[8] A study derived from chapter 3 is published in the proceedings of the 1999 International Conference on Patristic Studies.[9]

The research which is here reported was supported by Washington University in St Louis and Vanderbilt Divinity School. Grants from the National Endowment for the Humanities and the American Academy of Religion enabled the collaboration with other scholars in the study of North African Christianity – Graeme Clarke, Robin Jensen, Susan Stevens, Maureen Tilley, and William Tabbernee – which has shaped the appreciation of devotional practice in the development of theology. Finally, the hospitality of the Institute for Ecumenical and Cultural Research at St John's

University, Collegeville and the Jesuit Institute at Boston College supported the beginning and completion of the project. A final debt of gratitude is here acknowledged to the students who have shared the challenge and joy of reading these texts with me, confirming and developing the interpretations here offered.

ABBREVIATIONS

acta proc.	*acta proconsularia*, CSEL 3.3:cx–xiv.
bapt.	Tertullian, *de baptismo*, CCL 1:277–95.
CCL	*Corpus Christianorum, series latina*, Turnhout,1953–.
CSEL	*Corpus Scriptorum Ecclesiasticorum Latinorum*, Vienna, 1866–.
ep.	Cyprian, *epistulae*, CCL 3B–D.
fuga	Tertullian, *de fuga in persecutione*, CCL 2:1,135–55.
habitu	Cyprian, *de habitu uirginum*, CSEL 3.1:187–205.
h.e.	Eusebius of Caesarea, *Ecclesiastical History, Sources chrétiennes*, vols 31,41,56,73, Paris, Éditions du Cerf, 1952–60.
idol.	Tertullian, *de idolatria*, CCL 2:1,101–24.
lap.	Cyprian, *de lapsis*,.CCL 3:221–42
Letters	G.W. Clarke, *The Letters of St. Cyprian of Carthage*, translated and annotated, 4 vols, *Ancient Christian Writers*, vols 43–4,46–7, New York, Paulist Press, 1984–9.
mort.	Cyprian, *de mortalitate*, CCL 3A:17–32.
paen.	Tertullian, *de paenitentia* CCL 1:321–40.
PL	*Patrologia Latina*, ed. J.P. Migne, Paris, 1844–64.
Prax.	Tertullian, *adversus Praxean*, CCL 2:1,159–205.
pud.	Tertullian, *de pudicitia*, CCL 2:1,281–330.
rebap.	*de rebaptismate*, CSEL 3.3:69–92.
sent. episc.	*Sententiae episcoporum numero LXXXVII de haereticis baptizandis*, CSEL 3.1:435–61.
uita Cyp.	*uita Caecilii Cypriani*, CSEL 3.3:xc–cx.
unit.	Cyprian, *de ecclesiae catholicae unitate*, CCL 3:249–68.

1

HISTORY OF CYPRIAN'S CONTROVERSIES

In 248 CE, the Christian community in Carthage elected Thascius Caecilianus Cyprianus its bishop. This wealthy aristocrat, trained as a rhetorician, had become a Christian a scant two years earlier. Since he was still a neophyte, the laity seems to have overridden the objections of a majority of their presbyters in choosing him as bishop.[1] In ascending to office as bishop of Carthage, this Christian "new man" became the leader not only of the bishops of Proconsular Africa but of all Latin Africa, as far west as the Atlantic. At his summons, eighty-five bishops would converge on Carthage; at his prompting, they would speak with a single voice. His episcopate would prove foundational for the development of North African Christianity.

The Decian persecution

In December 249, the Emperor Decius, three months after defeating the Emperor Philip at Verona, and wishing to consolidate his position as well as to secure the good fortune of his reign, decreed that every citizen should join him in offering homage to the immortal gods, whose graciousness secured the peace and prosperity of the empire.[2] Each person was apparently required to appear before a locally established commission, to testify to having been always a worshiper of the gods protecting Rome and to demonstrate that piety in its presence by pouring a libation, offering incense and eating the sacrificial meats.[3] While Decius required participation in the Roman ceremonies, he did not specify the renunciation of other religious practices or loyalties.[4] Both continuing Christian practice and the clergy's access to the imprisoned recusants were apparently tolerated.[5] One of the imperial objectives seems to have been the elimination of the divisions of religious exclusivism.[6]

Christian bishops were targeted for early action when enforcement began in January 250: Dionysius of Alexandria was hunted down,[7] Fabian of Rome died in prison[8] and Cyprian of Carthage withdrew into exile.[9] When imperial commissions were established in various cities during the late winter and spring, many Christians voluntarily complied with the edict by actually offering sacrifice,[10] by using a legal subterfuge, or by bribing an official to obtain the certificate which attested to their having performed the rituals.[11] By the time the deadline for compliance with the edict arrived, a major portion of the laity and some of the clergy had obeyed.[12] Those who persistently refused the commissioners' demand were imprisoned and brought to trial; some were released and others sent into exile.[13] In April 250, the authorities introduced torture into the interrogations of Christian confessors and deprived them of food, water, fresh air and light in an attempt to force them to comply.[14] Although none were executed, some died under this regimen, the first martyrs of the persecution.[15] Others were worn down by the torture and reluctantly offered the required sacrifice.[16]

The repentance of the fallen

While the imperial prosecution continued, the clergy of the city of Rome urged the fallen, both sacrificers and certified, to begin purifying themselves through works of repentance.[17] They announced that the certified, who had not actually sacrificed, would be considered lapsed because they had failed to confess Christ.[18] Reconciliation and readmission to communion were delayed, however, until the end of the persecution, except for the traditional giving of peace to dying penitents.[19] The confessors in prison fully supported the clergy's insistence on sustained repentance.[20]

At Carthage, imprisoned confessors and the resident presbyters responded differently to the pleading of Christians who had failed. In expectation of entering into glory through martyrdom, the confessors granted letters of peace to the lapsed, in which they promised to intercede with God and win forgiveness for their sin of apostasy. Once a confessor died as a martyr and presumably entered heaven, the lapsed Christian presented the letter of peace to the clergy requesting or demanding readmission to the communion of the church on the strength of the martyr's intercession before God.[21] A group of presbyters decided not to await the end of the persecution but immediately to admit to communion the fallen who had received letters from the martyrs.[22] As a result, traffic in martyrs' letters soon developed: letters were distributed wholesale, with only the most general designation of the persons who were being recommended.[23] Some of the surviving confessors even claimed that they had been authorized by their fellow prisoners to issue letters of peace in their names after their martyrdom to any of the lapsed who asked for their help.[24]

The bishop of Carthage, however, refused to credit these letters of peace. He ordered the lapsed to undertake penance[25] and insisted that none of the fallen could be admitted to communion before God had granted peace to the church as a whole.[26] Cyprian recognized the authority of the martyrs by allowing the presbyters to give peace to any dying penitents who held their letter of intercession.[27] Shortly thereafter he extended this concession to all dying penitents, thus bringing his church's practice into line with that of the church in Rome where the confessors refused to issue such letters of peace.[28] Cyprian reminded the impatient, and apparently impenitent, lapsed that while the persecution continued they could immediately re-enter the communion of the church by recanting their apostasy before the imperial commissioners.[29] Finally, he pledged that general consultations would be held after the persecution had ended to establish a policy for restoring the repentant to communion.[30] Cyprian also began to build support for his position among the bishops of Africa.[31]

In Carthage, the confessors agreed to Cyprian's directive delaying the reception of the fallen into communion until the end of the persecution. Furthermore, they allowed that the bishop should review the conduct of each of the fallen.[32] In a proclamation intended for all the bishops, however, they extended the amnesty to everyone who had failed during the persecution.[33] Cyprian then instructed his clergy to inform the people that no action would be taken before the end of the persecution: the issue concerned all Christians and would require general consultation. Neither the confessors and martyrs, nor even the bishop, he explained, should presume to decide such a momentous and far-reaching question alone. He offered evidence, moreover, of growing support for his more stringent position among the bishops of Africa.[34]

Cyprian's firm stand provoked various responses from the lapsed in Carthage. Some, though they held letters from the martyrs, pledged their obedience, agreed to wait for general peace, and asked the support of the bishop's prayers.[35] The opposition, however, remained intransigent, insisting that the bishop had no right to delay the delivery of that reconciliation and communion which the martyrs had already granted: what had already been loosened in heaven could not be held bound on earth.[36] Cyprian sharply rebuked the rebels, recognizing a threat to the authority of the bishop and the unity of the church.[37]

At this juncture, the Roman clergy and confessors, under the leadership of Novatian, intervened forcefully to support Cyprian and his colleagues. They wrote to the clergy and confessors in Carthage and then to Cyprian himself for the first time since his voluntary exile. They asserted that the martyrs had no authority to grant peace to any of the fallen and implied that the presbyters of Carthage had instigated the rebellion.[38] Their own practice, the Roman confessors reported, was to deny the requests of the fallen for letters of peace.[39] Cyprian immediately distributed copies of these letters in Carthage and throughout Africa, thereby strengthening his position.[40] Despite the Roman support for their bishop's position, the rebels in Carthage held their ground.[41]

As his exile stretched to a full year, Cyprian worked to gain control of the church, assisted by other bishops who took shelter in Carthage and visited him in his place of retreat.[42] From among the confessors, he made three new clerical appointments.[43] He also commissioned two refugee bishops and two of his own presbyters, most and perhaps all of them confessors, to oversee the affairs of the church of Carthage, to review the merits of those who were receiving financial support from the community, and to identify loyal candidates for clerical appointment.[44] The work of this commission provoked an open rebellion in Carthage, led by a deacon and backed by five presbyters and a great number of the people.[45] These clergy threatened to deny communion to anyone who cooperated with Cyprian's agents, thereby signaling a complete break with the bishop. Cyprian's commissioners then moved to exclude the rebels from communion.[46]

As Easter 251 approached and the refugee bishops returned to their sees to celebrate the feast, Cyprian's position appeared particularly bleak. He could count on the support of only three of the eight presbyters remaining in Carthage and of a minority of the faithful laity; he dared not enter the city himself for fear of provoking an anti-Christian riot among the general population.[47] His Easter letter to the congregation warned that the continued admission of the lapsed and the division it provoked was the last and most dangerous trial of the persecution, which threatened to destroy the church utterly.[48] In the last weeks of his exile, he then completed the discourse, *On the Lapsed*, which was to be delivered upon his anticipated return.

Shortly thereafter, the imperial action had ceased and popular resentment of the Christians had subsided so that Cyprian could return to Carthage and resume direct governance of the community.[49] His first order of business was a division of the community into standing and fallen,[50] faithful and apostate. Cyprian praised all the standing as confessors of the faith: those who had withstood imperial interrogation, torture and exile; those who had voluntarily abandoned their property and fled; even those who had confessed only by allowing the edict's deadline to pass without complying.[51] To these standing, he contrasted all the fallen, whether they had acquired certificates without sacrificing or had actually sacrificed, either under coercion or spontaneously. He implored them to seek the forgiveness of God and the peace of the church through humble repentance.[52] The leaders of the schism he once again branded agents of Satan: in offering immediate peace to the fallen, they were actually preventing repentance and thereby blocking the only remaining access to salvation.[53] Finally, he warned all the rebels that unlike idolatry, the sin of splitting the unity of the church was unforgivable.[54] This conflict in Africa also set the context for the first version of Cyprian's treatise *On the Unity of the Catholic Church*.[55]

Later in the spring of 251, the bishops of Africa finally met in Carthage to work out a common policy for the reconciliation of the lapsed.[56] These leaders weighed the pastoral necessity of preventing wholesale defection by those who had failed in persecution and reviewed God's warnings of severity and promises of leniency in the scriptures.[57] In the end, they moderated the stance which Cyprian, the Roman presbyters, and others of their own number had taken during the persecution by reinstating the customary distinction between the sacrificers and the certified.[58] Those who sinned only by acquiring certificates and had been practicing penance might be admitted to communion immediately, upon the consideration of individual cases.[59] The sacrificers, in contrast, were to continue the regimen of repentance with the promise that they would be admitted to communion as death approached.[60] Anyone who refused to do penance would not be granted peace even at the time of death.[61] These decisions, to be enforced throughout Africa, were echoed by the council of Italian bishops meeting a few months later in Rome.[62]

Schism in Carthage and Rome

The leniency which the African bishops extended toward the certified was inadequate to heal the division of the church in Carthage and elsewhere in Africa. Insistence on extended penance for sacrificers and formal excommunication of the rebellious clergy of Carthage provoked the establishment of a rival communion with its own hierarchy in Africa.[63] Within the year, Privatus, who had been deposed as bishop of Lambaesis some years earlier, organized a college of bishops composed of some of his fellows who had failed during the persecution.[64]

At this same meeting in April 251, the African bishops had to address another troubling development: a disputed episcopal election in Rome. After the death of Bishop Fabian during the opening days of the persecution, the Roman church had decided not to elect a successor; it was governed only by its presbyters throughout the persecution. In March 251, a majority of the clergy and the people, with the assent of the attending bishops of neighboring cities, elected Cornelius bishop. On grounds which remain obscure, the presbyter Novatian organized a dissenting group which included many confessors. He then arranged his own ordination as bishop and established a competing communion.[65] Each of the rival bishops sent letters and representatives seeking the support of his colleagues abroad.

The letters and emissaries of the rival Roman bishops arrived in Carthage during the meeting of the African bishops. Each charged the other with various crimes and, it may be presumed, with having an improper policy regarding the reconciliation of the lapsed.[66] The bishops of Africa deputized two of their number to travel to Rome, interview their colleagues who were present at the ordinations, and recommend the proper candidate for recognition.[67] In the meantime, two other African bishops, who had happened to be in Rome when the election occurred, arrived home and reported on the conflict.[68] Only after the official delegates returned, however, did the Africans decide to support Cornelius. Soon thereafter, some confessors who had supported Novatian and joined his faction upon their release from prison negotiated a reconciliation with Cornelius.[69] The complex process of deciding which of the rival candidates was the true bishop resulted in a lingering uneasiness between Cyprian and Cornelius.[70]

At a synod in Rome during the summer 251, Cornelius and his episcopal colleagues adopted a policy for reconciling the lapsed

6

which paralleled that of the Africans.[71] In practice, however, Cornelius made two exceptions. A bishop named Trofimus and the entire congregation which he had led into apostasy were readmitted into communion though at least some had been guilty of sacrifice.[72] In addition, amnesty was granted to the confessors who had joined Novatian; they were admitted to Cornelius' communion without either public acknowledgment of wrongdoing or penance.[73] Although Trofimus was allowed to return to communion only as a layman, the schismatic presbyter Maximus resumed his place among Cornelius' clergy.

Novatian's party, in contrast, not only rejected this lenient policy of reconciling the certified lapsed but refused to grant peace to penitents even at the time of death.[74] This rigorist party then attempted to establish itself in Africa. While awaiting the return of the delegation sent to Rome to investigate the episcopal election, Novatian's emissaries to the African bishops sought support among the Christians of Carthage and other towns.[75] Upon the decision to support Cornelius, this first delegation was expelled but soon replaced by a second which included the bishop Evaristus.[76] Novatian's campaign against Cornelius and the policies for reconciling the lapsed which had been adopted in Carthage and Rome continued with letters circulated among the African bishops.[77] The following year, a former presbyter of the Roman church, Maximus, was ordained by Novatian and sent to challenge Cyprian as bishop in Carthage.[78]

At the same time, the laxist party in Africa continued to consolidate its position. Its leader, Privatus of Lambaesis, was able to form an alliance which grew to include four other deposed bishops. They appealed unsuccessfully for recognition by the synod of African bishops meeting in Carthage in April 251. When their second attempt was rebuffed in May 252, Privatus and his colleagues ordained Fortunatus, one of Cyprian's former presbyters, to be bishop of the laxist communion at Carthage.[79] The deacon Felicissimus, one of the leaders of the rebellion, was immediately dispatched to Rome to seek recognition for the new church. In apparent retaliation for the African bishops' extended review of his own credentials a year earlier, Cornelius allowed the delegation to present its case to the assembled clergy before refusing to accept them into his communion.[80] The experience taught Cyprian that charges of excessive rigor could be dangerous when presented to the Roman church which had rejected the policy of Novatian.[81] In response to this humiliation, he pointedly reminded Cornelius that

Novatian would exploit any apparent concessions which he made to the laxists.[82]

Cyprian and his colleagues were under assault from both sides. The rigorist bishop of Carthage, Maximus, charged that the purity of the church had been ruined. Not only were those who bought certificates admitted to the church but sacrificers who had recovered their bodily health after being reconciled at what had erroneously been judged to be the point of death were then allowed to remain in the communion.[83] The laxist bishop, Fortunatus, attacked the Catholic bishops for jeopardizing the salvation of the sacrificers by excluding them from communion until they were in danger of death.[84]

Reconciliation of the sacrificers

When the African bishops met again in May 253, they faced not only the recently united opposition of the laxists but the threat of renewed persecution by the government of the new emperor, Galerius.[85] They decided that those who had failed by sacrificing and had then persevered in the penitential discipline within the church should be admitted to communion immediately, instead of being delayed until the time of death.[86] In reporting this decision to Cornelius, they anticipated the objections which this policy would provoke from the Novatianists in Rome.[87] Their primary concern, however, seems to have been the charges of excessive harshness mounted by the laxists, which had been aired in Rome a year earlier.[88]

Cornelius was arrested in Rome a month later and escorted to the prison by his congregation in a massive display of solidarity.[89] Apparently convinced of the truth of Cyprian's predictions of a renewal of persecution, Cornelius adopted the African policy of reconciling penitent sacrificers before his own death in exile a few weeks later.[90] His successor Lucius, himself elected in exile, confirmed this practice upon his return to the city.[91]

In May 254, Lucius was in turn succeeded by Stephen who proceeded to clash with Cyprian on every other issue arising from the persecution. Stephen ignored appeals from Bishop Faustinus of Lyons for support in deposing Bishop Marcianus of Arles because he followed Novatian's policy of denying reconciliation to all penitent lapsed even at the time of death. Cyprian insisted that Stephen use the authority of his position to assist those penitents who would be lost eternally once they died outside the church's communion. No record has survived of a response by Stephen to Cyprian's entreaty.[92]

Next, two Spanish bishops, who had been deposed for acquiring certificates of compliance during the persecution and for other entanglement in the Roman religious cults, gained Stephen's support for their efforts to be reinstated in their episcopal office. The replacement bishops appealed to their African colleagues to intervene on behalf of their churches. Cyprian and his colleagues directed the Spanish congregations to stand fast in rejecting the apostates, asserting that Stephen had not only violated a policy accepted by his predecessors but would pollute himself and his own church by entering into communion with these idolatrous bishops.[93] Again, Stephen's response does not appear in the surviving record.

Rebaptism of schismatics

This series of disagreements set the stage for a bitter conflict between the Roman and African churches over the status of baptism performed in heresy or schism. Into the third century, the African church had followed a practice of accepting converts originally baptized in a separate community such as that of Marcion or Montanus with only the imposition of the bishop's hands.[94] In a council held in the 230s, however, the bishops had decided that henceforth they would require such converts to submit to the baptism of the true church.[95] The establishment of Novatianist and laxist churches, affirming Trinitarian faith and dissenting only in penitential discipline, now revived the question of rebaptism in Africa.[96] Should the bishops require that a person who had originally been baptized in one of these splinter communities submit to baptism again as a condition for admission to their universal communion?

In response to inquiries and objections from bishops spread throughout Roman Africa, Cyprian wrote a series of letters defending the practice of requiring rebaptism, some in his own name and some with his colleagues in Proconsular Africa.[97] The question might already have been under consideration for some time in Africa when Stephen was elected bishop of Rome in May 254.[98] A meeting of bishops in Carthage the following spring responded to an inquiry from their colleagues in Numidia on this question.[99] A year later, in spring 256, a council of seventy-one African bishops meeting in Carthage discussed the issue and confirmed their practice of rebaptizing. In reporting their decision to Stephen, however, they allowed that other bishops might act differently within the unity of the church.[100]

Stephen responded decisively to these letters sent by the bishops of Africa.[101] He rejected their decision as an innovation and claimed that his church's practice of receiving persons baptized in heresy as though they were penitent Christians, by the imposition of hands, had been established by the apostles themselves.[102] When a delegation of African bishops was sent to Rome to negotiate a resolution of the conflict, Stephen signaled a break in communion between the two churches – not only refusing to receive the bishops but forbidding them the customary hospitality and insulting Cyprian.[103]

In the face of this Roman challenge, the African bishops stood their ground. Cyprian called an unusual meeting on 1 September 256 and circularized influential colleagues outside Africa with dossiers of the relevant correspondence.[104] Whatever differences may have existed among the Africans in the earlier stages of the conflict had been resolved or set aside by the time of their vote. The bishops echoed Cyprian's arguments in their individual *sententiae*, unanimously affirming the rebaptism of heretics and schismatics.[105]

No record of the subsequent course of the controversy between Cyprian and Stephen has survived. When Stephen died early in August 257, he was succeeded by Sixtus, with whom the Africans enjoyed cordial relations.[106] At about the same time Cyprian was expelled from Carthage in the initial stages of the Valerian persecution. A year later he made formal confession of Christianity before the Roman authorities and was executed on 14 September 258, the first martyr-bishop of the African church. He became and remained its greatest hero.

The practice of rebaptism continued to be disputed even within the African church. After the Diocletian persecution at the beginning of the fourth century, it became one of the issues used by the Donatist church to identify itself with the heritage of Cyprian in opposition to the Catholic church in Africa which followed the Roman practice of accepting schismatics and heretics through the imposition of hands.[107]

Conclusion

The controversies of Cyprian's episcopate raised practical and theoretical questions which were to trouble the African church for another two centuries. His treatises and collected correspondence were carefully preserved and regularly cited by opposing sides, each claiming him as patron and guide. The scriptural texts which he cited and the symbols which he drew from them to establish and evoke the unity and purity of the church would serve as the currency of the conflict between Catholics and Donatists. The solutions which he drew from these premises, however, became the standards of a position which was rejected in the Latin church outside Africa. Thus, despite the scriptural foundation, theological coherence and religious power of his images, Cyprian's position did not prevail. This study proposes that Cyprian's theology succeeded in his own time and place because it was well suited to the social situation of that Christian community. After the Constantinian revolution, it no longer corresponded to the role of the church in the empire and the consequent structures of its communal organization. Attention, therefore, now focuses on the role of social organization in the development of Cyprian's response to the crisis of the Decian persecution.

2

CHRISTIANS OF CARTHAGE
UNDER PERSECUTION

The purpose of this chapter is to analyze the social culture and organization of the Christian community at Carthage under the impact of the Decian persecution. An analysis of the community structures prior to the onset of danger prepares for charting the disruption caused by the Decian edict, which then leads to cataloging the changes effected by the community's response to persecution. Finally, the cultural shifts in behavioral code, ritual practice and cosmology or theology which accompanied these structural changes will be noted. In this way, the scene will be set for the eruption of the first controversy, over the reconciliation of the lapsed.

The church in Carthage before the persecution

The study of this period in the life of the Christians in Carthage is restricted by the source of the evidence, which is found almost exclusively in Cyprian's later attempts to provide a cosmological or religious explanation for the persecution and the community's response to it. The letters which survive advance a certain justification for God's allowing the persecution and demand resistance to it. Yet to achieve the success that they did, Cyprian's exhortations had to reflect the actual conditions in the community. Fabrications, blatant lies or outrageous interpretations of events would have discredited Cyprian and failed to win the support of the clergy and laity who were in danger. Moreover, certain of the practices and dispositions which he reported would seem to have been necessary conditions for subsequent events. Under such a flag of caution, then, the analysis will begin with attention to the boundary separating the church from the city and then turn to the internal structures of the Christian community.

The Carthaginian church was voluntarily separated from the religious culture of the empire and appears to have been a fairly tightly bonded group. Although the Christians did not practice the renunciation of private property in favor of common ownership, they did contribute from their resources to a common fund.[1] The community seems to have owned its place or places of assembly, since mention is never made of its dependence upon any particular individual for these facilities.[2] Monetary gifts were made to the church itself and were channeled through a fund, from which expenditures were made in the name of the community as a whole rather than the original donors.[3] From these funds, the bishop paid the salaries of the clergy;[4] he also sustained the indigent, the enrolled widows, and those whose former occupations had been incompatible with a Christian commitment;[5] he ransomed Christians taken captive in raids[6] and provided support to confessors in prison.[7] Contributions to this common fund were urged upon the penitents as an appropriate means of demonstrating the commitment to Christ and the church which they had denied.[8]

Their religious commitment also served to draw the Christians together. They believed that sharing in the fellowship of the church and its ritual meal were necessary for attaining eternal salvation.[9] The eucharist could not be appropriated by each as a private good but remained common property. It was established by the very action of praying at a single altar, eating of a common loaf and sharing a single cup.[10] Moreover, the people as a whole exercised considerable control over the community's life and eucharistic celebration: they voted in the election of the bishop,[11] consented to his appointment and removal of other clergy,[12] were consulted in the admission of new members and the readmission of sinners who had been excluded from communion.[13] Voluntary interaction was apparently essential to the constitution of the assembly; deviating individuals were subjected to group pressure and in danger of being shunned.[14]

That same religious commitment established a boundary segregating the church from the dominant culture. Baptismal profession required the renunciation of all other religious practices, and in particular the avoidance of contact with the demonic idolatry which permeated Roman imperial society.[15] Christians had to use elaborate devices to avoid actually taking the oaths which were necessary for their business contracts with non-Christian associates.[16] They were to avoid touching or even looking at the statues of the Roman gods which dominated the public places in which they lived.[17]

They were required to avoid certain occupations which violated their moral standards or involved contact with idolatry.[18] Thus a pious Christian's relations with pagan neighbors would have been constrained even in time of relative peace.

Yet the church was not isolated: its members had numerous, routine interactions with the dominant culture. The wealthy, in particular, were engaged in the economic life of the empire: they had estates to preserve and enlarge, dependants to control and protect.[19] They seem to have enjoyed many of the public facilities of the city and to have followed the prevailing norms in clothing and personal grooming.[20] The working poor, as craftsmen or laborers, also lived on the Roman economy.[21] Only the indigent and the clergy, both of whom drew their principal support from the church, would have been more sheltered from polytheistic influence.[22] Although slaves whose masters were Christian may also have been more isolated, their Christian commitment might have been less voluntary than that of the free persons of the community.[23] Thus a reliance on the Roman economy for their livelihood and sustenance made the Christians of Carthage vulnerable to the challenge which the persecution would pose.

The pervading influence of Roman society is also indicated by the operation of its class system within the Christian community. The distinction between *honestiores* and *humiliores* among the free persons was largely based on inherited wealth and status.[24] Though it may have seemed natural to most of the members of the church, it was neither justified by the community's ideology nor integrated into its own differentiation of roles. Both church membership and office were assigned cosmic significance but neither had any formal relationship to the Roman class structure. Thus the class differentiation among Christians in Carthage tended to work against the unity and coherence of the group because it ran counter to the ideology of the community. Because Roman justice differentiated the coercion it imposed according to social class, this division caused tension among the church members during the persecution.[25]

Its particular behavioral requirements, therefore, along with its rituals of membership and its sharing of financial resources certainly established the Christian church as a voluntarily segregated group. It was not so highly bounded a group, however, as to provide its members independence from the demands of Roman society, whose institutions controlled their economic security and bodily safety.

The differentiation of religious roles, each with its rights and responsibilities, established a set of social classes peculiar to the

church community. Clergy, in the several grades, were d
from other communicants,[26] who were in turn separate
chumens, penitents and the excluded sinners.[27] The
fights among the Christians revolved around the p:
obligations attending different forms of membership, ┌──
the authority of the bishop and the right of penitents to full
communion. Thus the community's social hierarchy and the justifications for it require careful attention.

The surviving evidence consists almost exclusively of a bishop's
correspondence and deals primarily with conflict over his authority;
thus it provides more information about that office. Each community had only one bishop, who served for life. The bishop was
elected either by the community or by the bishops of neighboring
churches with the consent of the community he would govern; he
was then installed by other bishops. The election could be considered an expression of divine choice of a particular candidate.[28]
Normally, bishops could be removed from office for misconduct
only by the judgment of their fellow bishops; in extreme circumstances, however, a community might be required to refuse the
ministry of a failed leader.[29]

As the chief officer of the church, the bishop was expected to act
in the name of the community as a whole and to serve its interests
rather than his own.[30] As administrator, the bishop maintained relationships with other churches and supervised the community
funds.[31] With the advice and consent of the people, he appointed and
governed the clergy of his own church.[32] As bishop of the provincial
capital and chief city of Roman Africa, the bishop of Carthage
summoned and presided over synods of his fellow bishops which
formulated common policy and exercised discipline over the bishops
themselves.[33] He represented the entire college of African bishops in
its dealings with the bishops of Italy, Gaul, Spain and Asia.[34]

The bishop was also the principal judge in his church. He interpreted the behavioral demands of the gospel to the community and
punished those who failed to fulfill them. He supervised the repentance and reconciliation of sinners, acting as he claimed in the place
of Christ until the last day and final judgment.[35] The ritual life of
the community also revolved around the bishop, who himself
presided at the eucharistic service in imitation of Christ and authorized the presbyters to do likewise.[36] Through the imposition of
hands, he admitted newly baptized members and readmitted penitents.[37] Thus Cyprian would portray the local bishop as Peter, the
rock upon which the community was founded.[38]

The other clergy were distributed through several grades, including presbyters, deacons, subdeacons, acolytes and readers. Each had age requirements, specific duties and assigned compensation.[39] The clergy as a whole worked under the supervision of the bishop; the deacons may have been at the disposal of individual presbyters.[40] Like the bishop, the other clerics were expected to devote themselves to the concerns of the community; they were not allowed to engage in business or to serve as trustees of estates or guardians of children.[41]

Even among the laity, the community distinguished different ranks. The widows and indigent were enrolled to receive financial support.[42] The dedicated virgins were an established order within the community, whose bodily integrity was especially important for the church as a whole. These women retained their property but they refrained from marriage and were not to associate closely with men.[43] They were especially honored as symbols of the church's separation from the Roman world.[44]

In addition to these grades of full membership, the community had liminal classes, people who were neither outsiders nor full members of the group. Catechumens preparing for admission through the ritual of baptism were subject to behavioral restrictions but also had certain claims on the church, such as the right to immediate baptism and membership when they were in danger of death.[45] Baptized Christians who violated the behavioral code in some significant way were shifted into the class of penitents, where they were to give evidence of a renewed commitment through prayer, fasting and gifts to the common fund, under the supervision of the clergy. At a suitable time, they were examined by the bishop and ritually readmitted to the church.[46] Those who refused this discipline were excommunicated; although cut off and shunned, they retained a certain right to be admitted as penitents.[47] Clergy who failed in their offices might also be placed in a segregated rank, allowed to partake of the communion but not to regain office.[48]

Although this differentiation of roles and offices seems to have been formally established in the Carthaginian church, its functioning was severely tested even before the persecution. Cyprian was among the Roman *honestiores*, a wealthy and well-educated man; he had not yet been a Christian for many years when the bishop's office fell open and the people chose him to fill it, without his having passed through the lower clerical ranks.[49] A serious conflict arose between the people and the presbyters perhaps because the election was a slight to the other clergy and a frustration of the anticipated promotion of some prominent presbyter or deacon.[50] In any case, the dispute weakened the role differentiation since competition for control broke out as soon as Cyprian, as an *honestior*, withdrew into exile at the beginning of the persecution.[51] In addition, some of the presbyters and deacons neither accepted the restrictions of their status nor even followed the general morality; one of the deacons in particular had been stealing and mistreating his family.[52] The virgins themselves were not serving as appropriate symbols for the church's renunciation of the rewards of Roman society and for its heavenly aspirations.[53]

These conflicts and the operation of an unjustified distinction between wealthy and poor within the community lowered the strength of the system of social differentiation, in the same way that the members' dependence on the Roman economy weakened their group cohesiveness. Thus the community was vulnerable to the attack mounted in the Decian persecution, which forced the Christians to choose between the two societies, the two behavior patterns, and the two reward systems in which they continued to be involved.

Disruption by the Decian edict

The Decian edict challenged Christianity's accommodation to the demands of the Roman economic and legal system by requiring formal participation in its religious cult. The empire would not extend to Christian monotheists the religious exemption which it continued to concede to the Jews; instead it would require Christians to participate in the state cult. The Christians, however, were prepared neither to relax their religious exclusivism nor to attempt an economically and politically independent society. The church, therefore, had to look to its boundary, to the way in which it regulated its engagement with the dominant culture.

Because the edict was enforced in accordance with the behavioral norms of the Roman class system, it also challenged the role differentiation within the Christian communities. The Roman judicial system dealt in very different ways with the *honestiores* and *humiliores*. The nobility, based upon wealth, were more likely to be hailed before the imperial commissioners and required to comply with the edict; *humiliores* might never be called forward and required to take a stand.[54] Once they were engaged by the state apparatus, however, the *humiliores* were in greater danger of coercion and bodily harm.[55] Cyprian, as bishop and *honestior*, was in a particularly vulnerable position;[56] many of the other clergy were ignored by the imperial commissioners.[57]

In the enforcement of the Decian edict, wealthy Christians were allowed to abandon their immoveable property – which could have entailed a permanent loss of status – and voluntarily go into an exile which they hoped would be temporary. They could also avail themselves of a type of fictive compliance which was regularly used in doing other forms of business. Personally or through an agent, they could declare themselves unable to follow the prescriptions of the law, make a payment which they might interpret as a fine, and receive a certificate attesting to their participation in a sacrifice, which all knew they had refused to perform. In this way, they would avoid actual contact with idolatry, would preserve and even acknowledge their Christian commitment, and yet would avoid the loss of property and position attendant upon a more public confession of Christian faith.[58] Wealthy Christians could, of course, choose to comply with the requirements of the edict, thereby fully protecting their property and dependants.[59] They would then have to find some way to make an accommodation with the church.

Poorer Christians, the *humiliores*, faced a different burden. If they publicly refused to comply with the edict, they might be tortured or reduced to slavery. Since they did not have the moveable financial resources of the rich, voluntary exile would have made them refugees rather than exiles, dependent upon the support of Christian communities in larger cities.[60] Obtaining certificates through payments would have been more difficult in the absence of both financial resources and personal relationships with the governing class. Unlike the rich, however, the poor might hope to escape the attention of the commissioners charged with enforcing the edict. They could simply ignore the edict, restrict their activities, and hope that their neighbors and acquaintances would refrain from calling official attention to them.[61]

Thus the enforcement of the edict did not affect rich and poor Christians in the same way. Yet the differentiation of roles within the community did not make explicit provision for such a distinction in the fulfillment of the conditions of membership.[62] In upholding their baptismal oath, all Christians were, theoretically, equal.[63] To maintain its cohesiveness, the church would have to find some way to adjust for this difference, some system of dealing with success and failure which would maintain the standards of Christian life and justify the inequality in danger faced by its members.

The Christian clergy was also placed in a particularly difficult

position by the edict. The bishop, Cyprian, was p
city and his arrest was immediately demanded by
personal danger, moreover, drew attention to the en
thereby endangering the poor whose only defense
He withdrew into exile but did not allow such res
of the clergy, apparently most of whom were *humi*
byters and deacons had to expose themselves to the Roman
authorities in order to visit and care for the imprisoned confessors,
who required both religious encouragement and bodily sustenance.[66] Similarly, those charged with the care of the dead had to
claim and bury the bodies of confessors who died under torture.[67] If
the ministers made any compromise with the government, they
would invalidate the very authority by which they could strengthen
the community. Yet if they were discovered and hauled before the
imperial commission, their services would be lost.[68] The enforcement of the edict, then, did not fall evenly on the ranks of the
clergy. Legitimating the differentiation in danger would be
extremely important for the cohesiveness of the clergy and community.

Finally, the persecution created two new classes within the
community: the lapsed and the confessors. The very definition of
the lapsed would involve controversy: were those who had obtained
certificates without actually sacrificing guilty of apostasy; should
those who initially confessed but then failed under torture be
treated differently than those who volunteered to sacrifice without
even waiting to be called by the commissioners?[69] The powers and
privileges consequent upon the confessors' new relationship to God
also required definition: was their salvation secured, so that they
were no longer subject to the same behavioral restraints as other
Christians?[70] If they were to sit with Christ and judge the nations,
could they bind and loosen sinners within their own community?[71]

Through these challenges to the community's defining standards
of membership and its differentiated roles, the Decian persecution
endangered the cohesiveness of the Christian church and the established patterns of relationship among its members. The variety of
Christian responses to the challenge also threatened the church's
culture by questioning its moral, ritual and cosmological assumptions. Was fidelity properly defined as the avoidance of idolatry or
did it also require active confession of Christ once the opportunity
was given? Did this standard apply to all Christians equally? Was
flight or voluntary exile in time of persecution a confession or a
repudiation of faith? Did the rituals of the Roman state cult have

power to harm the Christian? Could the Christian ritual of penitence remove whatever pollution arose from idolatry and restore the sacrificer to the church? Most importantly, why was the persecution happening? Was the Christian God incapable of protecting the faithful? Cyprian and his colleagues would have to find a plausible a response to each of these questions in their efforts to restore the identity and order of the Christian community.

The church under persecution

The Christians of Carthage responded in different ways to the Decian edict. Some came forward voluntarily, with their dependants in tow, to offer the required sacrifice.[72] Others secured the certificates by payment, personally or through an agent, thereby protecting themselves and their households from prosecution.[73] Others sacrificed, in fear and trembling, under coercion.[74] A minority seems to have resisted. Following the example of the bishop, some abandoned their property and left the city.[75] Those who refused to sacrifice when they were called forward were imprisoned and eventually sent into exile.[76] Some of these remained outside the city but others defied the government and returned to the community illegally.[77]

After a few months, the imperial officials introduced torture into the interrogation process: they extended the imprisonment and deprived the confessors of food, water, light and fresh air. As a consequence, some of the confessors died as martyrs.[78] Others capitulated but then renounced their compliance and stood firm in a second test, either dying under torture or being sent into exile.[79] Some, of course, simply failed under the torture and harassment. The minority which remained faithful in secret lived in fear of being delated to the commissioners.[80]

All who failed to confess the faith were excluded from the peace of the church and participation in its eucharistic ritual. Those who agreed to repent of their apostasy before the community and to undertake penance were promised the peace of the church in the event of approaching death.[81] Thus the penitent lapsed were allowed to continue as members at the boundary of the community, with the hope of finally being readmitted and thus attaining eternal salvation. Some must have simply abandoned Christianity and returned to imperial society.[82]

Evidently, the community's mode of voluntarily segregating itself from the dominant culture had failed. To re-establish or to redefine its boundary would require a major effort to achieve consensus among the faithful and the fallen, which could not be undertaken before the end of the persecution. Cyprian called for patience and united prayer and proposed a broad consultation of bishops, clergy and people once God granted a return of civic peace.[83]

At this point, however, the authority structure within the church in Carthage also failed. The bishop was in exile, attempting to exhort the community and direct the clergy by letter and messenger. Because he was not facing the danger which beset the other clergy and the majority of the people, his own religious authority was weakened. Then news arrived that the presbyters in Rome had decided to delay the election of a replacement for their martyred bishop and to rule the church as a council. The majority of the presbyters in Carthage, who had opposed the election of Cyprian two years earlier, decided on a similar course of action. They treated Cyprian as fugitive from his responsibilities, ignored his letters and messengers, and took the situation into their own hands. They would draw upon the spiritual capital of the confessors to counteract the popularity and continuing influence of Cyprian among the people.[84]

The confessors and martyrs were a new category of membership in the church, a new position on the social hierarchy. Their rank seemed to have been achieved by their own initiative or by the direct assistance of God; unlike the clerical offices, it had not been conferred upon them by the action of the community. Thus the community experienced some difficulty in specifying the privileges and obligations associated with this public witness to Christ. When the first set of confessors was released from prison, some of them flaunted the behavioral standards of the church, asserting that their salvation was guaranteed by Christ's promise to acknowledge before God anyone who had confessed him on earth.[85] Despite these claims of cosmic privilege, the confessors continued to live in the community and could be subjected to personal pressure by the clergy and especially by their fellow confessors.[86]

With the introduction of torture into the process of interrogation came the deaths of some confessors as martyrs. They, it was believed, ascended directly to Christ and would sit with him in judgment. Thus, according to a disputed tradition, they might serve as intercessors to win forgiveness for the apostates. These martyrs escaped group pressure by dying; the privileges they enjoyed and power they exercised in heaven would prove even more difficult to control than that of the confessors. The fallen began to seek out the imprisoned and to secure letters which directed that the repentant sinners should be granted the peace of the church on the strength of the martyr's intercession before Christ.[87] So armed, the apostates expected to be readmitted to communion upon the death of the martyr. Some of the confessors provided such letters only to a few selected individuals but others gave general letters, including all of a recipient's dependants.[88] A few even authorized their fellow confessors to continue issuing the letters in their names after their deaths, to whomever requested them.[89] These letters were addressed to the bishop, as the officer charged with giving the peace of the church, but the martyrs seemed to be issuing commands rather than interceding for a favor or advising in a judgment.[90]

Thus was the stage set for a leadership struggle in the church. The martyrs were with God in heaven and were thus free from the face-to-face pressure which the community could use to establish and maintain rules and roles. The lapsed were understandably anxious to secure their readmission to the communion, and at the lowest personal cost; they could be trusted to uphold the authority of the martyrs.[91] The confessors enjoyed the honor in which they were held by the community and were ready to exploit their role as agents of the martyrs.[92]

In the ensuing struggle for control of the community, both the bishop and the ambitious presbyters would seek to gain the support of the confessors. When the martyrs first began to issue letters of peace, Cyprian tried to moderate rather than to stop the practice. He recognized the authority of the confessors but specified the way it should be exercised. Their letters should reflect their role, offering counsel to the bishop and community as individual sinners came up for judgment. Thus they should recommend individuals rather than indefinitely large groups, should base their advice on a judgment of the sincere repentance of the individual sinner, should require that peace be delayed until the end of the persecution, and must recognize the right of the bishop to examine cases individually before granting peace.[93] For the most part, the confessors seem to have complied with these provisions.[94] Some of the presbyters, however, ignored the restrictions of the letters: they admitted the lapsed to peace and communion immediately upon the death of the martyr, requiring neither confession of guilt nor public display of repentance.[95] Using the religious capital of the confessors, they challenged the authority of the exiled bishop and the community's right to control its membership and behavioral standards.

The situation was fraught with danger for the church. Some of the standing faithful were still in danger of being apprehended and tortured; others were safe before both church and empire because their guardian – husband, father, patron or master – had complied with the edict. The clergy and confessors were divided: some sharing the eucharist with the readmitted fallen and others shunning them.[96] Even the lapsed were divided: some undertook penance and awaited the return of the bishop at the end of the persecution; others enjoyed the peace of the church and the safety of the empire. By availing himself of the privilege of an *honestior* to protect his people, Cyprian had disabled himself as bishop: he could exert no face-to-face pressure to restore discipline or establish control.[97] The church in Carthage was in danger of disintegration.

The church culture at the end of the persecution

The social organization of the church in Carthage was shifting under the impact of the Decian persecution. Not only had the community failed voluntarily to maintain the regulations governing its relation with the imperial culture but the authority of the martyrs threatened to remove its defining characteristic – religious exclusivism – from the people's control. Some Christians had violated the standards of performance which defined membership and then been welcomed back into the communion without any indication of behavioral change or renewed commitment to the standards of the community. Moreover, the clearly defined lines of responsibility governing the actions of the clergy and people had been bent and broken by the presbyter's assertion of the martyr's privilege and repudiation of the prerogatives of both the bishop and the standing faithful to judge the sinners. In claiming the right to determine the conditions of membership, the coalition of rebel presbyters and confessors was asserting its autonomy and control over the people, both standing and fallen. Not only was the voluntary cohesion of the community being lowered but its differentiation of roles was changing. Some were breaking free of community control and exercising control over others.

The incipient shift in social organization to a lower level of group cohesion and internal differentiation was accompanied and facilitated by a corresponding change in religious culture. The formal, behavioral morality was giving way to negotiated rules of interaction based on the personally achieved authority of the martyrs. The assumption that rituals were efficacious was being called into question: contact with the demonic sacrifices of the Roman cult seemed to present no danger to individual or community; the Christian purification rites were either unnecessary or ineffective in comparison to the martyr's personal intercessory authority. The peace and communion of the church were becoming a possession acquired by rank to be conferred at the will of the powerful authorities – presbyters and martyrs – rather than the realization of voluntary fellowship among the members. Religious power was being appropriated by individuals and employed as an instrument of autonomy and control. Nor was this new power incorruptible: through the martyrs, the power of wealth and kinship could reach up into heaven and manipulate the judgment of Christ.

These shifts in the organization and practice of the church should have entailed a questioning of its cosmology, of the assumptions which provided the justification for its system of rules and roles. Among the most important of these was the assumption that the universe was governed by personal forces which were responsive to the moral actions and intentions of human beings. In fact, the instability of communal assumptions was manifest in the questioning of the cosmic efficacy of the church's ritual of reconciliation. This ritual will be considered in the next two chapters.

3

NECESSITY OF
REPENTANCE

The Roman Empire challenged the boundary by which the church had voluntarily segregated itself: Decian's edict demanded a violation of the baptismal oath in which Christians pledged allegiance to Christ and renounced every other religious cult. A significant number of the Christians – in Carthage and perhaps throughout Africa – complied with the imperial law either by sacrificing or by obtaining certificates attesting to their having sacrificed to the Roman deities. Because they had publicly violated the foundational condition of church membership, these failed Christians were a threat to the integrity and identity of the church. Because they had polluted themselves by contact with the demonic rites of the imperial cult, they were a danger to the purity of the communion. Because they stood under the threat of repudiation by Christ for refusing to confess him on earth, their participation could destroy the eucharist as a symbol and foretaste of the heavenly banquet.[1] Thus they were immediately excluded from the communion of the church. Under the threat of state sanctions, some of the sinners decided to abandon Christianity altogether and reverted to their former style of life in Roman society.[2] Many others sought to regain their membership and the hope of salvation on terms similar to those which they had enjoyed before the Decian edict. These posed a dilemma for the bishops.

The church had a procedure for purifying the faithful from significant sins. In place of the cleansing power of the Spirit-filled waters of baptism, the sinners used fasting, almsgiving and prayer to scour their souls. They pleaded that the community, in its identification with Christ, would intercede before God for their forgiveness. After an extended period of such penance, the purified sinners once again received the Holy Spirit through the imposition of the bishop's hands and were readmitted to communion. This procedure, however, was restricted to those sins which had been committed against the persons and property of fellow Christians.[3] Those who had sinned directly against God, principally by idolatry or murder, were permanently excluded from the church's communion;[4] by persevering in penance for the remainder of their lives, however, they would be readmitted to communion and commended to the mercy of God at the time of death.[5]

Faced with a life-time of penance and an uncertain acceptance by Christ, the lapsed turned to a more direct means of intercession: the power of the martyrs. When they died in the confession of Christ, the martyrs were believed to enter directly and immediately into paradise, where they could appeal to Christ himself for the forgiveness of their fellows.[6] What the lapsed sought, however, was not only an advocate to plead their cases when they appeared before the tribunal of Christ after death but a patron who would gain them readmission to the communion on earth. Thus the letters of peace provided by the martyrs and their deputies among the confessors were addressed to the bishops; they directed that the penitents be received into communion on the strength of the martyr's power to win forgiveness from Christ rather than on the basis of their submission to the process of penance and the intercession of the church.

The letters of peace granted by the martyrs threatened the community's identity by allowing the sinners to re-enter the communion without acknowledging their failure and recommitting themselves publicly to that exclusive loyalty to Christ which was the condition of membership in the church. The martyrs' authority also strained the traditional differentiation of roles within the church. The bishops asserted their responsibility and the community's right to require public repentance through submission to the established rituals and procedures. In exercising their judicial role as agents of Christ, however, the leaders were caught between conflicting pressures. As pastors, they could not fail to call the sinners to repentance. Yet they could hardly claim the authority to forgive a sin committed directly against God. Since Christ had threatened to deny in heaven those who denied him on earth, how could the church presume to loosen that sin on earth with any expectation, much less assurance, that it would be loosened in heaven as well? The bishops were also required to challenge the power of the martyrs, who claimed to intercede directly before Christ as he awarded them crowns of victory. Thus the bishops were faced with the apparently impossible task of rescuing the sinners without destroying the identity of the church or denying the glory of the martyrs.

A comparative overview

The challenge presented by the lapsed and their readmission to the church's communion can be analyzed in terms of the cohesiveness or identity of the church community and the differentiation of roles within it. The primary issue for identity was the group's power to specify and enforce the rejection of idolatry which segregated it from Roman society. The rights and responsibilities appropriate to the roles of bishops, martyrs, confessors, standing faithful, and fallen were also in dispute. The three different solutions to the problem of reconciling the lapsed actually adopted by competing Christian communities will be described in terms of group cohesiveness and role differentiation. Then each will be examined in greater detail.

The laxists

Fortunatus, Novatus and the other laxist presbyters in Carthage recognized the exalted status of the martyrs and accepted their power to secure forgiveness directly from Christ. The peace granted by Christ in heaven, they reasoned, could not then be withheld by the church on earth. The clients of these heavenly patrons, therefore, were not required to placate God or to demonstrate their remorse to the community by penitential lamentation and fasting, by depriving themselves of pleasures and possessions. Instead, the sinners for whom the martyrs had promised to intercede were returned to their former status, free of all taint of idolatry, worthy to share immediately in the communion, and subject to no continuing restrictions within the church.

This glorification of the martyrs and the use of their power by the confessors they had deputized and the laxist clergy who recognized their letters of peace entailed a diminution of group unity and cohesiveness. Control over its boundary passed from the community as a whole to the martyrs, the confessors who claimed to act as their agents, and the clergy. Since the martyrs were in heaven rather than present in the community, they could not be subjected to the face-to-face pressure which might have limited their exercise of power and allowed the members of the community to exert a counterbalancing force, as they had successfully curbed the first set of released confessors who had violated community moral standards.[7] By claiming that they had been authorized to act as deputies of the martyrs, the confessors and the rebel clergy also loosened the control of the standing faithful over their own decisions and actions. The peace of Christ, which the bishop had been accustomed to extend and withdraw upon the advice of the whole community, would now be granted by the martyrs or confessors and administered by the clergy without regard for or reliance upon any communally enforced standards of behavior. In breaking free of the limits of their roles in the church, therefore, the martyrs usurped and redistributed the power which had been differentially shared by Christians enjoying various types of church membership. Simultaneously, they undermined the voluntary cohesiveness of the community as a whole.[8]

The rigorists

In sharp contrast to the laxist program, the rigorist stance adopted by Novatian in Rome and his representatives in Africa relied exclusively on that behavioral morality which establishes and maintains a tightly bounded and segregated community. The widespread failure of Christians to uphold their baptismal commitment threatened the identity of the church as a gathering of the saints and its communion as an entryway to the kingdom of heaven. Because the rigorist church claimed to have no authority to forgive a sin committed against God after baptism, it could not associate the idolaters with itself even as penitents but could only commend them as outcasts to Christ's mercy as they appeared before him after death. The rigorists protected themselves from the contamination of idolatry by refusing communion with both the lapsed and any church which readmitted them to its fellowship.

The high and well-defined boundary which the rigorists voluntarily maintained protected their community as an island of pure holiness in the polluted sea of Roman idolatry. This defining concern for purity, moreover, suppressed any significant differentiation of roles which might have allowed varying degrees of separation from evil and thus created a place for the penitents, even at the fringe of the community. Faced with failure within the church, the rigorists expelled the evil and strengthened the voluntary unity and separation of their church. At the same time, they became a more egalitarian community by refusing to define classes of membership through differing expectations and privileges.

The moderates

Cyprian and his colleagues both affirmed a variety of interactive categories of membership and maintained a firm boundary which was defined by a behavioral standard of morality. They first expelled the fallen from the community and then required that the apostates submit to the ritual of reconciliation which demonstrated their repentance and recommitment in the presence of the entire church. Once reconciled, the lapsed were assigned to a specific status which restricted their participation in the communion and thereby prevented any residual contagion from adversely affecting their fellow Christians. Unlike the laxists, these bishops extended the peace of the church to the penitents as a necessary condition for their attaining the forgiveness of Christ in heaven rather than as a consequence of their having achieved it. They explained that only those whom the church had admitted to communion would come before the divine judge and thus could be considered for acceptance into the kingdom. Unlike the rigorists, they distinguished levels of purity appropriate to different types of membership and thereby integrated the sinners into the community.

By simultaneously affirming the definition of its boundary and asserting an internal differentiation of roles, Cyprian's church maintained the significance of its behavioral code and the efficacy of its rituals. It reintegrated the sinners without being polluted by their idolatry and sacrificing its own holiness. In the process, however, it had to redefine the cosmic or religious significance of its boundary: church membership no longer carried the presumption of salvation but only the right to appear before Christ and the promise of communal intercession. By thus limiting its claims to purity and its power to guarantee salvation, this church maintained both its cohesive separation from Roman idolatry and its internal differentiation.

Cyprian and his colleagues defended their moderate position on two fronts simultaneously. Against the laxist clergy and their allies among the confessors, they insisted that the fallen must submit to the judgment and rituals of the community in order to regain the peace of the church and the forgiveness of Christ. This issue will be considered in the current chapter. The following chapter is be dedicated to the battle against the rigorists, which began in Rome and spread to Africa, over the efficacy of the ritual of reconciliation to protect the purity of the church and win the forgiveness of Christ for the sin of apostasy.

The challenge of the martyrs and confessors

As the church in Carthage was shaken by the onset of the persecution and then by the introduction of torture to enforce the Decian edict, Cyprian took actions which would strengthen its unity and cohesion. His fundamental interpretation of the crisis and of the response required by the church was clearly established in the letters he sent to Carthage during the initial months of his exile. Once the martyrs had began to issue letters of peace and the clergy to grant immediate admission to communion, he then concentrated on upholding the rights of the community as a whole and restricting the privileges claimed by the martyrs, confessors and laxist clergy. Thus, from the beginning, he upheld the voluntary unity of the church.

Cyprian's actions and especially the justifications which he offered for them fostered certain attitudes and discouraged contrary outlooks; the motives and considerations he offered both reflected and shaped the worldview of his audience. In justifying his own withdrawal, he expressed concern for the safety of the community as a whole: his presence in the city would focus attention on the Christians and endanger all.[9] Similarly, he warned his clergy to assume a low profile when visiting the imprisoned confessors lest their presence stir up resentment against the church.[10] He directed that the financial resources of the community be used not only to support the members who had lost their means of livelihood as a consequence of the persecution but to pressure those dependent on the church to remain faithful: anyone who lapsed was to be deprived of assistance.[11] Similarly, care for the imprisoned confessors was declared essential[12] but aid was to be withheld from those who repudiated the church's moral standards after their release.[13] Most of the funds, including those which Cyprian himself contributed, were channeled through the clergy so that benefits were provided in the name of the community as a whole rather than by individual patrons.[14] Thus the financial resources of the church were mobilized and pooled to alleviate the economic hardships visited upon its members as consequences of their common religious commitment.

Cyprian's concern with the cohesiveness of the church was particularly evident in his initial attempts to explain the reasons for the persecution and the appropriate response to it. Illustrating God's use of moral standards in the governance of the universe, his exhortations assigned blame to the whole community and did not attempt to marginalize some members as scapegoats. Cyprian reminded his people that warnings had been given of the impending danger and the sins that provoked it. In a vision given prior to the beginning of the persecution, God had threatened the community with the consequences of its disharmony in prayer. Later, a dream had shown that the Father was preparing to allow Satan to savage the community because of its persistent refusal to obey Christ's commands. Just before the outbreak of persecution, a third vision admonished the church for inattentiveness in its prayer.[15] The persecution, Cyprian concluded, was a divine punishment intended to test, to correct, to sift the church.[16] When the community did not repent, when some of the first set of confessors sinned openly after they were spared by the imperial officials, God had intensified the persecution. By divine permission, the Roman government had begun to imprison and torture the confessors rather than sending them into exile.[17] Thus Cyprian called the whole community, both the standing and the fallen, to repent and appease God by fasting and tears, by vigilant and persistent prayer.[18] That prayer must be harmonious and unified; each must petition God for the peace of the entire community rather than for private safety.[19]

This overriding concern with the solidarity of the community also appeared in Cyprian's glorification of the martyrs and his attempt to control the released confessors. While the first set of confessors was still under interrogation, he praised them as friends of Christ, who would reign and judge with him.[20] Once they were released and some had began to violate the law of both God and the empire, however, he called upon their fellows to correct and even to shun them.[21] Their public confession was only the beginning of salvation, he warned; like everyone else, they must continue to guard against the intensified assault of the devil.[22] The martyrs who had stood firm against torture and deprivation even unto death, he proclaimed to be the glory of the whole church, in whom Christ himself had fought and conquered.[23] The community must take particular care to recover their bodies and to mark the days of their victory for its future celebrations.[24]

Thus from the beginning of the persecution, Cyprian warned that the church was being punished for sins against group solidarity, that all must join together in repenting, and that deliverance would be granted only to the church as a whole. In contrast, the lapsed who had voluntarily abandoned Christ and the community by obeying the demands of the emperor were even then attempting to secure a private peace with God through the intercession of the martyrs.[25]

Cyprian's early explanation of the nature and causes of the persecution clarifies his reaction to the conspiracy of the confessors and the rebel clergy which allowed the lapsed to return to communion before the danger was removed and peace restored to the church. The imperial action was itself God's chastisement of the community, by which the deserters had been tried, found wanting, and expelled from the church. To accept them back into communion even while the testing continued, therefore, would be to reject God's warning and even to obstruct the divine purpose. By reconciling the sinners without requiring even a semblance of repentance, the laxist clergy would certainly provoke divine outrage and delay God's granting peace to the church. Danger threatened not only the individual sinners who had further offended God by usurping the eucharist but the confessors who promoted this sacrilege and even the standing faithful who tolerated it.[26] Calling upon his visions once again, Cyprian warned that the church's safety required that unity and discipline be restored and preserved.[27]

The exiled bishop called upon the different members of the community to apply personal pressure to the clergy, the confessors and the lapsed.[28] The confessors were to curb those among their number who abused their honored position, to remind the presbyters of the responsibilities of their office, to restrain the lapsed, and to halt the growing traffic in their own letters of peace.[29] The clergy were reminded of their duty to instruct the people, maintain discipline, and accept their particular role within the church;[30] the rebels among them were threatened with suspension from office and trial before the entire community for usurpation of the bishop's authority.[31] The faithful people were exhorted to challenge and shun the unrepentant lapsed. By ordering that his letters addressed to the confessors and the clergy be read out to the laity as well, Cyprian used the people to pressure their leaders to conform to the bishop's directives.[32] All were again enjoined to unite in vigilant and insistent prayer so that God would give repentance to the fallen and peace to the church.[33]

Cyprian also outlined a procedure by which the whole community would regain control over its standards of membership by determining the proper course to follow in reconciling the fallen once God had granted peace to the church. In keeping with what he claimed had been constant practice throughout his episcopate, he promised to seek the counsel of all in making any decision which affected the whole church.[34] When it was safe for the bishop and other exiles to return, all would meet to consider the recommendations made by the martyrs and to judge the individual lapsed.[35] To bolster his position in Carthage, moreover, he immediately sent copies of these letters to some episcopal colleagues in Africa, seeking their support for his policy.[36]

A month later, Cyprian wrote to his clergy again, to make provision for any lapsed who might fall sick during the summer months. He conceded first that those who held letters from the martyrs should be granted peace as death approached,[37] and then, in a later letter, extended this benefit to all the penitent lapsed.[38] On the healthy, however, he remained adamant: they were not to be admitted to communion as long as God withheld peace from the church as a whole. He suggested that those demanding immediate reconciliation should reverse their earlier denial of Christ by a public confession of faith before the imperial authorities.[39] This form of repentance would certainly satisfy both God and the church. Some of the lapsed seem to have undertaken just this form of repentance and were promptly reinstated.[40] The only alternative was for the lapsed to be patient and penitent, confident that they would share whatever remedy God provided to the community as a whole.[41] While making concessions to the dying, Cyprian insisted that the lapsed would be admitted into the living community only with the consent of its members, thereby maintaining the voluntary and personal character of the church.[42]

As the conflict over the admission of the lapsed developed, the focus shifted to the privileges which were attached to the role of the martyrs and their agents among the confessors imprisoned in Carthage. Cyprian had admonished the confessors that if they were to judge with Christ, they must judge as Christ would, recommending for reconciliation only individual sinners whose true repentance they had personally witnessed.[43] When the confessors responded by granting a general amnesty and ordering him to broadcast it among the bishops, Cyprian broke off attempts to negotiate with them. Instead he turned for support to his episcopal colleagues in Africa and then to the clergy and the confessors in Rome. In a daring attack on their authority, he charged the martyrs and confessors with violating the explicit commands of Christ: sins could be remitted without works of repentance only in baptism, which was given in the name of the Trinity, not that of a martyr.[44] In refusing to respect Christ's threat to condemn in heaven those who failed to confess him on earth, he asserted, the martyrs had undercut the very foundation of their own authority – Christ's parallel promise to recognize and reward their confession.[45] The church, Cyprian insisted, must repudiate the martyrs' attempt to exercise power contrary to the gospel's explicit teaching.

As the persecution continued into the autumn of 250, the divisions within the Carthaginian church hardened and the rising influence of the imprisoned confessors and their clerical allies threatened to overwhelm the established hierarchy and splinter the community. Although some of the lapsed submitted to Cyprian's demand for full public repentance, others adamantly claimed the peace which, they asserted, the martyrs' prayers had already secured for them in heaven.[46] Over the winter, the clergy in Carthage did expel one laxist presbyter who had granted communion to the lapsed.[47] He, however, was a refugee from another city. They proved unable to control the dissidents within their own ranks. For this purpose, Cyprian had to appoint a commission of exiled bishops and presbyters whose own status as confessors enabled them to confront the rebels and excommunicate some of their leaders.[48] He also prepared himself for the personal struggle with his challengers in Carthage which would come the following spring.

Reconciling the lapsed

Shortly after Easter 251, Cyprian was able to return to Carthage and address the assembled church. His masterful oration, *On the Lapsed*, reasserted his own interpretation of the persecution and reiterated the demand for repentance. Within a month, the bishops of Africa met in Carthage to determine the program through which they would admit the fallen and exclude the rebels. They gathered again in the spring of the next two years to review progress and adjust policy. By the summer of 253, they had regained control of the church in Africa and decided to restore all the penitents to communion. The methods employed in each of the three stages of this process will be examined in turn.

Cyprian's return to Carthage

Cyprian's opening statement to his community in *On the Lapsed* recalled the explanation of the meaning of the persecution which he had advanced in his letters to them a year earlier. The Christians had renounced the Roman world in word but not in deed; they had failed to fulfill the promise made in baptism to follow the way of Christ alone. Instead, they had compromised their Christianity by preferring the property and protecting the position which had then enslaved them to imperial society. They retained Roman fashions of dress and ornamentation; some married their daughters to non-

Christians. Even the clergy had neglected the Christian commitment in order to pursue wealth and advantage.[49] The entire community was at fault and had brought God's corrective anger down upon itself in the form of imperial persecution.

So God had acted to correct the church, to arouse and liberate the people from the bondage into which they had fallen. When faced with the stark choice between Christ and Caesar, Cyprian recalled, many Christians awoke and reformed themselves. Some immediately abandoned their possessions to imperial confiscation and protected their faith by withdrawing into exile. Others were apprehended and upheld their commitment to Christ at the risk of limb and even life. Still others confessed in secret: by refusing to obey the edict within the appointed time, they had resisted the attack and privately stood ready to confess publicly in case they were denounced to the authorities. All these faithful constituted the church and Cyprian proclaimed them confessors of Christ.[50] Those unfortunates who had bravely confessed Christ but had eventually been overcome by torture and deprivation he judged deserving of pity and God's mercy. Though they failed to win the crown, still they too had been corrected by God's thrashing; their spirits bewailed the weakness of their flesh; their wounds pleaded eloquently for forgiveness. In some cases, God had accepted their repentance, strengthened them, and granted them the crown of martyrdom in a second trial.[51] Still others among the faithful admitted that they had been preserved only because they were not discovered and required to sacrifice. Recognizing the weakness of their resolve, they also sought God's forgiveness.[52] All of these Cyprian welcomed – some with joy and others with compassion. Because they had heard and heeded the call to reform and repentance, they might expect Christ's commendation or hope for his forgiveness. Yet these were the minority.

The majority of Christians in Carthage, Cyprian charged, had failed openly and freely. Many had lined up to comply with the edict on the first day of its enforcement, encouraging their friends and dragging along their dependants. So eager were they to protect their property that they refused to be delayed, forcing themselves on the imperial commissioners until late in the evening. Others waited, bound to their possessions, until they were called forward and then they denied Christ. Though some had subsequently submitted to the discipline of penitence, many of the apostates refused to repent as openly and fully as they had sinned.[53]

Yet Cyprian did not turn away from these recalcitrant fallen.

Picking up the themes of his last letter from exile, he addressed them as the wounded who could yet be revived and healed by repentance. He warned them of the second and graver persecution which now threatened to destroy them completely. The sin to which the lapsed were now tempted – to share the laxist communion without having repented of their idolatry – he branded as more offensive to God than the prior sin of participating in the demonic sacrifice.[54] In exile, he had compared the five rebel presbyters to the five commissioners who supervised the enforcement of the imperial edict in Carthage.[55] In *On the Lapsed*, he called them false surgeons who closed and covered a wound which would then always fester and never heal.[56] Thus Cyprian asserted that in denying the community's right to require public penance of those members who had failed to uphold their baptismal oath of loyalty to Christ and the church, the rebel clergy and confessors had taken up the devil's own work.

Having clarified the danger posed by the laxist offer of communion, Cyprian turned to the rights and responsibilities of the martyrs, in whose intercessory power the lapsed had placed their trust. No human being could forgive a sin which was committed against God, he asserted; the servant could not write off a debt owed to the Master. The martyrs, like the other faithful, would indeed have the opportunity to intercede for their fellows but only when Christ himself returned to sit in judgment at the end of the world.[57] In the meantime, the bishops would accept their counsel and certainly accede to any request they made which corresponded to the law of God. If the martyrs' petition was not grounded in the scriptures, however, the bishop should await some sign of God's willingness to grant it. The scriptures clearly show, he reminded the community, that God did not always grant what the saints asked – not Moses, Jeremiah, Daniel, Noah or Job, or even the martyrs under the altar in the Book of Revelation.[58] In granting peace to the lapsed, moreover, the martyrs were promising what was actually contrary to the law of God. Their general amnesty blocked that very conversion and repentance which had been the divine objective in allowing the persecution itself.[59] Moreover, by ignoring Christ's threat to denounce those who refused to confess him, Cyprian recalled, the martyrs were undercutting the very foundation of the authority they claimed – Christ's contrasting promise to reward those who did acknowledge him.[60] Thus, Cyprian concluded, the martyrs had no authority to forgive the sin of idolatry and were wrong in demanding that the bishop grant the peace of the church to the fallen.

The church could indeed accept the lapsed, Cyprian reminded his people, but only as penitents. Those who refused to submit to the discipline of repentance were in the greatest danger. They had refused to be reformed by the persecution itself and now they were further provoking divine anger by violently demanding the eucharist.[61] As he had cited dreams and visions as indicators of God's will during the persecution,[62] Cyprian now pointed to the terrible punishments which divine wrath had already visited on some of the sacrificers who had grasped at the eucharist: one was struck dumb, another bit off her tongue, a child vomited up the holy blood, a girl collapsed in convulsions, others were possessed by unclean spirits and broke into frenzies. These few were warnings to all of the danger of provoking divine anger.[63] The rebels, however, declined to heed these threats. Refusing to do penance, they went on living in the Roman manner – feasting regularly, ornamenting their persons in fine clothes and jewels, dying their hair and painting their faces, just as they had before the persecution.[64] Their blindness, Cyprian explained, was itself a punishment for sin, a hardening of their hearts. The only appropriate response for the community was to exclude and shun such persons, since their very presence among Christians was a danger to the faith.[65]

The fallen who could still hear God's call must, Cyprian concluded, turn and repent. The sacrificers, the certified, even the secretly fearful must beware the divine wrath, for God judges not only action but intention.[66] Let them embrace the role of penitents, he urged, by confessing their sin while they were still in this world, while penance and the intercession of the bishop might still be acceptable to God. Let them place their trust not in the power of the martyrs but in the prayer and rituals of the church.[67]

Cyprian's treatise *On the Lapsed* bears witness to his extraordinary skill as a leader and an orator. Analyzed from the perspective of the social organization of the community, it reveals a shrewd program through which he moved the church both to affirm its protective boundary and to realign its system of offices and roles which had been distorted by the martyrs, confessors and laxist clergy. The ritual of penance was the key element in his plan for restoring the church.

Cyprian's interpretation of events stressed the shared status of the church before God. The entire community, not just the individual lapsed, was being subjected to divine correction in the persecution itself. Subsequently, the faithful assembly was endangered by sharing the eucharist with the unrepentant lapsed. The ritual of reconciliation itself strengthened the bonds uniting the community. Individual lapsed were required to reaffirm repeatedly and before the entire assembly their separation from Roman society and adherence to the church. They must confess their sin before the community; abstain from the pleasures offered by the city; give a portion of their property to the community in alms; fast, weep and pray for God's forgiveness in the sight of all; submit to judgment of their conduct by the assembly; and if they persevered, receive the imposition of the bishop's hands readmitting them into communion at the end of their lives. Their repentance re-established in practice the voluntary commitment of each Christian to a shared faith and moral code. Those who would not make such an open repudiation of apostasy and such a submission to the community were to be shunned by all. The participation of the faithful, as witnesses to penitential works and in their prayer for the repentant, strengthened their own commitment to Christ and to the behavioral standards of the community. Thus the practice of penitence increased the voluntary cohesion of the whole church.

Cyprian also restored the differentiation of privileges and responsibilities. The troublesome martyrs were disenfranchised: their influence was suspended until Christ himself returned in glory. The glorious confessors were placed alongside the standing faithful, ranked with the exiles and all those who had hidden in the city. All of these had confessed Christ and all would assist the bishop in judging the fallen. The repentant lapsed were welcomed into the role of penitent; they were promised the peace of the church before death and the intercession of the faithful when they came to face the final judgment of Christ. The clergy were forced to accept the limits of their authority – since not even the bishop could forgive sins committed against God.

This restoration of the church's social structure was accomplished by an insistence on behavioral standards proper to the community as a whole and to each of its classes of membership. The moral code was enforced by personal pressure in the community and by divine governance of the universe itself.[68] The boundary separating the church was further buttressed by demonstrations of the efficacy of the eucharistic ritual. Although the Roman cult was portrayed as an effective contaminant, the power of the Christian ritual was shown to be even stronger in the harm it worked on those who approached it unworthily. Thus Cyprian argued that the greatest danger to the community lay in provoking divine wrath by the refusal to repent and reform, rather than through the pollution of idolatry.

Bishops' meeting, spring 251

An agenda for the reconstruction of the African church was set in Cyprian's treatise *On the Lapsed*. When the bishops met in Carthage late in April 251, they brought forward a variety of scriptural passages which would indicate one or another course of action for reconciling the lapsed and responding to the challenge of the martyrs. They were concerned to maintain the discipline of the church but they recognized that denying or setting too stringent requirements for granting reconciliation would actually drive the lapsed, and all their dependants with them, into the schismatic community being established by the laxists.[69] The episcopal decision included five provisions. The certified might be admitted to communion immediately, upon the consideration of individual cases.[70] The sacrificers were to continue as penitents, with the promise of reconciliation before their deaths.[71] The lapsed who refused to submit to penance were to be denied the peace of the church even at the time of death.[72] The excommunication of the rebel clergy was reaffirmed.[73] Finally, the bishops located control of the communion in the individual churches: all cases were to be judged where the crime had been committed.[74] No mention was made of those who had sinned by intention alone.[75]

Thus the African bishops upheld the church's right to require submission to its behavioral standards and the entire community's right to enforce these conditions of membership. In agreeing to readmit the certified without delay and requiring no public penance of those who had failed only in intention, Cyprian abandoned the more rigorous position he had taken in *On the Lapsed*, just as he had acquiesced in the more lenient policy of the Roman clergy toward penitents dying during the persecution. Evidently, Cyprian could not enforce a standard which did not win the support of his people and colleagues. The power of a voluntary community over its officers is evident in these concessions.

Bishops' meeting, spring 253

When the bishops met two years later in Carthage, they judged that the time had come to gather the church into a closer unity by admitting the penitents to communion.[76] Warning signs of a renewed and intensified persecution convinced them that the eschatological struggle itself had begun. This new persecution, they judged, was not to be another chastising of a sinful church but its final testing in anticipation of the judgment of Christ.[77]

The standards had, of course, been announced in advance: those who confessed Christ would be crowned; those who denied would be damned.[78] In preparation for this final battle, the bishops mustered the whole people, arming both the faithful and the penitents for the coming struggle.[79]

In this crisis, the bishops sought to delineate the church's boundary most clearly by integrating its marginalized members, the penitents who had remained faithful to the church.[80] They would thereby clearly segregate their communion from the schismatic gathering which had raised itself in opposition.[81] In so doing, they would also assert the efficacy of the rituals which maintained that boundary. Though they continued to recognize the limits of their ability to forgive the sin of idolatry, they forcefully asserted the efficacy of their excommunication: to be refused membership in the communion was to be excluded from the kingdom. Only those whom the church had admitted to communion on earth could be freed by Christ in heaven; all others were bound.[82] Furthermore, they asserted that the rituals actually provided the strength to follow Christ and win the crown of martyrdom. Only those who had received the Holy Spirit in the ritual of reconciliation would be prepared to confess Christ publicly.[83] Only those who shared the eucharistic blood of Christ would be ready to shed their own blood.[84] Finally, the bishops even implied that penitents who confessed Christ through voluntary exile would not gain salvation outside the communion.[85] The bishops so clearly overreached Cyprian's prior teaching because they intended to mark the church's communion as a boundary between those who might expect to be saved and those who definitely would not.[86]

The development of Cyprian's position during the three years following the outbreak of the Decian persecution is remarkable. Initially, it will be recalled, he had insisted that those who had failed could re-enter the communion immediately only by public confession of faith.[87] Under pressure from the Roman clergy, he recognized the importance of the church's peace by admitting all penitents at the time of death. At the end of the persecution, under pressure from his African colleagues, he agreed to admit the penitent certified immediately and the penitent sacrificers at the time of death so that they might be presented to Christ. Two years later, Cyprian and his colleagues again focused attention on the unity of the church and the benefits of its eucharistic fellowship by admitting all the penitent sacrificers into communion. They even drew the baptism of blood inside the communion, implying that the martyrs could win glory only by fighting from within the body of the church.[88] In this, they effectively denied that the schismatics could be saved, even by public confession of Christ.

The bishops of Africa had made their point. Those who deserted during the persecution had been required to acknowledge that they had violated the conditions of church membership. They had to accept a marginal position in the church for three years and then individually submit before being admitted to communion. They had to declare, moreover, that they were prepared to stand firm in the anticipated renewal of persecution.[89] By bowing to the demand for public repentance, the penitent lapsed effectively asserted that those who had relied on the authority of the confessors and joined the laxist communion in opposition to the unity of the church would never be accepted by Christ, even if they died by confessing him on earth.[90] The cohesion of the church, threatened by the desertion of the apostates and the authority of the martyrs, had been effectively restored and maintained.

The bishops may have realized that to continue to exclude the penitents and to allow them to die in the ambiguous condition of martyrs outside the church might have undercut the church's claim to provide exclusive access to the kingdom of God. The penitents had proven their commitment and were ready to defend it in the face of threatened persecution. This was all that the bishops could, and the laity would, require of them.[91] They were joined into the peace of the church.

The stance of the laxists

The principal opposition to Cyprian's position in Carthage, that of the rebel clergy, relied on the authority of the martyrs for restoring the lapsed to communion. By dying in a public confession of faith, the martyrs had guaranteed their immediate entrance into heaven, where they received the crown of their victory from Christ.[92] While they were struggling on earth, the martyrs had been filled with the power of the Holy Spirit and Christ himself had been fighting in them.[93] Enthroned in heaven as friends of Christ, they would judge the nations with him.[94] As his associates, therefore, they seemed to be empowered to intercede with Christ and to win his forgiveness for the sin of idolatry committed by their fellows.[95]

The community's confidence in the martyr's intercession was based upon the belief that a public confession of faith, even without death, was a fully efficacious repentance which satisfied the anger of

God.[96] Those who were assured of this assistance, therefore, were not required to supplement the martyr's authority by their own prayer to Christ and by the works which would demonstrate their repentance.[97] Indeed, some of the imprisoned confessors so trusted the power they would attain by their anticipated martyrdom that they granted letters of peace to their friends, benefactors and all their dependants, so that Cyprian could charge that they were allowing a market in letters of peace to develop.[98] Some authorized their fellows to continue distributing letters of peace in their names after their deaths, even to persons whom they had never met.[99] Finally, these designated agents declared a general amnesty in the name of the martyrs.[100]

Although the martyrs did not require the sinners to follow the normal penitential discipline of prayer, mourning, fasting and almsgiving, they themselves did set certain restrictions on the use of their letters of peace. The fallen were to await the end of the persecution when they could appear before the bishop; they were then to confess their sin and to submit to an examination of their conduct subsequent to the fall; only then were they to receive the peace of the church from the hands of the bishop.[101] The rebel presbyters, however, ignored the traditional limits of the martyrs' authority, the specific conditions they had set in the letters of peace, and the responsibilities of the bishops. Relying on the efficacy of the martyrs' intercession, they not only dispensed with penitential works and prayer to God for forgiveness[102] but admitted the lapsed who held letters of commendation immediately upon the death of the martyr, without the specified rituals of confession of sin, examination of life, and imposition of hands.[103] When certain presbyters balked at this irregular procedure, the lapsed insisted that they be admitted to communion immediately and unconditionally,[104] arguing that the peace which had already been granted by the martyrs in heaven could not be withheld by the clergy on earth.[105]

Cyprian's stratagems prevented their taking over the church in Carthage, so the rebel presbyters and their allies among the confessors and lapsed established a competing community.[106] Their confidence in the power of the martyrs was apparently unlimited: after the persecution, they entered into communion with bishops who had themselves been guilty of sacrifice during the persecution.[107] One of their number was ordained as rival to Cyprian and attempted to win recognition by the church of Rome.[108]

Its distinctive stance on the proper means of winning forgiveness for sins was reflected in the organizational structures of the laxist church. The community's ceding control over its boundary to the confessors and clergy, as well as the unjustified inequality in the treatment they accorded different members of the community, resulted in the loosening of the voluntary bonds which linked the members to one another. The martyrs initially accepted favors, presumably from the wealthy, in exchange for authorizing these sinful benefactors to return to the communion of the church.[109] The faithful were thereby deprived of the right to require that the lapsed demonstrate a higher level of commitment to the church as a whole.[110] The sharing of goods between rich and poor which had been mediated through the common fund was also undermined when the lapsed bribed the confessors.[111] Next, the presbyters – without consulting the community as a whole – proceeded to allow the lapsed back into communion even while the persecution continued. Thus some of the confessors were still in exile and all the faithful were still in danger while these sinners were safe from the power of the empire and the sanctions of the church.[112] The community of life was undermined by the acceptance and even promotion of this private evasion of a common danger.

The patterns of role differentiation were also changed through the abuse of the martyr's power by the clergy and confessors. Those confessors who had been deputized by the martyrs exercised a religious authority which gave them control over the community's boundary, independent of the clergy and the people. The authority granted to the presbyters by the community for performing the eucharistic ritual and thus giving or refusing communion was also turned into a private means of exercising control over the people.[113] The laxist clergy also made distributions of church funds to the poor who had fallen during the persecution and then threatened that any of the faithful who objected to this irregular procedure would themselves be deprived of further financial support.[114] In a similar way, the fallen bishops led by the condemned renegade Privatus of Lambaesis broke free of the control of their colleagues and people; they used the power originally conferred by their community office to establish a competing church.[115] Finally, wealth gave some of the lapsed an influence over the confessors and martyrs.[116] In contrast, the poor were not in a position to negotiate for themselves and consequently fell under the control of the clergy and confessors.

As the personal forms of restraint and interaction which constitute a cohesive voluntary organization began to break down, the opportunity was presented for some members of the community to exercise autonomy and deprive others of even a limited voice in the affairs of the church. When this happened, some who had followed the confessors into the laxist church in Carthage became disenchanted by their dependent status; they deserted their patrons and returned to Cyprian.[117] As group cohesion evaporated in the laxist community, trust in the efficacy of its other rituals seems to have faded. By questioning the power of penance, the laxists had undermined the efficacy of the eucharist as well.[118]

Reconciliation of the lapsed and unity of the church

Since Cyprian and his supporters were attempting to maintain both the cohesiveness and internal differentiation of the church in Africa, they assigned a religious or cosmic significance to the communion of the church. They asserted that the church and the kingdom of God had related boundaries and that God would enforce the same cultic and moral standards as the church. To die outside the communion of the church was to lose the opportunity of entering the kingdom of God. The church's approbation could not guarantee acceptance by God because the community and its leaders could not judge the interior dispositions of the initiant and penitent. The church's rituals were necessary but might prove insufficient in establishing a person's status in heaven as well as on earth.

The ritual of baptism initiated the catechumen into a new relationship with God and the church. Converts made an oath of fidelity to Christ and renounced all that was opposed; God purified them from all sin and sanctified them by the indwelling of the Holy Spirit. The baptized were then admitted to full participation in the eucharist and promised both the financial and religious support of the community. In return for adhering to the moral and cultic norms of the church, Christians expected entrance into the kingdom of God. In baptizing, therefore, the community brought the divine power to bear and effected both earthly and heavenly changes in the recipient.[119] As a result, violation of the baptismal commitment entailed both social and cosmic consequences. The sin of idolatry was directed against God's honor; by breaking an oath of exclusive fidelity, it incurred the threat of eternal damnation. The sin also violated the cultic standard by which the community defined its boundary and thus carried the penalty of exclusion. To justify expelling the sinner, the bishop cited not only the church's need to maintain its identity but more importantly the cosmic significance of the sin: voluntarily associating with an idolater risked bringing down the divine wrath on the whole community.[120] The exclusion of the sinner and the elaborate ritual of readmission also restored the boundary by which the community separated itself from the religious culture of the empire.

Thus the Christians who complied with Decius' order to participate in the Roman cult were immediately excommunicated and required to do penance. Soon, however, pressure began to build to allow the penitents to return. On the cosmic level, the lapsed claimed the intercessory power of the martyrs and appealed to the compassion of Christ, arguments which the bishops could not ignore. Organizational considerations must also have played a part in the bishops' deliberations: a majority of the Christians had failed and a competing church was welcoming them into full and unrestricted membership. Many who had remained faithful, moreover, were sympathetic to the lapsed: the confessors provided letters of peace; some of the faithful admitted that they too would have failed had they not escaped detection; those dependants who had been shielded by the apostasy of their patrons spoke up for them. To allow the sinners to return to communion without destroying the church as a social organization, however, the bishops had to require a voluntary and public commitment to the traditional conditions of membership; the boundary had to be reaff.....ed by the returning sinners and their sponsors. The bishops also had to establish the cosmic significance of their giving of peace: the church's ritual had to be shown capable of changing the apostate's status in heaven as well as on earth. That, however, proved to be the sticking point: the church had not claimed for itself a ritual power to forgive sins committed against God after baptism; specifically, it acknowledged Christ's threat to disown in heaven those who failed to confess him on earth.[121]

The laxists had solved the problem of cosmic efficacy by relying on the martyrs who linked earth to heaven. While in prison, they promised to intercede for the sinners; once they died and were crowned in heaven, they presumably won the forgiveness of the sin of idolatry and the granting of the peace of Christ. The sinner could then claim the peace of the church. In the social realm, however, the martyrs brought too much power to bear: the confessors and their clerical allies did not require the sinners to submit publicly by repenting their violation of the behavioral norms and pledging future allegiance to the community. Thus their method of reintegrating the apostates further weakened that defining boundary

lready been undercut by the original fall into idolatry.
could not adopt this laxist solution: to maintain the
religiously segregated, cohesive society, they had to
control the authority of the martyrs and their agents.[122]
Cyprian's attack on the martyr's power and its abuse by
the presbyters was framed in cosmic and religious terms, its objective and effect was clearly social and organizational as well. Neither the church nor any human being, he asserted, had the power to forgive a sin committed against God, such as idolatry. The church did have a ritual of reconciliation, through which sinners could express their repentance to God and recommitment to the standards of the community. In that ritual, the whole church did intercede for the penitent before Christ. In the case of offenses against human beings, the prayers of the church were presumed to be effective in winning divine forgiveness, so that the sinner could be reintegrated into the church without its incurring the divine wrath.[123] In the case of sins committed directly against God, however, neither the intercession of the church nor the judgment of the bishop could be assumed to be effective in heaven. Thus the bishops could not presume to admit the fallen back into communion.

Although the church could not assert the efficacy of its intercession in winning forgiveness of sins committed against God, still it could not refuse to grant its peace before the penitent's death. The African Christians gave full evidence of believing that unless they died in the peace of the church they could not win a favorable hearing when they appeared before the tribunal of Christ.[124] This belief constituted the popularly accepted cosmic significance of the church's social boundary and the bishops could not ignore it. To refuse to allow the penitents to recross the church's boundary into the realm where salvation was at least available would have undermined the Christians' commitment to the religious significance of the boundary, and to the moral and cultic standard which defined it. In practice, to define a boundary so that it cannot be negotiated by the rituals available to a community is to undermine the significance of the boundary itself.

To maintain the cosmic significance of membership in the church's communion, therefore, the bishops had to find a means of publicly identifying those idolaters who would appear to the community as likely to win divine forgiveness in the judgment of Christ, in whose cases the church's intercession might prove effective, and thus whose presence within the community would not arouse divine wrath. In addition, the process had to restore the integrity of the community itself through the voluntary submission of the sinners to its standards. In the scriptures, the bishops found adequate evidence that God would grant forgiveness to those who sincerely repented of their sin and reaffirmed the standards of the community. Unlike God, however, they could not read the penitents' hearts and discern the truly converted from those who only appeared to repent and reform. By requiring behaviors which manifested interior repentance, however, the church could both identify the sinners whom God might forgive and simultaneously reaffirm the identifying standards of the community itself. Thus the bishops extended the ritual of penance to the sin of idolatry but restricted its heavenly efficacy. The penitents would be admitted to the church, there to be reserved for, presented to, and commended before the judgment seat of Christ. By admitting the idolaters under these conditions, the church granted sinners access to divine mercy without condoning their failure or guaranteeing the success of their appeal. The success of this solution will be examined in the next chapter.

The conflict between the bishops and the laxist clergy focused on the necessity of ritual behaviors by which the penitents would voluntarily re-establish their commitment to the church community. The laxists did not require such a public confession of guilt and a penitential submission: the power of the martyrs had suppressed the control of the community over its own standards of membership. Cyprian and his fellow bishops, in contrast, maintained the voluntary character of the church: the sinners were required to plead their cases before the assembled community, which advised the bishop on accepting them as penitents. In professing repentance before the community and begging God for forgiveness, the sinner affirmed the heavenly import of the behavioral standards which defined the boundary of the church. By performing penitential works and submitting to the imposition of the bishop's hands, the sinner also professed belief in the cosmic efficacy of the church's intercession and ritual of reconciliation. In return, the penitent was granted admission to the communion and promised the church's intercession before the tribunal of Christ.

To fulfill the social and cosmic requirements identified by this analysis, the ritual of reconciliation focused on begging for the divine pardon and on demonstrating submission to the standards of the community. The bishops, of course, articulated these requirements in terms of the satisfaction necessary to meet God's judgment on the repentance in the heart. In actual practice, however, they also upheld the community's need for a demonstration of allegiance and a commitment to prescribed behaviors.

Cyprian's explanation of the process of repentance and reconciliation met both these criteria. The penitent attempted to exercise a personal pressure on God which would result in the granting of forgiveness. Thus the terms which he most often used express insistent asking: *deprecari, orare, exorare, rogare*.[125] The penitent must gain God's favor[126] and win God's mercy.[127] The term *satisfacere* is most often used in connection with these notions of begging.[128] To gain God's forgiveness, the penitent must mourn and pray not simply internally but in action, by fasting, weeping and beating the breast.[129]

In the final sections of *On the Lapsed*, moreover, Cyprian clearly demonstrated the social significance of the practices of penance. The clients of the martyrs, he pointed out, had never ceased to live in the grand manner: feasting, enjoying the public baths, grooming and dressing in the most exquisite manner. How differently they would be acting, he suggested, if one of their loved ones had died.[130] Obviously, they were flaunting the standards for which the martyrs died, the confessors endured torture, the exiles abandoned their patrimony, and the poor lived in fear for more than a year. Clearly, he concluded, the laxists had been blinded and cursed by God so that they would not even perceive their peril.[131] In contrast, the behaviors which Cyprian demanded of the truly penitent would not only placate God but rebuild the community. Days in sorrow, nights in tears, sackcloth, ashes, and fasting were to be the lot of the penitents. They should give themselves to good works, particularly alms-giving. By generous giving, they would not only put God in their debt but emulate the first Christians who held all things in common. The wealth which had been the occasion of failure could become a privileged means of demonstrating solidarity with the community.[132]

Conclusion

The conflict between Cyprian and the laxist presbyters in Carthage might be viewed as a successful popular rebellion against the traditional discipline of permanently excluding all Christians who fell in time of persecution. In such an interpretation, the laxists would have credited the martyrs with the authority to win forgiveness for the sin of apostasy and eventually forced the bishops to claim and exercise similar authority themselves. The fight would be over authority but the consequence would be the lowering of moral standards to a more realistic level. Analyzed in the categories adopted for this study, however, the bishops appear to have adopted a strategy designed to restore community acceptance and enforcement of the behavioral standards defining the boundary of the church. The community retained both the structures through which authority was shared and the traditional conditions of membership. The confessors and the laxist clergy, on the contrary, subverted the received structures and secured exclusive control over the boundary of the community, deprived its members of the authority to enforce it, and thus lowered the level of social cohesion.

The bishops maintained the voluntary character of their churches by encouraging the interplay of personal influence and pressures among the members. Cyprian claimed significant authority for the bishop but recognized the community's right to choose, advise and, in extreme circumstances, depose its leaders. Thus he had to convince the community that the standards he attempted to enforce were appropriate. The community supported the demand that the lapsed do penance and agreed, more reluctantly, to admit even penitent schismatics. In the face of their pressure, however, Cyprian had to allow the reconciliation of the dying during the persecution, the forgiveness of the certified shortly afterwards, and the readmission of the sacrificers in anticipation of renewed persecution. Thus the behavioral moral code provided a clear and accepted boundary demarcation, which was strengthened in the ritual of reconciliation by the penitent's confession of failure, the community acceptance of the signs of recommitment, and the bishop's granting of peace.

Each of the community's actions was justified by a cosmic correlative. In exercising personal control over the universe, God was responding to the moral successes and failures of the church. Negligence had occasioned the persecution; reform and renewal had brought peace; requiring penance forestalled further suffering; making satisfaction might win forgiveness; sympathy for the wounded would be approved but leniency toward the impenitent courted condemnation. The rituals of reconciliation and peace changed the standing of the penitent lapsed both on earth and in heaven, though it could not guarantee their acceptance by Christ.

The laxist presbyters, in contrast, actually undercut the cohesion of the community by acceding to the declarations of the confessors and the demands of the lapsed. They shifted responsibility for the enforcement of the boundary from the whole community to the martyrs, whose authority had been personally achieved rather than granted by the community. By appeal to the privileges of the martyrs, the laxist presbyters and bishops also isolated themselves from the pressures which the faithful, even the dissenting confessors, might have exercised to curb their policies. Without regard for the rights of the other communicants, they extended participation in the eucharist to apostates who refused to appear as penitents before the assembled church. The only counterbalancing power seems to have been that of wealth, employed by the lapsed to gain assistance from the martyrs and confessors. The cosmic justification for this system concentrated power in the hands of the martyrs and confessors. It failed to account for the authority of the clergy, which was derived from the community but exercised autonomously. The impoverished, both faithful and fallen, were disenfranchised and dependent upon the religiously powerful confessors and clergy or their wealthy allies among the lapsed.

Although the laxist rebels attempted to organize an independent communion of bishops and churches, Cyprian and his colleagues successfully turned aside the threat and discredited these foes. The laxist community failed to establish itself outside Africa and did not prosper or survive even at home. The rigorists, as shall be seen, mounted a more sustained threat to the policies of the bishops. Attention now shifts to that challenge.

4

EFFICACY OF THE
RECONCILIATION RITUAL

Cyprian's dispute with the confessors and their supporters among the clergy in Carthage focused on the necessity of the ritual of reconciliation for winning God's forgiveness and receiving the peace of the church. Placing their trust in the intercessory power of the martyrs, these laxists did not require penance or use the ritual of reconciliation in admitting the lapsed to communion. When the African bishops rejected their practice, the laxists established a rival church with its own college of bishops. Though they failed to attract followers outside Africa, the availability of this alternative communion influenced the policies adopted by Cyprian and his colleagues for the reconciliation of the lapsed.[1]

A faction headed by Novatian in Rome took a rigorist stance, refusing to grant reconciliation and communion to the lapsed who submitted to the ritual of penance, even at the time of death. This party made some headway in Italy and Gaul but in Africa it never won a level of popular support sufficient to threaten either the laxists or the Catholics. Still, Novatian's letters and envoys raised questions which forced Cyprian to justify his refusal to maintain the more rigorous positions which he had followed during and immediately following the persecution.[2] In the process of defending the policies adopted in consultation with his African colleagues, Cyprian not only attacked Novatian for the sin of dividing the church but developed an explanation of the power of the ritual of reconciliation to forgive the sin of idolatry – or at least to affect the standing of the apostates before God – and thereby to protect the purity of the church from contamination.

This chapter will begin with a consideration of Novatian's rigorist position and analyze his assumptions about the nature of the church. It will then trace the development of Cyprian's own stance and the basis for his trust in the efficacy of the ritual of reconciliation. Then the role of the social structures of the two communities in the development of their conflicting positions will be examined.

The rigorist rejection of penitents

After the death of Bishop Fabian at the outset of the Decian persecution, the Roman clergy decided to delay the election of a successor and act as a council to guide the church through the period of trial. Their first communication with the clergy of Carthage, in spring 250, offered instruction to a sister church which was also forced to operate without the leadership of its bishop.[3] After exhorting their colleagues to follow the magnificent example which they were themselves providing in strengthening the faithful against the terror inspired by the persecution, the Roman presbyters laid down certain policy directives. Although the lapsed had brought a severe sentence upon themselves, they observed, the extreme fear under which they had acted should be taken into consideration in judging their religious condition.[4] Thus the lapsed should be urged not to lose heart but to undertake penance in hope of winning forgiveness from God. Thus encouraged, they explained, the lapsed might reform themselves and stand firm in the faith if they were brought to trial a second time. They asserted, moreover, that penitents and catechumens should be granted communion when they were in danger of death.[5]

The letter of a Carthaginian layman who had confessed under torture at Rome bears witness to the implementation of these policies by the Roman clergy. Celerinus reported that both the sacrificers and the certified were required to engage in penitential works until a new bishop was appointed and a decision could be made about readmitting them to communion.[6] Having failed to win any concessions in Rome, he appealed to his associates among the confessors imprisoned at Carthage to come to the assistance of mutual friends who had sinned in Rome.

In Carthage, it will be recalled, Cyprian had directed his clergy to follow a parallel but somewhat more restrictive policy, granting peace at the time of death only to those who had letters of peace from the martyrs.[7] Those who had not secured these letters were to continue in penance and trust in the mercy of God.[8] Anyone who found this course of action too risky, or too tedious for the ardor of a revived faith, and insisted upon immediate admission to communion was directed to approach the imperial authorities and recant prior compliance with the edict.[9] Upon receiving a copy of the letter which the Roman presbyters had addressed to his own clergy, however, Cyprian agreed that peace should be given to all the penitents who were in danger of dying.[10] He also wrote to the Roman clergy, assuring them that he had not abandoned the responsibility of governing his church. In evidence of his efforts to guide his people from exile, he forwarded copies of the letters by which he had attempted to stop the abuse of the intercessory power of the martyrs, correspondence which indicated that he had promoted a practice parallel to that of Roman presbyters.[11]

In summer 250, the Romans addressed a series of five letters to Carthage, expressing dismay at the rebel presbyters' practice of immediately reconciling the lapsed who had letters of intercession from the martyrs. The Roman clergy and confessors each addressed their counterparts in Africa; then they each addressed Cyprian; finally the clergy responded to a further letter from Cyprian. Novatian was involved in the composition of some of these letters[12] whose style is notably different from the one sent from Rome earlier in the spring.[13] In the first pair of letters, the Roman clergy not only condemned the sacrificers but accused the certified of having violated their baptismal oath by attempting to evade the Christian commitment to confess Christ.[14] For their own part, the confessors still imprisoned at Rome pointed out that martyrs who undermined the discipline of Christ's gospel within the church would thereby lose the glory of having confessed him before the imperial authorities.[15] Next, the Romans addressed Cyprian himself for the first time, supporting the determined stance taken in the letters he had forwarded to them. The clergy stressed the just severity of the gospel, which their church had always maintained, as well as God's own zeal in enforcing the commandments.[16] They specified that only a penitent whose death was certainly imminent, who was expected to appear before God's judgment immediately, should be admitted to the church's communion.[17] In their own letter, the confessors objected to the practice of the rebel clergy in Carthage, which allowed the fallen to return to the peace of the church even while those still standing continued to suffer persecution. The lapsed, they observed, should remember that they could have retained that place in the church which they so eagerly sought to recover.[18] Furthermore, the confessors accused the laxist clergy of casting the sacred body of Christ to swine in granting communion to the apostates.[19] Finally, the Roman clergy argued that as defenders of the gospel, the Carthaginian martyrs were the least appropriate authors of letters granting peace to the fallen; indeed, such martyrs stood in danger of being classed with the lapsed whom they championed.[20]

The Roman clergy claimed that they and the refugee bishops who had joined their deliberations were attempting to define a moderate course which avoided the extremes of compliance and cruelty.[21] They encouraged all the faithful, including the lapsed, to confess the faith. In response to the challenge of the letters emanating from the martyrs and confessors in Carthage, however, both clergy and confessors were increasingly troubled by the signs of impatience and even impenitence among the lapsed.[22] Novatian may have objected to abuse of the privilege accorded dying penitents and refused to perform the ritual himself.[23]

After the persecution ended, Cornelius was elected bishop and tension between Novatian and his fellow clergy came to a head. Supported by some of the confessors who had spent more than a year in prison, Novatian rejected communion with all the lapsed and established himself as bishop in a rival communion.[24] In consultation with his colleagues in Italy, however, Cornelius adopted the African policy of reconciling the certified immediately and granting peace to the penitent sacrificers before they died.[25] Bowing to pastoral necessity, moreover, he immediately admitted an entire local church community which had been led into sacrificing by its bishop, Trofimus, who was himself received as a layman.[26] Other sacrificers had survived the illness during which they had been granted peace and were allowed to remain in the communion of the church.[27]

The evidence provided by their opponents indicates that Novatian and his allies believed both that idolatry committed by a Christian after baptism could not be forgiven by the church and that the admission of the apostates would make the entire communion a party to their sin.[28] In protecting the holiness of the communion, they focused on the failure to confess Christ and thus distinguished neither the certified from the sacrificers nor those subjected to torture from others who voluntarily complied with the imperial edict.[29] Although the letters Novatian earlier prepared for the clergy and the confessors in Rome had recommended the healing power of repentance to the lapsed and acknowledged the possibility of their attaining salvation,[30] after peace had been given to the church, he refused to grant the fruit of that repentance by reconciling the penitents at death.

Ambiguities in the evidence leave Novatian's interpretation of the situation of the lapsed uncertain. Some indicators suggest that he might have taught that the lapsed were already eternally condemned and that their attempts at repentance were futile. In attacking Novatian's letter to an African colleague, for example, Cyprian argued that the lapsed must be given an opportunity to repent.[31] In addition, a contemporary treatise explained that the rigorists believed that Christ's threat to deny those who had failed to confess him on earth meant that the apostates could not be saved.[32] Thus, after the persecution ended, Novatian may have reached the judgment that the lapsed would never be forgiven by Christ and that as a consequence they could not be admitted to the church.[33] Other evidence, however, implies that Novatian may have continued to urge the lapsed to do penance, and thus that he believed they might obtain from Christ himself the forgiveness which the church could not mediate. Cyprian, in particular, accused the rigorists of inconsistency in exhorting the lapsed to do penance even while refusing them the fruit of that repentance, admission to communion.[34]

A key to understanding Novatian's position might be found in the first letter of the Roman clergy to their colleagues in Carthage. The African presbyters were urged to exhort even their fallen charges to correct their hearts by penance, so that the sinners might reverse their apostasy by confessing Christ if they were put to the test again.[35] A second clue can be discerned in the African bishops' defense against an anticipated rigorist attack on their later policy of reconciling even the penitent sacrificers in expectation of a renewal of persecution. At the end of their letter to Cornelius, the Africans observed that their common rigorist opponents would argue that, in view of the coming persecution, the penitents did not need the peace given by the bishop: God was about to give them the opportunity to confess the faith, to be baptized in the blood of martyrdom, and thus to win not only peace but a glorious crown from Christ himself.[36] A third indicator: when the penitents at Rome joined in parade escorting Cornelius to his arrest, Cyprian extolled their action as a confession of faith, which demonstrated God's acceptance of their repentance.[37] These three observations, spread over three years, suggest that the rigorists might have believed that the proper function of repentance was to strengthen the fallen in faith so that they could actually reverse their sin. By failing to affirm Christ, the lapsed had fallen under his threat of condemnation; by confessing Christ they would win forgiveness and even his commendation before the Father.[38] Once the lapsed had allowed the opportunity for confession during a full year of persecution to pass, however, the rigorists might have judged them bound by Christ's sentence. Cyprian, on the contrary, would find new opportunities for them to bear witness to Christ.

Whatever their beliefs about the possibility of regaining salvation, Novatian and his supporters must have insisted that the bishops had no authority to release the apostates from the sin committed against God. The fallen who had refused the opportunity to raise themselves up by confessing could only be regarded as beyond the assistance of the church.[39] Thus the anticipated renewal of persecution, which Cyprian and Cornelius used to justify admitting the sacrificers to communion, might have been viewed by the rigorists as a divine mercy allowing the fallen a second chance to recover salvation by confessing the faith before the Roman authorities. According to this hypothesis, Novatian could have urged repentance while refusing to offer the peace and communion which the penitents could secure only by publicly confessing Christ.[40]

Whatever Novatian's estimation of the possibility of attaining salvation after once failing to confess Christ during the persecution, his understanding of the nature of the church was clear to Cyprian: only those who were free of the taint of idolatry could participate in the communion. Novatian would have judged that only baptism, in water or in blood, could effectively cleanse a candidate from the sin of idolatry and protect the communion of the church from impurity.[41] Those who had polluted themselves in the demonic rituals had ruined their baptismal purity and would contaminate all who consented to share the eucharist with them.[42] The warning of Christ, therefore, indicated the only remaining means of rehabilitation: anyone who confessed him before his enemies on earth would certainly be acknowledged in heaven.[43]

During the persecution, Cyprian's position had been considerably strengthened by the support of the Roman clergy's opposition to the Carthaginian laxists. At the time of the schism in Rome, he gave Novatian's claim a fair and extended hearing before deciding in favor of Cornelius on procedural grounds.[44] After the split, however, he adamantly opposed not only Novatian's attempt to divide the church but his refusal to grant reconciliation to the penitents, especially at the time of death. To answer the rigorist charge that he had betrayed his principles,[45] he had to elaborate an argument for the efficacy of the church's ritual of reconciliation in the case of the sin of idolatry.

The efficacy of repentance

Cyprian seems to have assumed from the beginning that the sin of idolatry could be forgiven, at least by Christ, perhaps through the intercession of the martyrs, and that the penitent lapsed could be reconciled to the church. Then in dealing with the immediate threat posed by the confessors and the rebel presbyters, he insisted on the necessity of public repentance. As the subsequent controversy in Rome developed and Novatianist envoys argued their case in Carthage, he had to build an argument for the efficacy of the ritual of repentance and find a means to safeguard the purity of the communion.

During the Decian persecution, Cyprian insisted that the lapsed must undertake penance and attempt to win the divine favor through prayer and good works. He initially followed the precedents of the African church which gave the martyrs the privilege of recommending penitents to the bishop for reconciliation.[46] As the summer approached, with its outbreaks of disease, he directed that the lapsed who had been promised assistance by the martyrs should be given the peace of the church if they were in danger of death.[47] Still, Cyprian appealed to this traditional practice primarily to restrain the growing abuse of the martyrs' letters of peace.[48]

Toward those who did not have the support of the martyrs, Cyprian adopted a more restrictive stance: they were to undertake penance and trust in the divine mercy.[49] He refused, moreover, to recognize any meaningful difference between the certified and the sacrificers: both had refused to confess Christ and must undertake penance in patience.[50] Any of the lapsed who genuinely repented their failure and were impatient to regain the communion of the church could, he suggested, win the crown of martyrdom by publicly confessing the faith.[51] Once the Roman clergy had announced its policy of reconciling all the penitent lapsed at the time of death,[52] however, Cyprian's position became untenable and he agreed to follow the common practice.[53] Still, he regarded the public confession of faith as the privileged form of repentance, praising his colleague Caldonius for admitting to communion the lapsed who had washed away their sin by standing firm in a second trial.[54]

As opposition to restrictions on the readmission of the lapsed developed among the laxist clergy, Cyprian began to attack the authority of the confessors and martyrs. In declaring a general amnesty, he argued, the confessors had claimed for their victorious friends a power which only Christ could exercise, which was at work in baptism.[55] Next, he adopted the Roman assertion that a martyr who acted against the discipline of the gospel by granting peace to the unrepentant thereby forfeited all authority before God and the church.[56] Upon his return to Carthage, he repeated and developed this argument by demonstrating from scripture that neither the martyrs nor even the closest friends of God always received even the legitimate favors which they asked.[57] Once again, he refused to distinguish between the certified and the sacrificers, warning both of Christ's threat to denounce them before the Father in heaven.[58]

Novatian had reason to expect, therefore, that Cyprian could be counted upon to uphold the severity of the gospel.[59] Cyprian, however, was faced with a different kind of challenge and developed the principles enunciated by the Roman rigorists to conclusions which they did not anticipate or accept. The revolt and schism led by the laxist clergy made available a new way to confess Christ publicly, reverse their earlier failure, and thereby regain a place in the communion of the church. In his last letter from exile, he identified the revolt of the presbyters in Carthage as a new form of persecution, a second demonic assault on the faith of the community.[60] By undertaking penance, he explained, some of the fallen had begun to rise and were almost ready to stand again. Now the devil was tempting them to give up their penance and accept the false peace offered by the rebel clergy under the patronage of the martyrs. By cutting off penance – the only means of healing – Satan would not only prevent their rising again but destroy them completely. The rebels' offer of immediate reconciliation was the last trial of the persecution, Cyprian warned, in which the lapsed were given the opportunity to persevere in faith and in the hope of winning forgiveness according to the directives of the bishops appointed by God.[61]

In *On the Lapsed*, which he delivered upon his return to Carthage, Cyprian began to build his case for the efficacy of the penance undertaken by the lapsed and the church's ritual of reconciliation in removing the sin of idolatry. The argument had two components: setting limits to the intercessory power of the martyrs and interpreting submission to the discipline of the church as a form of confession of faith. First, Cyprian attacked the authority of the martyrs. If the martyrs asked for something which was in accord with the gospel, the bishop would certainly grant it; if they ordered something contrary to the command of God, the bishop must certainly refuse it.[62] When the martyrs asked for something that was not written in the law of God, however, the bishop must ascertain whether God had granted the favor before acting on their request.[63] The problem they all faced, then, was to discern God's intention for the reconciliation of the lapsed. Was God responding to the petitions of the martyrs or to the works of the penitents and the prayers of the church? In evidence of God's intention, Cyprian recalled his earliest explanation of the persecution as a divine testing of the Christians, intended to draw them from their indifference to a more perfect practice.[64] Some of those who failed had repented their apostasy, had undertaken the works of penance, and had then been found worthy of the crown in a second trial.[65] When other apostates had refused to reform their lives and tried to force their way into the communion of the church under the patronage of the martyrs, terrible punishments had been visited upon some of them as a warning to the rest.[66] Thus, Cyprian concluded, God's intention had been revealed: the sin of apostasy might be forgiven in those who submitted to the penitential discipline of the church but not in those who relied on the intercession of the martyrs alone. Buttressing his argument with the exhortations to repentance which abound in the scripture, he asserted that God could indeed relent and forgive the sin of those who did penance but would surely condemn and destroy those who refused.[67]

The second step of Cyprian's argument showed that submitting to the church's authority was a form of confession of Christ. In his last letter from exile, as noted above, he had identified the revolt of the laxists against the bishops' demand for penance and submission to the ritual of reconciliation as the last and most dangerous stage of the persecution itself. Having wounded the lapsed, the devil now sought to destroy them completely by preventing their repentance. Both the standing and the fallen must resist this final demonic attack.[68] In *On the Lapsed*, he took up this theme again: by resisting this new assault of the devil, by rejecting the false promises of the laxists, by placing their trust in the command of the Father and the warning of Christ, the lapsed were actually defending their faith. Such repentance would win God's favor.[69] Indeed, he concluded, the prayer and good works of the fallen might so move the Lord that they would not only be pardoned but rearmed and strengthened to win the crown of victory by martyrdom.[70]

Thus, Cyprian continued to follow the principles he had shared with Novatian but he developed them differently by exploiting the opportunities provided by the laxist schism within the African church. By identifying the revolt of the laxists against the community's right to judge the apostates as a form of demonic temptation and persecution, Cyprian showed that accepting the imposed penance was a form of resisting the devil and confessing Christ which was both necessary and effective. During the next two years of turmoil, Cyprian developed his argument that protecting the church's unity and defending its boundary against the attacks of both rigorists and laxists was a rehabilitating confession of faith in Christ.

The African bishops met in Carthage in April 251, to determine a common policy for reconciling the lapsed. A delegation seeking support of Novatian's challenge to Cornelius arrived during that extended discussion.[71] Although Cyprian later sought to give Cornelius the impression that the accusations made against him had been rejected without a hearing, the evidence suggests that Novatian's points were considered.[72] The bishops sent their own delegation to Rome to investigate the charges and countercharges before deciding to enter into communion with Cornelius.[73] Although they judged that pastoral considerations ruled out Novatian's program of withholding peace from the penitents, they were apparently sympathetic to his concerns.[74] The African bishops finally decided to relax the standards which they had imposed during the persecution by offering immediate reconciliation to penitents who had obtained certificates without sacrificing. They imposed life-time penance on sacrificers, however, determining that reconciliation would be granted only at the time of death.[75] They refused, moreover, to yield to pastoral necessity as Cornelius had done for Trofimus: they rejected the plea of a bishop who had led his entire congregation into sacrifice.[76]

Though the decisions of his episcopal colleagues relaxed the stand which Cyprian had taken on the certified, they confirmed his rigorous demands that the sacrificers submit to public penance. Thus, in writing to the Roman confessors who had provided invaluable support to him at a critical moment during the persecution and then to Novatian after it, Cyprian challenged not their stance against the admission of penitents but their violation of the gospel by defending it in schism against Cornelius.[77]

During this time, Cyprian addressed the schisms in Carthage and Rome in his treatise *On the Unity of the Catholic Church*.[78] Once again, he attacked the authority of the confessors who had refused to submit to the bishops, comparing them to Judas.[79] Schism, he reiterated, was actually the more ancient and dangerous form of persecution, in which the devil transformed himself into an angel of light and led Christians away from the church, under the deception that they were following the path to salvation.[80] Yet this deadly assault, like the imperial persecution, served Christ's own purposes by testing Christians and separating the good from the evil. Once again, Cyprian exhorted the penitents to seize the opportunity provided by this assault on the church to confess Christ and regain salvation.[81]

Cyprian also defended against Novatian's attack on the decisions of his colleagues in Rome and Africa by focusing on the role of public penance in preparing fallen Christians for public defense of their faith.[82] During the persecution, he recalled, the efficacy of penance had been demonstrated by the subsequent confession and even martyrdom of some Christians who had failed in their initial trials.[83] Clearly, God had heard the groans of these penitents, had rearmed them with faith, and had granted them the crown of victory. He charged that Novatian's practice of denying reconciliation actually discouraged penance and effectively deprived the lapsed of the very means by which they might be restored to faith and rearmed for martyrdom.[84] Thus he concluded that both the laxist and rigorist programs effectively cut off the way to salvation for the lapsed.

Cyprian seems to have found a contemporary, peace-time indication of the efficacy of repentance in the unforeseen effects of reconciling penitents on their death-beds. Novatian objected that this practice was being abused as a loophole through which the sacrificers were being allowed to return to the communion of the church: though not seriously ill, they were reconciled as dying; then not unexpectedly recovering, they were allowed to remain in the communion. After pointing out that the clergy could not murder the penitents as soon as they had granted them peace, Cyprian suggested that their recovery of health should be attributed to God's own kindness and mercy, as a sign that their repentance had proven acceptable.[85]

In defending the agreed policy against Novatianist attacks, moreover, Cyprian argued that other forms of loyalty to the church also had a salvific value for the lapsed. Even as they were apparently denying Christ, for example, some of the lapsed had actually demonstrated a commitment to their fellow Christians. By performing the required sacrifice, some family heads had sheltered and protected the faith of their wives, children and dependants. They had then provided safe haven to exiled confessors and to refugees who had preserved their own faith by flight. Further, many of the certified had openly asserted that they were Christians, had refused to perform the required sacrifice, and had offered to pay a fine instead.[86] The bonds of gratitude joining the faithful to their penitent benefactors effectively undercut the charge of apostasy and put intense pressure on the bishop to assure them eventual admission to the communion. Clearly, the people judged that these demonstrations of loyalty to the community would win God's forgiveness.[87]

This same sensitivity to the fidelity which the lapsed had demonstrated to the church in the face of schism is evident in the bishops' decision to offer reconciliation to all the penitents, in their meeting in spring 253. First the leaders noted that amidst signs that the persecution would soon resume, the lapsed gave evidence that their repentance had been effective: they declared themselves ready to stand and fight for the name of Jesus and so to win salvation.[88] Sound pastoral practice, they judged, required that the bishops strengthen these penitents with the blood of Christ and impart to them the gift of the Spirit.[89] The explanation the bishops offered, however, indicates the pressure to which they were being subjected and the excuse which would justify capitulation to it. The day of judgment, they decided, was fast approaching; they anticipated facing charges of cruelty and harshness if they forced the penitents to fight and die for Christ outside the church.[90]

Finally, the public demonstration of support for Cornelius which the faithful of his church staged at the time of his arrest provided Cyprian yet another opportunity to point out the efficacy of their penitence. The Roman penitents had been restored to communion by parading their faith before the persecuting emperor.[91] Clearly, he proclaimed, God had accepted the repentance of the lapsed and had thereby approved the program followed by the bishops.

Although Cyprian had asserted that the bishops and the church did not have the power to forgive the sin of idolatry, since it was committed directly against God, the laxist schism in Africa did provide the opportunity for him to identify loyalty to the church — to its officers and faithful — as a form of confession of faith in Christ under persecution. Like the imperial action, Cyprian explained, the schism was allowed by God to test and prove the devotion of the standing and the fallen. Those who had withstood the open assault had then to guard against this insidious one. Those who had failed in the first conflict, however, could rise to claim victory in this second battle against the devil. In rejecting the policy of extending the peace of the church to the persevering penitents, he asserted, Novatian and his rigorist followers were obstructing the reforming work of Christ, just as the laxists had done by granting forgiveness too freely.

Still, Cyprian and his colleagues did not claim that they could grant full rehabilitation to the penitents who remained faithful to the church. Resisting the temptation to schism could not be assigned the same efficacy as a public confession of Christ under imperial interrogation and torture; nor had it the cleansing power of baptism. The penitent lapsed, therefore, were neither declared pure nor assured acceptance by God. Yet the granting of the church's peace in the ritual of reconciliation did affect the heavenly status of the penitents. They were promised an appearance before the tribunal of Christ and the entire church's intercessory support, as they pleaded there for mercy and forgiveness. Thus Cyprian contrasted the victorious martyr, who approached the throne of Christ confident of an earned reward, to the reconciled penitent, who came forward trembling and fearful of the judgment which would scrutinize the intentions of the heart.[92] The schismatics and others who remained outside the church in death, however, would be subject to summary condemnation.[93] Fear of such a rejection was evident in the pressure which the lapsed and their supporters exerted to gain readmittance to the church's communion before death.[94]

In the face of overwhelming pressure from the faithful as well as the lapsed, Cyprian and his colleagues found a means of asserting the real but limited efficacy of the church's ritual of reconciliation. Christ had promised to acknowledge those who confessed him and threatened to disown those who had denied him. The apostates, therefore, could be certain of Christ's acceptance only by reversing their prior failure, as confessors or martyrs. Yet, their loyalty to the church under demonic assault might also be accepted by Christ as a rehabilitating renewal of faith. The penitential works, moreover, responded to God's reforming purpose in allowing the persecution and thus had won not only rehabilitation but the crown of martyrdom for some of the fallen. In this way, the bishops argued that the penitents should be brought into the church, there to be preserved for judgment by Christ. The ritual of reconciliation was effective in moving them from certain damnation to a hopeful ambiguity which might issue in salvation.

The purity of the church

Novatian apparently believed and convinced his followers that Christians who had failed to confess Christ during the persecution must not be admitted to the communion of the church. Christ had clearly asserted, he argued, that those who denied him on earth would be condemned by him in the judgment. The ritual of reconciliation, unlike baptism, did not have the power to remove the pollution of idolatry and could not be trusted to cleanse the sinners. He charged, moreover, that the apostates would contaminate the entire church communion. Thus Novatian not only refused to admit the penitent lapsed to communion, even at the time of death, but broke relations with any bishop who had been infected by sharing in communion with them.[95] He insisted that the church could retain its purity only by enforcing the behavioral morality which defined its protective boundary.

As has been seen, Cyprian remained sympathetic to Novatian's insistence on the limits of the church's power to forgive the sin of apostasy. In his initial attacks on the presumption of the martyrs, he upheld the prerogative of Christ and the singular power of the invocation of his name in baptism. The sure and certain way to remove the taint of idolatry, he reminded the lapsed, was the repetition of that baptism by public confession of faith. After the persecution ended, he interpreted submission to the ritual of reconciliation within the church as a form of confession of faith which might win forgiveness of the sin. Because he could not assure the faithful that the pollution of idolatry had actually been cleansed, however, he still had to address Novatian's second charge: that the communion would be contaminated by any contact with unforgiven idolatry. This seems to have been accomplished by a further differentiation of roles within the church.

Initially the idolaters were offered association with the church in the role of penitents. They were required to acknowledge their sin before the community, to beg for the prayers of the faithful, and to perform works or make offerings in support of the church. Although they were excluded from the eucharist during their lifetimes, they had the right to be admitted at the time of death, so that they might appear before Christ's judgment as communicants. As penitents, the lapsed presented no immediate danger to the purity of the communion. The protection provided by their exclusion was lost, as has been seen, when some of the penitents survived the illness which brought them to death's door and thus into the eucharistic fellowship. Since they enjoyed the full peace of the church after their recovery, Novatian charged that they were a source of contamination within the community.[96]

The policies for dealing with the lapsed which were adopted by the Italian and African bishops provided the rigorists with further ammunition. In their meetings immediately after the persecution ended, the bishops had admitted the penitents who had obtained certificates of compliance without actually sacrificing. Cornelius and his colleagues, moreover, had accepted the bishop Trofimus and the entire community he had led in offering incense to the imperial deities. Two years later, in anticipation of a renewal of persecution, the bishops opened the way of peace and reunion for all the repentant sacrificers. Thus the rigorists charged that in accepting the apostates into communion, the bishops had approved their sin and contracted their contagion.

In defending the decisions of his colleagues, Cyprian first appealed to Christ's charge to the pastors to care for the flock. The shepherds could not allow the wounded to be destroyed by the devil.[97] Next, he countercharged that the rigorists were themselves tolerating adulterers in their communion, whose sin violated the temple of God and served in the scriptures as the very symbol of idolatry and cultic infidelity.[98] Having asserted that the rigorists could not elude the charge they mounted against the Catholic bishops, Cyprian then attacked the assumption that the sin of one person could harm another.[99] Most importantly, however, Cyprian exploited a category of membership to isolate the reconciled apostates within the communion and thus protect their fellows from contamination.

Cyprian's community assigned a cosmic or religious significance to the differentiation of roles and categories of membership within the church: the bishop, the clergy, the confessors, the dedicated virgins, and the poor, for example, stood before God in ways which reflected their various rights and responsibilities within the community. The church was already using a special status for members who failed to meet the requirements of their roles. Thus bishops and other clergy who might otherwise have been subject to permanent excommunication were allowed to remain in the communion among the laity.[100] By imposing this permanent disability, the community formally distanced itself from their failure even as it allowed them to share its fellowship. Similarly, the dedicated virgins who had been inappropriately familiar with men but could prove that their physical integrity had not been corrupted were placed in a probationary status.[101]

A distinct station within the communion seems to have been developed for the reconciled apostates as well. The sacrificers admitted to communion were treated as probationers and warned that they must distinguish themselves in the anticipated persecution.[102] Their marginal status within the communion corresponded to the ambiguity of their own relationship to Christ, who had threatened to disown them.[103] None of the lapsed, moreover, was allowed to retain or receive positions of leadership, to be ordained or serve as clergy.[104] As passive participants in the communion and recipients of the church's charity, the reconciled idolaters would not pollute the communion.[105] Thus the bishops seem to have applied a new differentiation in classes of membership recognized within the church and to have given it a cosmic significance.[106] In so doing, they segregated the lapsed within the church and thus safeguarded its purity. In this way, the community was able to arm the penitents for defending the faith and to intercede for them before the bar of Christ's judgment, even as it continued to repudiate their treason and to suspect the sincerity of their repentance.

By elaborating the differentiation of roles within the church, Cyprian and his colleagues were able to uphold the relevance of the behavioral moral standards which had defined the boundaries of the community while recognizing the limits of their power to apply that norm. The intentions of the heart were significant to the salvation of its members but the church could not judge them. The bishops were responsible for guarding against unconverted hearts but only through their outward manifestations. Thus the bishops would distinguish one sin from another by focusing on the actions performed: accepting a certificate was not equivalent to performing a sacrifice; sacrificing under coercive torture was not the same as rushing forward to comply with the imperial edict; offering incense was not equivalent to eating tainted meat.[107] They accused Novatian of following pagan philosophy in judging all sins equal.[108] In a parallel way, the bishops had to credit penitential behaviors on the basis of actual performance: patient and enduring prayer, giving away the possessions which had led to sin, serving the needs of the community, parading behind an arrested bishop, demonstrating loyalty to the church and the bishop. As one behavior formed the basis for excommunication, the other provided a basis for reconciliation. As open apostasy had excluded the lapsed from communion, confessing their sin before the assembly gained them the status of penitents, and continued fidelity to the church eventually won them acceptance as communicants. Yet none of these actions could be assigned the same efficacy as a public confession of faith before the imperial authorities, which would wash away all sin.

In order to maintain the voluntary unity of the Christian community and the moral standards which identified its social boundary, Cyprian and his colleagues focused on the behaviors of the lapsed penitents. Distinction could be made between different types of sins; penitential actions could win the peace of the church. Still they warned the apostates that Christ would judge their intention in both sinning and repenting, that Christ would review and might revise the decision of the church. Thus they admitted the penitents but in a probationary status which permanently restricted their rights within the communion. Distinguishing their own power to judge and to forgive from that of Christ, they recognized that while the earthly church should not attempt to attain that holiness which would be fulfilled in the kingdom of heaven, it did maintain itself pure from the contamination of the idolatrous empire.

The role of social structures

The communities led by Cyprian and Novatian both had a well-demarcated sense of identity. The two churches attempted to enforce a clearly articulated and behaviorally defined boundary separating them from the dominant religious culture of the empire. These were both intentional communities which established and maintained their identifying boundary definitions by voluntary assent of their members. The preceding analysis has suggested, however, that Cyprian, his colleagues and their people were able to reintegrate the apostates into the church through a redefinition of their communal identity which was unacceptable to the rigorists. A review of this procedure may permit comparison with the choices made by the rigorist church led by Novatian. The influence of the social structures of each community can be discerned in their responses to the apostates.

The social structures of Cyprian's church

Cyprian's church at Carthage seems to have been a voluntary community in which the members themselves enforced a boundary defined by fidelity to Jesus Christ and rejection of all competing forms of religious practice, as well as by standards of moral action.

The church used the efficacious ritual of baptism to cleanse its members from the contamination of the idolatry of the Roman state and other cults, as well as from all other sins. Participation in the communion seems to have served as the basis for a presumption that the Christian would be admitted to the heavenly kingdom of Christ. As a consequence, those whose acceptance by Christ appeared unlikely would have been excluded, by episcopal action and common consent, from the communion. Such were any of the virgins – and their male partners – who had violated their consecration to Christ.[109] Such were members of the clergy who had proven unworthy of their office.[110] Such also were the apostates, at least those who had voluntarily sacrificed.[111] In order to protect the distinct reality of the religious community, these persons all had to be excluded from communion until they were purified again through a ritual of public repentance. In the case of some sins, such as voluntary apostasy, reconciliation and readmission to communion were granted only at the time of death.[112] When a majority of the Christians failed during the persecution, however, the community found its established procedure overwhelmed and its identity shaken. Could only the minority of a church's members maintain a communion, from which the majority were permanently excluded as penitents? Cyprian and his African colleagues seem to have led their churches to a solution of this problem by reconfiguring both the external boundary and the internal differentiation of roles.

The community was uncertain that its ritual of reconciliation could be used for readmitting the apostates, because the sin of idolatry was committed directly against God and could not be forgiven by a human agency.[113] The violation of the baptismal oath had ruined the sanctification originally produced by this ritual, which by established tradition could not be repeated. Christ, moreover, had threatened to denounce in heaven anyone who had failed to confess him on earth. As has been seen in the prior chapter, the laxists appealed to the intercessory power of the martyrs in order to win forgiveness directly from Christ. In the process, however, they gave up community control over the behaviors defining their boundary. The rigorists, in contrast, enforced the boundary condition by refusing to credit their ritual of reconciliation with the power to purify and thus qualify those guilty of idolatry for readmission to the communion. They apparently experienced difficulty in maintaining the plausibility of this rigid boundary condition, however, in the face of the sinners' persevering repentance. Cyprian and his colleagues found a way to retain the community's voluntary establishment of the boundary and its behavioral definition, as well as to credit the ritual of reconciliation with a cosmic efficacy which both the laxists and rigorists denied. The elements of his program will be detailed here in a logical order rather than the temporal sequence of their appearance in his letters and treatises.[114]

Cyprian focused attention on the cosmic meaning of the boundary which separated his community both from the Roman world and from the competing Christian groups. He reasserted the community's belief that all who died outside the church would certainly be lost, without any opportunity for salvation. The schismatics who had rebelled against the church, Cyprian consigned to damnation even if they died while appearing to confess Christ.[115] Similarly, he argued that the apostates who had refused to do penance and relied instead on the intercession of the martyrs had already been abandoned by God and were certainly lost.[116] Even Catholic penitents unreconciled at death would presumably have been rejected by Christ.[117] Only those found within the church's communion at the time of the judgment would actually appear before Christ and his saints; they alone would have the opportunity to plead for and gain salvation.[118] Being in the communion was, therefore, a necessary but not a sufficient condition for admission into the kingdom of heaven. Even once reconciled, therefore, the apostates could not be confident of being accepted as they approached Christ's judgment.[119] This interpretation of membership in the communion, moreover, explained the traditional practice of readmitting penitents to communion before they faced the judgment of Christ.

When a threat of renewed persecution arose, the bishops decided that the same privilege had to be extended to the penitent apostates who professed themselves prepared to confess Jesus before the authorities. Their dying as martyrs outside – but not in rebellion against – the church would have given rise to ambiguities in the significance of the boundary as the line of demarcation between those certainly lost and those who might be saved. Clearly, the bishops could not expect to convince their people that Christ would reject penitents who had publicly confessed his name and died as martyrs. In presenting their decision to readmit all the penitents, of course, Cyprian and his colleagues avoided any reference to such a dilemma; instead they focused on the plight of penitents who might suffer accidental death as voluntary refugees.[120] Thus the popular understanding of both the church's boundary and the efficacy of martyrdom may have moved the bishops to avoid the problem altogether by granting immediate peace to all the penitents.

The power of the face-to-face pressure which can be brought to bear in a tightly bounded group is also evident in the bishops' earlier dealing with the reconciliation of apostates. During the persecution, Cyprian insisted that the entire community would have to be consulted in developing a policy for the readmission of the lapsed.[121] The protests of those who had accepted certificates won them the right to immediate reconciliation at the first meeting of the African bishops.[122] The faithful made their influence felt on behalf of the sacrificers as well: many confessed that they also would have fallen under the coercion; others owed their fidelity to the protection provided by a patron who had himself sacrificed. The demonstrated loyalty of the penitents also lent force to their pleas: they had submitted to the authority of the bishop and rejected the communion offered by the laxist presbyters; they had persevered in penitential prayer and good works.[123] Anticipation of a renewal of persecution made this pressure irresistible: could the penitents be expected to abandon their property and risk the dangers of exile without being accepted once again into the community?[124] A refusal to reciprocate the penitents' commitment would have been unacceptable to many of the faithful and resulted in defections from the church.[125] Under pressure from both the faithful and the penitents, therefore, the bishops redrew the church's boundary to include the penitents and provide them the opportunity for salvation. In contrast, Cyprian had to labor to convince the people that returning schismatics, once arrogant and rebellious, might be admitted even into the class of penitents.[126] Though these pressures were exerted and felt within the face-to-face confines of the community, their influence was justified by reference to cosmic realities, particularly the judgment which Christ himself would soon pass on the bishops.[127] Thus Cyprian articulated the community's own understanding of the meaning of its boundary definition and the cosmic significance of both admission and exclusion.

The community's belief that the loyal and submissive penitents ought to be readmitted to the communion so that they could be presented with its prayers to Christ for judgment was also the basis for its trust in the power of the ritual of reconciliation to effect the purification necessary for crossing the church's boundary. When Cyprian interpreted the laxist rebellion as a renewal of the demonic attack on the community's religious identity, he provided a way for understanding submission to the bishop and loyalty to the faithful as a form of adherence to Christ under persecution. This in turn linked the ritual of reconciliation to the cosmic efficacy of public confession of the faith. Thus the imposition of the bishop's hands, the offering of the penitent's gift, the sharing of the eucharist could free even one who had sinned directly against God from the certainty of condemnation and guarantee a hearing before Christ. Those whom the bishop and people loosened on earth might indeed be loosened by Christ in heaven; those whom they held bound, however, would certainly be held bound.[128]

Such ambiguity as remained in the interpretation of the church's boundary and the power of its ritual of reconciliation to cleanse the stain of idolatry arose from a clearly articulated difference between the standard of judgment which the community could enforce and that which only Christ himself could apply. The bishops and people, as Cyprian explained, could judge only on the basis of behavior: those who had submitted to penance and professed themselves prepared to defend their faith must be accepted. Christ, however, could read and judge the intentions of the heart: he would detect and reject those who had dissembled and deceived the church in order to gain its peace.[129] In the same way, the standing faithful who volunteered that they had intended to comply with the imperial edict had they been questioned were not excluded from communion or treated as fallen but were warned to repent and ask Christ's forgiveness.[130] Still, the church's behavioral standard itself retained a certain priority which Christ was expected to confirm: no martyr need fear being found unworthy on the basis of hidden intentions; penitents whose bishops dissented from the common policy and refused them the church's peace were lost, though the bishops themselves would answer to Christ for their lives.[131] In thus making provision for an additional standard of judgment, based on intention, which would be administered by Christ alone, the church limited and thereby justified the efficacy of its ritual of reconciliation and accounted for the difference between its boundary and that of the kingdom of heaven.

Against the objections of the rigorists, as has been seen, Cyprian's church had to satisfy itself not only that its granting of peace on earth might extend to heaven but that its ritual of reconciliation could purify the sinner and protect the church from pollution. For this purpose, it used a differentiation of roles. Communities which espouse not only a well-defined boundary but a hierarchy of rights and responsibilities tend to use their rituals as powerful tools not only for defending against external evil but also for controlling conflict and contagion within the group. The church, as has been seen earlier, had a set of well-differentiated roles and could deal with sin by shifting members from one status to another. The clergy who took to flight during the persecution, for example, were suspended from office for conduct which won praise for the laity.[132] Dedicated virgins who failed to maintain their status were urged to join the ranks of married women within the communion.[133] The reconciled apostates, like Christians who had been guilty of other kinds of serious sin, were assigned a restricted role within the communion. In this probationary status, they were more easily expelled for a subsequent failure and, in particular, were excluded from leadership roles in the ritual life of the community. These restrictions clearly dissociated the community as a whole from their sinful behavior and signaled the ambiguity of their religious status. Christ, who judged intention as well as action, could be trusted not to hold the entire community responsible for the sin which it so clearly condemned even in extending its support to the penitent sinners.

Further evidence of the efficacy of this role differentiation in limiting the spread of the pollution of idolatry within the church can be seen in the power which Cyprian assigned to both the demonic and the Christian rituals. Although contact with idolatry, even involuntary, might harm and even destroy individual Christians, its power could not be compared with that of the church's ritual, the eucharist. During the persecution, it will be recalled, the Roman confessors charged the laxist presbyters in Carthage with throwing pearls to swine by admitting the lapsed to communion.[134] In contrast, Cyprian subsequently pointed out that the real danger was to the swine rather than the pearls: those tainted by idolatry were burned by the consecrated bread or choked when they drank from the cup.[135] Later, the purified penitents were allowed to receive the precious blood so that it might strengthen them to shed their own for Christ.[136] Unlike the rigorists who seem to have regarded their rituals as vulnerable and liable to serve as carriers of pollution, Cyprian and his people viewed them as powerful – cleansing or destroying – but incapable of themselves being polluted or of transmitting contamination.[137]

Analysis of the social structures of the African church indicates the means which the bishops and people used to solve the problem of readmitting the lapsed into the communion. The boundary was so defined as to allow the inclusion of Christians who had proven themselves worthy of being presented to Christ for judgment, even if his own approval of them could not be presumed. The various stations in the church were so specified as to isolate those whose overt behavior had created doubts about their religious status. The community was able to limit its judgment to the behavior of sinners and penitents; it left the intentions of the heart for Christ to assess. Thus it could trust its rituals – baptism, eucharist and reconciliation – to achieve their earthly purpose and to effect a real – though less complete and secure – change in heaven.

The social structure of the rigorist church

The correlation which has been established between the social organization of Cyprian's church and its successful response to the problem of reconciling the lapsed raises the possibility of a similar analysis of the rigorist community led by Novatian. Such an investigation, however, is hindered by the quantity and quality of the evidence. Novatian's surviving writings on the subject are limited to the letters he drafted for the clergy and confessors during the persecution, two of which have been preserved. His rebellion against Cornelius and his stance on the status of the apostates was reported only by his opponents. Unrelated treatises and the exhortations which he addressed to his community might provide some indication of the attitudes they shared. Even from such meager evidence, however, some points are clear.

Novatian's community was an intentional and exclusive group. Each of its members made the decision to break away from the established Christian church in Rome, protesting the admission of the lapsed into its communion. For the purpose of preserving a community free of contact with idolatry, they set aside the significance of church unity and of the established procedures for the selection of church leaders. For the most part, they maintained this commitment to purity even when some imprisoned confessors who had originally supported them abandoned the cause and in spite of the continuing attacks of the bishops who supported Cornelius and his policy of reconciling the lapsed.[138] The community may even have used its eucharistic services as a ritual of renewing commitment to the church and its ideals.[139] Thus Novatian's community may have been more intentionally cohesive than that of either Cyprian or Cornelius.

This rigorist church defined its boundary by an active fidelity to Christ. In the letter he drafted for the Roman clergy during the persecution, Novatian asserted that the baptismal commitment forbade all stratagems by which a confession of faith might be avoided.[140] No distinction, therefore, could be made between those who had employed legal fictions to obtain certificates and those who had actually sacrificed, either voluntarily or even under coercion.[141] To Christians of this persuasion, Cornelius' decision to readmit the bishop Trofimus and his entire community despite the fact that they had been guilty of sacrifice would have provided adequate cause for rebellion.[142] Furthermore, the decision of the council gathered in Rome to grant peace to the certified would have confirmed Novatian's followers in their opposition. This church then steadfastly refused to readmit anyone who had been tainted by idolatry after baptism, denying even the traditional deathbed reconciliation to penitents.[143] The community's concern with the pollution of idolatry was also evident in Novatian's later exhortations. His treatise on the Jewish food law singled out the prohibition of food offered to idols as the one element of these regulations which had not been abrogated by Christ. Dedication to the demon, he explained, ruined the goodness which the Creator originally bestowed upon these meats.[144] Novatian and his people, it seems, established their individual and communal identity on a commitment to Christ which tolerated no compromise with competing religious practice.

The particular cosmic significance which the Novatianist church assigned to its boundary remains somewhat ambiguous. Certainly, the community believed that it could retain its saving relationship to the kingdom of heaven only by excluding idolaters. Further, it asserted that communion with idolaters had destroyed the sanctifying power of the rituals of the other communities.[145] While the rigorists believed that the church had not been given the power to forgive the sin of apostasy, they might have believed that Christ himself could release the penitents from their bondage at the judgment.[146] A number of indicators of such a view can be identified. During the persecution, it will be recalled, Cyprian himself had enunciated just such an understanding of Christ's sovereign freedom to judge what the church could not.[147] Later, he charged the Novatianists with inconsistency in exhorting the apostates to penance but refusing them communion.[148] The Novatianists might also have expected that repentance would lead to the reversal of idolatry by public confession of Christ or even martyrdom. Cyprian offered this as a motive for repentance while he was still denying reconciliation.[149] In defending their decision to readmit the sacrificers, the African bishops anticipated what may have been a

Novatianist objection that the penitents could win the crown of martyrdom even outside the communion.[150] These rigorist Christians, therefore, may have assumed that idolaters excluded from the church could still be saved by actions performed outside the unity of the church. Unlike Cyprian's community, therefore, the Novatianists might have recognized that the kingdom could extend beyond the communion of the church.

Whatever heavenly significance the rigorist church assigned to its earthly boundary, concern for its definition and defense tended to suppress the significance of the differentiation of roles within it. Novatian did retain the hierarchical structure of the church: he had himself consecrated bishop by the requisite three colleagues and then sought recognition and sharing of communion with other bishops; he subsequently ordained and sent out bishops to establish faithful communities in cities where he judged the existing churches as having failed. Still, Novatian and his supporters subordinated the cosmic significance of the church's offices and the procedures for filling them to the overriding value of fidelity to Christ. Although he had agreed to a broad consultation of bishops, clergy and laity to establish a policy for dealing with the lapsed, he refused to credit the resulting consensus when it opposed his own convictions on the demands of Christian faith.[151] He then violated the procedure established for selecting a new bishop by arranging his own ordination after Cornelius had been elected and installed. Though he sought an admission into the communion of other bishops, his objective seems to have been gaining adherents to his own position rather than extending recognition to bishops who disagreed with him.[152] When his initiatives were rejected, he ignored the practice of local control of church office by choosing, ordaining and sending out replacements for established bishops who opposed his policies.[153] Novatian also seems to have denied the religious significance assigned to role differentiation by other bishops. From his viewpoint, Trofimus' having been shifted out of his episcopal role seems to have been irrelevant: no sacrificer could be admitted to communion.[154] Finally, in his exhortation to modesty, Novatian urged a similar practice of sexual continence on all the members of the church and did not differentiate a greater reward to be gained by the virginal state. In all its forms, he explained, chastity divides the Christian from the Roman culture.[155] In all these ways, Novatian's rigorist community seems to have suppressed the traditional significance of differentiated roles.

In comparison to Cyprian's community in Carthage, therefore,

Novatian's church seems to have been slightly higher on the group-identity scale and lower on the role-differentiation one. The rigorists might be expected to have focused the power of their rituals on maintaining the boundary and to have made an appeal to intention as much as behavior in defining standards of morality within the community. As shall be seen in a subsequent chapter, Novatian did protect his church's boundary by repeating baptismal purification when a convert came from a rival Christian community. Unlike Cyprian, moreover, his analysis of the sin of idolatry highlighted the pollution of the conscience which preceded the defilement of the hands and lips by sacrificing. Thus he asserted that sacrifice and certificate were religiously equivalent forms of failure, each betraying an unfaithful heart.[156] Finally, his treatment of the Jewish food laws used an allegorical method, finding the approval and prohibition of various animals in the moral symbolism of their modes of life rather than in contact with a contaminating evil.[157]

Novatian's fear of contamination of the church by the evil of idolatry seems, then, to be related to the tightly bounded but internally undifferentiated social structure of his community. A voluntary community which is focused on maintaining its boundary as a defense against the encroachments of a threatening evil will tend to be egalitarian in applying the behavioral code which defines its border. In the absence of differentiated roles, with the variety of behavioral standards and rituals which establish them, it would be unable to isolate and check the spread of contagion within the community. Its only option would be the radical one of permanent expulsion. Its concern with the internal purity of the community would help focus its ethical codes on the inward intention as much as the outward practice of its members. In such a group, evil may therefore be transmitted simply by consent, even the tacit consent of allowing a sinner to share the eucharist.

Conclusion

Analysis of the process by which the Christians who failed during the Decian persecution were reintegrated into the churches demonstrates that the African bishops relied on both the community's boundary and its internal differentiation of roles. They established that the ritual of reconciliation could provide an effective means of crossing the boundary when both the penitent's action and the community's judgment affirmed the cosmic significance and the voluntary definition of the boundary. In the face of the laxist schism, submitting to the church could be understood as confessing Christ. Segregating the reconciled penitents in a limiting role within the communion could also protect the community from participating in their failure.

By maintaining its behaviorally defined boundary and class structure, Cyprian's church also strengthened the efficacy of its rituals. Not only did the imposition of hands in reconciliation and sharing in the eucharist modify the standing of the penitents before Christ but these rituals conferred the Holy Spirit and empowered the Christians to repel the attacks on their faith and secure the victory which had earlier eluded them.

Finally, the community was able to assert a behavioral or performance-based morality through which it could actually enforce its boundary and class structure without neglecting all considerations of intention and purpose. Because Christians believed that Christ had reserved to himself judgment of interior dispositions, they could tolerate a level of moral and religious ambiguity among fellow communicants which apparently proved impossible for the rigorists.

The rigorists, in contrast, viewed themselves as vulnerable to contamination from a threatening evil which was held at bay only by strict enforcement of the behavioral standards which defined their boundary. Refusing to assign cosmic significance to internal role differentiation, they enforced purity rules in an absolute and egalitarian manner. Thus this church insisted on the efficacy of baptism and distrusted the ritual of reconciliation. Novatian's eucharistic ritual served as a focus for expressing and renewing interior commitment to the ideals of the community but it was vulnerable to contamination and lacked the cosmic power to repel evil. The tightly bounded, egalitarian community seems to have feared the presence of evil hidden in its midst; it sought constant reassurance of the interior dispositions of its members. Thus the rigorists attempted to enforce an intentional as well as a behavioral moral standard.

Given the differences in their social structures and corresponding religious assumptions, it should be anticipated that Cyprian and Novatian would have had different reasons for their common stance on the necessity of rebaptizing converts from competing Christian communities. Before the analysis turns to this issue, however, the competing views of the unity and organization of the local church must be considered.

5

INDIVISIBILITY
OF THE CHURCH

Cyprian's interpretation of the laxist schism as a demonic attack on the church turned the revolt into an opportunity for the penitents to exhibit their loyalty to Christ and thus reverse their failure in the imperial persecution. This identification of submission and fidelity to the church as a form of confession of Christ rested upon a belief that Christ had conferred the power to bind and loosen upon Peter and his successor bishops. Thus the laxist altar and eucharistic communion set up against that over which the bishop presided was a rejection of divine ordinance. The rigorist schism at Rome, in which the church divided between Cornelius and Novatian, raised the question of legitimate succession from one bishop to the next. As these two schisms developed, moreover, Cyprian was faced with first a Novatianist and then a laxist rival, each of whom claimed to be the true bishop of Carthage. The unity of the local church, built upon its bishop and the eucharistic communion gathered under his leadership, became the focus of the debate. The understanding of the universal communion of bishops, its common power to sanctify, and its shared responsibility for governing the church grew out of the debate about the local church; it will be considered in chapter 8. The present study will consider first the divisions within the church in Carthage during and immediately after the persecution. Attention will turn next to the problem of competing bishops in a single city which began in Rome and then spread to Africa. A statement of Cyprian's understanding of the unity of the local church will conclude this chapter.

The crisis in Carthage

During and immediately after the Decian persecution, Cyprian had to deal with four issues which affected the unity of the Christian church in Carthage. He provided an explanation of the persecution itself which called the community to greater cohesion and avoided singling out any one group for blame. He also had to exert control over the exiled confessors who proved to be a divisive force within the church. His major problem, however, was the usurpation of the roles of the community and its bishop in the penitential process by a group of presbyters. Then, as he returned to Carthage from his own exile, Cyprian labored to re-establish the structures which guided the common life of the Christians in face of the challenge to his leadership and the division in their eucharistic fellowship.

Reasons for the persecution

Discord and division within the church provided the earliest recorded explanation which Cyprian offered to his community for the suffering its members were undergoing in the persecution. Shortly after his flight from Carthage, Cyprian claimed a vision in which the church refused God's order to pray in concord for certain of its members.[1] The only conflict attested in the surviving evidence which might offer an interpretation of this prophecy had arisen when a group of presbyters opposed the election of Cyprian as bishop but were overruled by the people. Cyprian's biographer claimed that the bishop's patience and goodness later won over his opponents but Cyprian himself asserted that they consistently worked against his administration and were eventually excluded from the church.[2] One of the presbyters, Novatus, had already been accused of various crimes and the outbreak of persecution forestalled the hearing which had been expected to result in his removal from office.[3] Whether the vision Cyprian reported referred to this division, so that members of one faction in the community were refusing to pray for their bishop or clergy, cannot be determined. Still, the causes of discord within the church were widely enough known for Cyprian to allude to them in such veiled terms and significant enough to provide a plausible explanation for the catastrophe which God had allowed to descend upon the church. Cyprian's primary concern, however, was the danger of discord and disintegration of the community under the imperial pressure. As the persecution continued, he attempted to secure the unity of the church by urging others to join him in contributing funds to aid their fellows who were suffering from loss of property or livelihood.[4] During the year its bishop was in exile, however, the divisions within the church at Carthage became more active.

Return of the exiled confessors

The first set of Christian confessors were not subject to torture by imperial officials but instead were deprived of their property and sent into exile. Some of them returned to Carthage in triumph and apparently considered themselves unrestricted by either Roman law or the behavioral standards of Christian faith. They may have considered their salvation secured by their confession of Christ. When their conduct was reported to Cyprian, he proposed to return to the city himself to deal with the conflicts. His advisers convinced him, however, that his presence would be far more dangerous for the community,[5] so he asked the clergy to take responsibility for the church in his stead.[6] He also took the precaution of writing directly to the confessors as a group, urging that they not only support the efforts of the clergy but use the considerable influence of their own status to control their disruptive fellows who were dishonoring the good name of all confessors.[7] In this and subsequent conflicts he enlisted the active engagement of all members of the community in enforcing its standards rather than asserting his episcopal authority alone.

The revolt of the presbyters

The problem which was to dominate the period of the persecution and several following years involved a usurpation of episcopal and community authority by a group of clergy, some of whom had originally opposed the election of Cyprian. Using their position as delegated leaders of the eucharistic ritual,[8] they welcomed back into communion those of the lapsed who had secured letters of peace from the martyrs.[9] They neither required the penitential ritual nor awaited the return of the bishop at the end of the persecution, as they had been instructed.[10] In response, Cyprian cautioned the confessors that the assistance they provided to the lapsed was being abused and threatened to suspend the clergy for violating the directives they had received.[11] Cyprian again tried to defend the rights of the community as a whole and to secure broad support for the established structures of authority, even when he had to assert the privileges of his own office against those claimed for the martyrs.

Cyprian's contention that the lapsed must not be allowed back into the eucharistic communion until God had ended the persecution and thus granted peace to the whole church seems to have won broad agreement.[12] He argued that those who had secured their persons and property from the imperial threat by performing the idolatrous sacrifice should not be welcomed into communion while the confessors who were upholding the community's fidelity to Christ were still suffering in exile or prison, having forfeited all their goods.[13] The confessors themselves picked up this point and specified that the clergy should act upon the letters of peace they were granting only at the end of the persecution.[14] Even some of the lapsed recognized its force and agreed to await the cessation of danger and the return of their bishop before petitioning for the church's peace.[15]

Next Cyprian argued that the reconciliation of the lapsed on recommendation of the martyrs was a change in the policy and practice of the church, which would affect everyone in the community. His constant practice in such matters, he recalled, was to act only upon the advice of the clergy and consent of the people.[16] Any decision made in Carthage, moreover, would have repercussions throughout the churches of Africa and thus would require consultation with the other leaders.[17] A delay would thus be necessary until the danger had passed and the bishops could safely assemble with the clergy and the people. Although the confessors did not concede that the consultation of the bishops was necessary for the implementation of their directives, they did recognize that the crisis was not a local one. After being petitioned for letters of peace in favor of the lapsed in Rome,[18] they issued a general declaration of forgiveness for all the lapsed and directed Cyprian to inform his fellow bishops of their decree.[19]

When some presbyters began to welcome the lapsed into communion on the basis of the letters of the martyrs alone, Cyprian objected that this procedure violated the right of the people to advise on the reconciliation of individuals who had been excluded for public sin. The lapsed, he pointed out, should have confessed their sin before the assembled community; their penitence should have been publicly enacted to demonstrate their repentance and recommitment; their conduct would then have been judged by the bishop with the advice of the people. Only after these communal actions might they have been readmitted to communion through the ritual of imposition of hands by both the bishop and the clergy.[20] In usurping the authority of the bishop and in trampling the rights of the clergy and people, the offending presbyters had not even respected the restrictions which the martyrs and confessors had themselves placed upon their patronage.[21] In their decree of general forgiveness, if not in their earlier letters for individuals, the martyrs and confessors had specified that the lapsed were to acknowledge their sin before the community and submit to the judgment of the bishop on their conduct since the time of their failure.[22] Though they made this concession to the authority of the bishops, Cyprian observed, the confessors had made its exercise extremely difficult.[23] The lapsed would demand that the peace which the martyrs had won for them in heaven should be granted on earth without either delay or restriction. In some towns, he reported, mobs of sinners forced the clergy to admit them to the eucharist.[24] Cyprian appealed directly to the people to enforce their rights to receive an apology and to exact satisfaction for the betrayal of the shared commitment.[25]

In claiming his own rights as bishop, Cyprian tried to present himself as acting on behalf of the community as a whole. On one significant point, however, he clearly distinguished the episcopal authority and power. The confessors were willing to recognize the parts played by the community, clergy and bishop in actually conferring the peace of the church. The power to forgive the sin of apostasy, however, was not only claimed by the martyrs themselves and the confessors serving as their agents but acknowledged by the lapsed seeking the letters of peace, those clergy accepting them, and those people who tolerated the readmission of the apostates. Cyprian was willing to concede the right of the martyrs to intercede before Christ and to advise the bishop in judging individuals.[26] He insisted, however, that within the church only the bishop had been given the power of binding and loosening.

This conflict between the privilege of the martyr and the authority of the bishop developed in three stages. First, Cyprian asserted the point which the rebel presbyters were contesting: the bishop is appointed by God for the governance of the church during the present time; judging belongs to him and submission to his authority is a necessary sign of repentance.[27] Second, groups of lapsed wrote to Cyprian, presuming to speak for the church and demanding that he recognize the peace granted them by the martyrs.[28] Instead of undertaking public penance and petitioning for reconciliation, they laid claim to the status on earth which the martyr Paulus had promised to secure for them in heaven immediately.[29] In response, Cyprian cited Mt. 16.18–19, as a justification of the structure of authority in the church: Peter was appointed the first bishop, upon whom Christ laid the foundation of the church; the power given to Peter by Christ was passed to his successor bishops, who then held and exercised it within their individual communions.[30] In his last letter from exile, he repeated the text and drew out its implications: the bishop, not the martyr, was autho-rized by Christ to forgive sins; no sinner could find sanctification and salvation through another source.[31] Third, Cyprian began to question the intercessory influence of the martyrs. How could they claim to sway the judgment of Christ because they had professed the faith when they were advising others to disregard Christ's teaching in the gospel.[32] Cyprian would focus this battle on the bishop's status as the successor recipient of Christ's commission to bind and loosen within the unity of the church and on the limita-tions of the martyr's power to intercede before Christ.

To prevent his own isolation from the community in a stand-off against the confessors, Cyprian began to form alliances with some who had actually suffered for their faith and thereby countered the rebel presbyters and their supporters. He appointed four of them to clerical office and promised them promotions in the future.[33] He established a commission including two exiled bishops and two of his own presbyters; of the four at least three can be identified as confessors.[34] These commissioners were to determine whether all the impoverished Christians supported by community funds had indeed remained faithful during the persecution.[35] They were also to recommend candidates for ordination, presumably to replace both lapsed and rebellious clergy.[36] This action precipitated an open conflict with the rebels, who countered that anyone who maintained communion with Cyprian would be excluded from their own fellowship and denied its funding.[37] The excommunication of some rebel leaders[38] was supported by a minority of the clergy and a portion of the faithful, including some penitent lapsed.[39] Cyprian was provoking strategic divisions in order to secure a larger unity.

The rebels proceeded to establish a rival communion, headed by five presbyters, which included other clergy and confessors, many lapsed, and some faithful who followed the guidance of the confes-sors. This group did not, however, elect and ordain its own bishop. Instead, the dissidents apparently intended to maintain pressure on Cyprian and force him to admit the entire group into communion on the terms specified by the confessors.[40]

In his last letter from exile, Cyprian analyzed the rebellion as a series of attacks on episcopal authority. First, the dissidents had refused to recognize God's own providential government of the church in the people's original selection of Cyprian to be their bishop.[41] When the persecution broke out, these same rebels sullied the glory of the confessors and set the people against their bishop by granting the lapsed immediate admission to the eucharist, contrary to the directives of both.[42] Once the imperial persecution finally ended, they took up the devil's work by impeding the repentance and restoration of the fallen and hindering the efforts of the bishops to govern the churches.[43] Finally, they had attempted to set up a separate altar and establish a new priesthood.[44]

Cyprian asserted that the unity of the communion rested upon a heavenly foundation: as God is one and Christ is one, so must the church be one. The union of church and bishop was also based upon divine ordinance: the Lord himself established a single church upon a single bishop, signified by Peter. To reject the bishop's authority and gather a rival communion around a second altar served by an opposing priesthood, therefore, violated the order which God had established. Such insurrection must, therefore, be branded as adultery, impiety, sacrilege, and even idolatry.[45] The rebels, therefore, carried a contagion which could spread disease throughout the entire body of the church.[46] Thus he insisted that every Christian must resist this attack on the unity of the church. The faithful should shun the rebels, flee their pollution, and continue to stand fast in the faith. The lapsed, who had been deceived by the wiles of the devil in the first trial, now faced an even more insidious temptation: the false communion offered by the rebels was actually another denial of Christ. In revolting against the bishops established by the Lord, the fallen would make themselves permanent exiles from the church and would never be forgiven by God.[47] Whoever gathers apart from the bishop and the church, Cyprian reminded the people, was scattered and lost.[48]

Even though he remained separated from Carthage in his exile, Cyprian had managed to meet the threats which might have resulted in the dissolution of the community or his own isolation. He had characterized the misbehavior and usurpations of the confessors and presbyters as violations of the rights of the other members of the community as well as the bishop. He had won the support of a number of confessors and the acquiescence of at least a minority of the lapsed for his policy. He had asserted the rights of his office within the context of its service to the whole church. Most importantly, he had won the delay necessary for building a coalition which would isolate the rebels and allow him to confront the problems in person.

Restoring the structures of the church

In returning to Carthage, Cyprian faced the task of reviving the processes through which the community regulated its life and

justifying the procedures which had been challenged by the persecution and the usurpations of the clergy. He clearly demarcated the
membership of the church and insisted on the marginalized status
of the lapsed. He then specified the privileges of the confessors
within the community and reclaimed the roles of the bishop and
people in the process of reconciling penitents. He also advanced an
interpretation of the conflict and division within the church as a
form of persecution, in which Christ could again be confessed or
denied. Finally, he brought the communal authority of the bishops
to bear within local churches.

In the treatise *On the Lapsed*, which Cyprian seems to have delivered as an oration to the assembled community upon his return to
Carthage, he clearly marked the line dividing the core community
from those who were at the margins. Though he recognized the
achievements of those who had suffered for their faith, he classified
them with all the rest who had avoided public apostasy, honoring
all as confessors. Thus he asserted that a passive protection of
Christian commitment by allowing the imperial decree's deadline
for performing the sacrifice to pass unheeded or by voluntary flight
into exile to avoid confrontation with the authorities was as effective a witness to Christ as public proclamation, even under
torture.[49] By honoring all the standing faithful as confessors, he
continued to undercut the special status claimed for those who had
actually been apprehended and tried.[50] His classification of the
fallen was equally global: any who had voluntarily obeyed the edict
by sacrificing, or capitulated under torture, or acquired certificates
of compliance either personally or through an agent without actually sacrificing.[51] All these he placed at the margin of the
community and urged to undertake penance in the hope of
attaining God's mercy.[52] By acknowledging that they would have
fallen if actually confronted by the imperial officials, some of the
standing faithful challenged this stark classification scheme.[53]
Though Cyprian praised their forthrightness and urged others to
imitate their confession, he required only private repentance of their
weakness.[54]

In this same oration, Cyprian further attacked the claim that the
martyrs could win forgiveness for the sin of apostasy. He recognized
that they could intercede for the fallen but specified that this would
be done before the tribunal of Christ himself, when he returned to
judge all. They had no role in the meantime, however, while the
bishop judged in Christ's place within the church.[55] Elaborating his
earlier argument, he observed that since their power to petition was

based upon Christ's promise to acknowledge those who confessed him, it must be limited by the corresponding threat to deny those who had denied him. To ignore the threat was to abandon the promise.[56] Unlike the bishop, then, the martyrs had no scriptural basis for an authority to bind and loosen, or even assurance of effective intercession.[57] Cyprian would later argue that the intercessory role of the martyrs was shared by other Christians; even those who had remained standing only through the protection of others could intercede with God for their excommunicated benefactors.[58]

The competition between the episcopal and presbyteral communions within the church at Carthage evinced the overriding value which the African Christians set upon participation in the unity of the eucharistic fellowship. During and immediately after the persecution, many confessors and a majority of the clergy refused to support the bishops' policy of withholding this essential means of salvation or granting it only at the moment of death. All apparently believed that even the intercessory power of the martyrs in heaven would be salvific only if the apostates were first admitted to the church's communion on earth.[59] While sharing this belief in the efficacy of eucharistic participation, Cyprian denied its saving power to the competing altar set up for the rebel presbyters' fellowship. In Peter, he asserted, Christ had established the bishop as the foundation of the church's communion; altar, priesthood and bishop's throne were consequently inseparable. Any communion gathered against the bishop was opposed to the church, to Christ and to God; sharing in it would prove an obstacle rather than an aid in gaining access to heaven.[60]

By reclassifying the penitents and confessors, by devaluing the influence of the martyrs, and by insisting on the authority exercised by the bishop, Cyprian moved to re-establish the processes of public repentance and reconciliation within the church. In the meeting they held in Carthage after Easter 251, the bishops of Africa decided to begin this process immediately: those who had acquired certificates of compliance without actually sacrificing might be readmitted as soon as individual cases could be reviewed; those who had sacrificed could be enrolled as penitents and granted peace as death approached them.[61] The bishops' claim of authority to deal with the sin of apostasy and their subjecting the lapsed to the established ritual proved a great boon to the community. A process of reintegration began by which all the sinners could acknowledge their failure and be accepted by the whole community as penitents, with the promise of full membership either in the near future or at least before their deaths. Cyprian described the process of public examination of individual candidates and the exhortations through which the members of the community were convinced to accept back even schismatics who had assaulted the unity of the church.[62] Admission of the certified also resolved at least partially the perceived unfairness of excluding some who had acted as protectors and shields, thereby enabling their dependants to remain standing within the communion.[63] In publicly performing the rituals of repentance and reconciliation, moreover, the entire church could acknowledge the failures and divisions which had led to the persecution and resulted in its losses.[64]

As has been argued earlier, Cyprian justified the efficacy of the ritual of repentance by interpreting the division of the church initiated by the rebel clergy and their supporters as a second phase in the persecution which then presented a new opportunity for the lapsed to confess Christ and thereby reverse their earlier failure. Submitting to the authority of the bishop and the intercession of the community rather than relying on the influence of the martyrs and accepting the false peace of the schismatics was identified as an adherence to Christ in the face of temptation.[65] After having argued this case to the lapsed, Cyprian made a similar appeal to the confessors and those of their followers who were splitting the church. In sections of On Unity which clearly pertained to this stage of the conflict, Cyprian warned that the devil could tempt not only to idolatry but to a false form of Christianity.[66] As he had exhorted his community early in the persecution to pray with united hearts, so he now affirmed that the efficacy of Christian prayer depended on the unanimity of the community. Those who broke from their fellow Christians could not assemble separately in the peace of Christ and thus could not expect God to heed their prayer.[67] Nor could anyone who had violated the solidarity of the church on earth hope to enjoy the peace of the kingdom of heaven. Those who refused to love their brethren on earth could not be rewarded by admission to their company in heaven, even if they had died for confessing the name of Christ.[68] He concluded that the unity of the church derived from God and that the community was thus indivisible; anyone who abandoned the people glued together in harmony lost God, Christ, faith and the hope of salvation.[69]

During the persecution, Cyprian had begun to build a coalition of bishops who supported his opposition to the confessors and the rebellious clergy.[70] The meeting of bishops from the provinces of Roman Africa in Carthage after Easter 251 to determine a policy for the reconciliation of the lapsed[71] strengthened the position of each bishop in his own church. First, the individual bishops could appeal to the council's decision as a justification for the actions which they took or refused to take in their individual churches. Cyprian, for example, met the Novatianist charge that he had changed his own rigorous position after the persecution by appealing to the decree of the council allowing the certified to be reconciled immediately and the sacrificers on their deathbeds.[72] Second, the adoption of a rule requiring that each sinner's case be heard in the church where the crime had been committed meant that no bishop could undermine the authority of another by overruling his decision on an individual.[73] Third, the bishops reviewed and affirmed the removal of the rebel clergy at Carthage and further agreed to enforce the excommunication of any clergy who reconciled the lapsed without penance,[74] again strengthening the authority of the local bishop over his clergy. Fourth, individual bishops retained the right to refuse reconciliation of the lapsed, as they had been given freedom to deny the peace of the church to adulterers by an earlier council.[75] The council of spring 251 responded to the revolt of the laxists by reasserting the role of the local bishop in organizing and governing the church.

One bishop in a church

In the spring of 251, the Roman clergy decided that a successor to Bishop Fabian, who had died a martyr at the outset of the persecution, could be safely chosen. Cornelius was elected by the clergy and people, then ordained by sixteen bishops from the surrounding area.[76] Novatian, who had shaped the policy of delaying reconciliation of the lapsed during the persecution, objected to the choice and, with the support of a number of recently released confessors, secured his own ordination as bishop in opposition to Cornelius. Both Cornelius and Novatian then solicited letters of recognition from their colleagues throughout the world. Novatian's emissaries remained in Carthage, trying to build support for their cause, while an African episcopal delegation traveled to Rome to investigate the conflicting claims.[77] This commission found in favor of Cornelius and he was universally recognized by the African bishops. Undeterred, however, Novatian worked to establish his rival church in Africa. He sent the bishop Evaristus and a deacon Nicostratus over to Carthage from Rome.[78] He also directed letters to the African bishops attacking their delegates' decision, impugning the qualifications of Cornelius, and seeking recognition for himself.[79] A year later, the presbyter Maximus, who had headed the original party seeking African support for Novatian, was ordained bishop and sent to contest Cyprian's position in Carthage.[80] Novatian ordained other new bishops from among his followers and sent them out to challenge the established bishops who held to communion with Cornelius and practiced the reconciliation of the lapsed.[81] Although they won some support, the rigorists did not pose a significant threat to Cyprian and his colleagues.[82] The primary problem in Africa was rather the development of the laxist opposition into a separate church.

At the first meeting of African bishops after the persecution, in May 251, a group of lapsed bishops led by Privatus, the previously deposed bishop of Lambaesis, presented themselves for recognition. Though they were condemned and excluded from fellowship, they appeared again in May 252, apparently hoping to be admitted to communion along with their congregations.[83] Rebuffed a second time, the five bishops proceeded to ordain Fortunatus bishop of the laxist community in Carthage and to establish a rival college of bishops in Africa, claiming some twenty-five members in the province of Numidia.[84] The rebels immediately sent a delegation to Rome to seek recognition.[85] Initially, Cornelius refused to receive them but when they threatened to make the whole dispute public, he granted a hearing in which letters attacking Cyprian and his colleagues were read out. Although the Roman church denied the laxists' demand that Cyprian be deposed and Fortunatus admitted to communion, Cornelius then had to deal with Cyprian's outrage at the proceeding itself.[86]

The analysis will consider first the process by which bishops were selected as a basis for understanding Cyprian's teaching that they received the authority Christ had conferred upon Peter. Next, the composition and revision of the treatise *On Unity* and its characterization of the structure of the local church must be explored. Third, the role of the bishop as the guarantor of the unity of the local church will be specified. Finally, the justification for granting peace to the lapsed who had sacrificed because of their confession of the unity of the church will be reviewed.

The succession of bishops

The issue between Cornelius and Novatian in Rome, and later between Cyprian, Maximus and Fortunatus in Carthage, was not whether a local church might be served by more than one bishop. Neither the history of Israel nor the Roman political system nor even the Trinitarian theory of the third century church provided a model of shared *imperium*.[87] Each of the rival bishops in Rome sought the exclusive recognition of his fellow bishops.[88] Cornelius denied all legitimacy to his opponent and reported that Novatian was requiring a loyalty oath from his communicants and a vow not to return to Cornelius.[89] When a group of schismatic confessors did rejoin Cornelius, each was required to affirm that there could be only one bishop in a Catholic church.[90] Novatian sent out bishops to other cities, intending to supplant the existing bishops who had refused to recognize him, just as he had attempted to overthrow Cornelius in Rome.[91] Similarly, the laxist bishop of Carthage sought the approval of the Roman bishop as the replacement, not the colleague, of Cyprian.[92] Displaying a prejudice against the multiplication of bishops, many of the laity who had joined the laxist schism in Carthage refused to support Fortunatus as a rival bishop and returned to Cyprian's communion.[93] The bishops of Africa had themselves drawn up a list of all approved bishops and sent a copy to Rome, so that no one would unwittingly recognize a schismatic or lapsed pretender.[94] All parties assumed that only one bishop could preside in a local church.

Neither in practice nor in theory did Cyprian provide any indication of the manner in which new churches and bishoprics were established, though his theory of episcopal succession to Peter and the other apostles of Jesus clearly required the expansion of the college. His explanatory efforts were focused instead on the disputed cases in which rivals fought over succession to existing sees. The procedure for the succession of bishops was designed to establish a single bishop in each town or city and to secure his status through recognition by other bishops in an episcopal college of indefinite extension. A bishop was replaced only upon his death or deposition, so that no bishop had a role in selecting his successor and handing on his episcopal power and responsibilities.[95] In most instances, bishops died in office. Those who voluntarily resigned after a public sin were often allowed to remain in communion among the people.[96] When a bishop had to be removed by the action of his colleagues, exclusion from communion seems to have resulted, as in the cases of Privatus of Lambaesis and some of the bishops who sacrificed or did not require penance of the lapsed in Africa.[97] Cornelius achieved the removal of the three bishops who had consecrated Novatian, though one confessed his fault and was allowed to remain in communion among the laity.[98] The church was not in a position, as it would be after the Constantinian toleration, to utilize the assistance of the government in removing a bishop who had been deposed. Successful action, therefore, might require extensive collaboration among a wide range of bishops, in order to render an obstinate bishop ineffectual. Thus Donatus of Carthage and Fabian of Rome were needed to endorse the deposition of Privatus of Lambaesis.[99] The removal of Marcianus of Arles was beyond the power of the bishops of his province, so that the support of the bishops of Carthage and Rome was being sought.[100] In extreme cases, the bishops had to urge the congregation to withdraw and abandon its deposed leader.[101]

Following a death or deposition, a new bishop was elected by the laity, and perhaps the clergy, with the approval of the neighboring bishops.[102] Cyprian appealed to the precedents set in the selection of a replacement for Judas, the choice of the seven deacons, and the installation of the Israelite priests to justify the role and responsibilities of the community in securing a worthy candidate for the office.[103] The election need not have been unanimous – it was not in the choice of either Cyprian or Cornelius. The successful candidate may not always have been a member of the community he would head: in inscribing the confessor Numidicus among his presbyters, Cyprian indicated that this confessor was destined for higher honors, presumably outside Carthage.[104]

A newly elected bishop was installed in office and given his authority not by his predecessor, who was dead or deposed, but by the bishops who supervised the election and performed the ordination. The surviving evidence indicates that Cornelius was consecrated by sixteen bishops,[105] Novatian by three,[106] and Fortunatus by five.[107] No bishop or Christian community, therefore, was autonomous; each was necessarily part of a broad network of bishops and their churches.

The number of consecrators could be important in securing the recognition of other episcopal colleagues, without whose acceptance a new bishop could not function effectively. Cyprian argued that once an election had been completed and the candidate installed by the attending bishops, no other bishop could be elected as a replacement. Any dispute over the succession had only to establish which of the claimants had first completed these two stages of the process.[108] In Novatian's challenge to Cornelius, however, the argument was advanced that Cornelius was unworthy of the office because he lacked integrity[109] and had entered into communion with sacrificers.[110] Cyprian defended Cornelius against the charges themselves[111] and argued that a different procedure had to be followed if he were to be removed from office.[112]

Letters of communion were apparently granted routinely to the new bishop by his colleagues upon announcement of his election in a particular church, on the supposition that the selection was undisputed and consecration had been proper.[113] The consecrators, particularly the principal bishop of a province, may have had an important role in testifying to the regularity of the process. When Cornelius and Novatian competed for the recognition of the bishops of Africa,[114] for example, those bishops sought the testimony of their colleagues who had been present at the election.[115] The process of approval also seems to have been mediated through the churches in the major cities, with those bishops taking responsibility for informing and coordinating the responses of their colleagues.[116]

Significant elements of Cyprian's theory of episcopal office can be correlated with the process of electing, installing and recognizing new bishops. He argued that divine providence would not abandon the church in the important process of choosing a bishop, so that the election by the people actually reflected the prior divine choice of a particular candidate.[117] He then inferred that anyone who opposed a candidate once elected and established was contesting the decision of God.[118] Furthermore, he asserted, this refusal to submit to the judgment by which God had declared a particular candidate suitable for office was the origin of heresies and schisms within the church, and by implication the work of the devil.[119] The experience of having the presbyters who steadfastly opposed his own election end up as rebels against the church seems to have served as a foundation for his judgment.[120] It would have been confirmed by the unworthiness which the previously trusted Novatian displayed once passed over by the people of Rome in favor of Cornelius.[121] Thus he argued that even had Novatian been properly elected and installed as bishop of Rome, he would have lost his place in the episcopal college when he sent out replacements for other bishops who had been properly installed in other cities.[122] Cyprian later observed that only Cornelius was later arrested by the imperial government: Satan had not attacked Novatian, who was already one of his own.[123] Despite his appeal to a divine sanction for elected candidates, Cyprian also argued that congregations had to act responsibly in electing or retaining a leader and that bishops had to be careful in approving and entering into communion with colleagues. The laity must neither select an unworthy bishop nor act in false loyalty to a fallen one.[124] Though he chided Antoninus for indecision about Cornelius, Cyprian carefully answered all the questions raised about his suitability for office.[125] Later he intimated that Stephen was in danger of communicating in the apostasy and blasphemy of Basilides and Martialis through his negligence in investigating the charges which had led to their being deposed and replaced.[126] The process of electing, approving and confirming bishops indicated that they were chosen by God and functioned as members of a collegial body.

On the Unity of the Catholic Church

The episcopal commission sent by the African bishops to Rome was charged not only with determining which of the candidates had been properly elected and installed but was to attempt to resolve the conflict and restore unity.[127] Caldonius and Fortunatus may well have carried a version of *On Unity* which Cyprian had originally directed against the laxist schismatics in Carthage.[128] When their efforts failed, Cyprian tried to convince the confessors who had followed Novatian into schism to return to the unity of the church.[129] Acknowledging their desire to defend the gospel of Christ against the laxists as they had against the persecutors, he warned that they must guard their holiness within the unity of the church.[130] To demonstrate his sympathy for their insistence on the purity of the church, he also sent along copies of *On the Lapsed*, in which he had both demanded penance without promising reconciliation until the time of death and *On Unity*, in which he upheld the indivisibility of the church.[131] His efforts were successful: the formula in which Cyprian had asserted the unicity of God, Christ, church and bishop was incorporated into the statement by which the confessors publicly submitted to Cornelius and were received into his communion.[132] He then congratulated them on their confession of the unity of the church.[133]

Cyprian's treatise *On the Unity of the Catholic Church*, which was used against both the laxist and rigorist schisms, summarized his thinking on the church. The text has been transmitted in two manuscript versions which differ principally in chapters 4, 5 and 19.[134] The contrasting versions of these chapters are generally referred to as the *Textus Receptus* (*TR*) and the *Primacy Text* (*PT*), which latter was at one time considered an interpolation into the former but is now recognized as an alternate version deriving from Cyprian himself. At least one version of *On Unity* was certainly produced by the middle of 251, when Cyprian recorded the sending of the treatise to the Roman confessors.[135] Moreover, portions of the common text clearly reflect the issues under debate in Africa and Italy at that time.[136] Cyprian warned that the confessors were in greater danger after their triumph and that they were being tempted under the guise of the Christian gospel rather than solicited to engage in idolatry.[137] He asserted that not even martyrdom can bring salvation to the schismatic.[138] He elaborated these points through a number of other scriptural citations which also appeared in contemporary letters:[139] Jer. 23.16–17 warns of the danger of false prophets;[140] Mt. 15.14 characterizes the leaders of the opposition as blind guides;[141] 2 Tim. 2.17 compares the speech of heretics to cancer;[142] Mt. 12.30 asserts that those who do not gather with Christ scatter.[143] The text of Eph. 4.4–6 well illustrates Cyprian's objective in 251: he alluded to the text to link the unicity of God, Christ, faith, church and throne founded on Peter but passed over the text's reference to baptism.[144]

The specific variants in the *Primacy Text* version of *On Unity* seem to indicate that Cyprian introduced these changes when he sent the text to Rome to try to effect a reconciliation between Cornelius and Novatian, or to influence the return of the Novatianist confessors to unity. The reference to the primacy of Peter in chapter 4 might have served the same function as the later reference to the Roman church as the chair of Peter, the source of the unity of the church, which Cyprian used as an accusation of the laxists when they sought recognition for a second bishop in Carthage.[145] The Roman church should certainly have recognized that in giving power to Peter first, Christ had demonstrated the unity of church and chair. To desert the unity and chair of Peter, therefore, was necessarily to abandon the church.[146] The more specific reference in chapter 19 to the penance being undertaken by "those who had sacrificed" accurately described the situation in the time between the African councils in 251 and 253 when only the certified had been reconciled and the sacrificers continued to do penance.[147] The more inclusive reference to the "lapsed" would have been part of an earlier version prepared for Cyprian's own church in Carthage or presented to the African council in spring 251. It did not describe the situation at any time after spring 253.[148]

The specific variants in the *Textus Receptus* version of chapters 4 and 5, as well as the issues which were addressed and scriptural passages which were adduced in support, clearly belong to the later period of the controversy on rebaptism, as shall be argued below.[149]

Thus *On Unity* seems to have been written for delivery in Carthage in spring 251, and then revised when it was sent to Rome that summer, either with the episcopal commission investigating the election or later when it was sent to the Novatianist confessors. It was then substantially rewritten during the rebaptism controversy in 256 not only to remove ambiguities in the statements made about Peter in the version sent to Rome but to forge a clearer link between the unity and sanctifying power of the episcopate itself. The text will be used to interpret Cyprian's justification of the unity of the local church against the laxist and rigorist schisms of spring and summer 251, except as it clearly indicates a later revision.

The most striking image of the unity of the church Cyprian introduced in *On Unity* was the tunic of Christ, which had been woven in one piece from the top to the bottom and remained undivided. The unity of the church, symbolized by that garment, comes from the Father and from heaven; it cannot be divided. In contrast, the Prophet Ahijah divided his cloak into twelve parts to symbolize the division of the kingdom and people of Solomon. Christ's people cannot be torn apart; some may leave but the church remains whole and undivided.[150] This exegesis may have been directed at the laxist presbyters. Nor could the schismatics appeal to the words of Christ in Mt. 18.19–20 that where two or three gathered in his name and prayed together, he would be among them and the Father would hear their prayer. This promise applied, Cyprian contended, only to those who were joined in harmony with the whole community and prayed in unanimity, not to those who separated themselves off in opposition.[151] He added a second image aimed at the Novatianists: when Christ himself had proclaimed one flock and one shepherd, how could they pretend to establish two flocks and two shepherds in the same place?[152]

The two levels of composition seem to be revealed in the successive commentaries on those leaving the church. Apparently referring to the conflict which had characterized the presence of the opposing presbyters in the church at Carthage, Cyprian explained that only the evil leave the church, like chaff from the threshing floor, because they never belonged within it. Their loss has been our gain, he exclaimed.[153] The following argument might have been aimed at Novatian and the confessors supporting him. The coming of schism within the church was a divine judgment before the end time,[154] in which people were judged not by the bishops but by the exercise of their own freedom. The resulting division revealed the true faithful and unmasked the hidden traitors.[155] This barb could only have been aimed at the Roman situation, and the outstanding presbyter who revealed his true colors by usurping the name of bishop by irregular ordination.

The first version of *On Unity* was directed against the schismatics in Carthage and in Rome, attacking them for attempting to divide the church. In it, Cyprian advanced the thesis that the church was indivisible because its unity rested upon a divine foundation. Those who left separated themselves from Christ and his church; they took nothing of its sanctifying power with them and had no access to salvation. The images employed in the treatise broadened Cyprian's earlier emphasis on the role of the bishop by stressing the integrity of the community itself.

The bishop in the local church

Against the assaults of rigorists and laxists alike, Cyprian asserted that the bishop was first and foremost the leader of a local church, fulfilling the role which Christ had assigned to Peter as the rock of foundation.[156] Relying on the Petrine authority to bind and loosen, he concluded that the bishop had been appointed by Christ as judge and leader in the time between his ascension and return in judgment.[157] In reflecting on Peter's response when Christ challenged his disciples in the Bread of Life discourse of John's Gospel, Cyprian explained that what Peter had said of Christ himself applied to the church: the Christian could find no other way to salvation.[158] That church, therefore, was itself in the bishop and the bishop in the church, so that to abandon the bishop was to lose the church and Christ himself.[159]

When the African laxists consecrated a bishop for Carthage and applied to Cornelius in Rome for the deposition of Cyprian and recognition of their own candidate, Fortunatus, their principal charge was that Cyprian was himself guilty of dividing the church through his refusal to accept the schismatics into communion. In defense, he asserted that he regularly labored to overcome the animosity which he found within his own people against the rebels who had arrogantly despised their communion and the religious standards they upheld.[160] This attack on a bishop who required repentance of those who had publicly denied Christ by sacrificing was in fact an assault on the church itself. Cornelius, he implied, was being derelict in his own duty when he entertained the petition of these people who would force their way into the church by threats rather than be welcomed by repentance.[161]

In explaining why unworthy bishops must be removed from office, Cyprian pointed to the episcopal role of offering the community's oblation and interceding for its welfare.[162] He also found the unity of the local church symbolized in its eucharistic celebration. The irreversible mingling of water into wine symbolized the inseparable unity of the people with Christ. The joining together of the many grains of wheat through grinding, moistening and baking signified the unity of the church itself as the body of Christ.[163] The crushing of many grapes and mingling of their juice into the one cup carried the same significance.[164] Concretely, he argued that the eucharistic celebration could not be dispersed into private homes but required the assembly of the entire community.[165] In Cyprian's way of thinking, the local church was a specific social group with an identifiable membership, sharing eucharistic fellowship under a bishop. To refuse to adhere to such a community under the leadership of a legitimate bishop was to be outside the church and by implication ineligible for participation in the kingdom of Christ.

Reconciling the sacrificers

The division between Cyprian's community in Carthage and its rivals, both laxists and rigorists, had been thoroughly hardened by the attempts to establish bishops for each of the schismatic groups. As has been argued above, this presented Cyprian and his colleagues with an opportunity to justify the reconciliation of the sacrificers who had persevered in penance in submission to the bishop of the Catholic church rather than accepting the peace of a competing communion.[166] The reconciliation of the certified among the lapsed and the admission of the sacrificers as penitents in 251 had relieved conflicts within the community. Tension had been building again, no doubt, through the admission of penitents during the seasons of summer illness.[167] Some of the sacrificers admitted to communion on what were taken to be their deathbeds had then recovered and remained in communion while their fellows continued as penitents.[168] These disparities are evident in the questioning of the earlier decree. One bishop proceeded with the private reconciliation of a former presbyter though he was not in danger of death;[169] another urged that those who had failed under torture should be given preference over others who had volunteered to sacrifice.[170]

When the bishops met in council in spring 253, they decided to authorize admitting all the penitents into communion without further delay. The bishops argued that signs and warnings of a new outbreak of persecution had moved them to act. The decision was justified, however, by the loyalty which the penitents had consistently demonstrated toward the church.[171] Unlike the many who had abandoned the Christian life completely or had taken up arms against the church as schismatics, these penitents had never wavered from their determination to regain the communion of the church.[172] They had accepted the connection Cyprian had made explicit between the authority to forgive sins and the one bishop in the one true church.[173] In welcoming the penitents back into communion, he and his colleagues recognized the confession of faith in the unity of the church which the penitents had made, a confession which they believed would be approved by God and crowned with martyrdom.[174]

Later, during the controversy over rebaptism, Cyprian would reassert this foundational link between the office of bishop, the unity of the church, and the power to forgive sins. Then he would use two premises to invalidate the rituals of schismatics. First, in practice everyone agreed that only one bishop could be found in a local church. Second, all should recognize that this one bishop held and exercised the power to sanctify. Thus for a bishop to recognize the power of a rival to baptize was necessarily to give up his own claim to the authority and the office of bishop; it was also to concede the title of church to the competing assembly and place oneself outside the kingdom of God. Because the bishop received and held the powers given to Peter, he was the foundation and guarantee of the unity and holiness of his communion.[175]

The unity of the local church

By the end of the council of African bishops in the spring of 251, the main lines of Cyprian's theory of the unity of the local church were already clearly established. In response to the Novatianist and laxist attempts to establish competing churches, the theory was applied and developed but not changed. The church was a concrete unity, a particular group of people sharing eucharistic fellowship and exclusive faith in Christ, under the leadership of their elected and recognized bishop. The common welfare had to take precedence over the religious good of any individual and no Christian's standing before God might be separated from that of the community as a whole. Those who violated the explicit or implied behavioral code of the community were excluded and might be readmitted only through a renegotiation of that code – as in the case of the certified – or a public acknowledgment of their failure to follow the agreed practice and a commitment to do so thereafter – as in the case of the sacrificers. Both procedures involved the community as a whole. This community could tolerate disagreements, tensions and rivalries among its members but not a break in eucharistic fellowship. If a division occurred, only one of the parts actually remained a church. The others were deprived of all connection with God and Christ; they were demonic shams, no better than the idolatrous gatherings of imperial society.

Cyprian provided two different justifications for the unity of the local church: the indivisible unity of the community and the unity deriving from its leader. The bishop elected leader of the church was actually a successor to Peter, upon whom Christ had founded the unity of the church and through whom each church received its power to sanctify by forgiving sins. The bishop must not act independently of either the people in his own church or the leaders of other churches. Cyprian's people believed that they had the right to be consulted and heard both on major policy changes and in significant decisions about persons, such as the selection of officers and the admission of penitents. The selection and installation of a bishop demonstrated that no community was autonomous; it must coordinate its decisions and practices with those of other churches. The bishop's inheritance of Peter's authority to bind and loosen, to judge and forgive, could enable him to serve as a unifying foundation of the local church.

The community itself was established as indivisible through the divine will. Like the tunic worn by Christ, the church could not be torn apart and divided into pieces. As the flock of Christ, it must be united and thus have only one pastor in each town. The unity of the members of the community with one another was sacramentally symbolized in their union with Christ in the one loaf and one cup of the eucharistic celebration.

Both these positions would be revisited in the conflict over the rebaptism of schismatics and purity of the church. Finally, they would grow into twin foundations of a theory of the church spread throughout the world.

6

INITIATION INTO UNITY

The division of the Christians in Africa into three competing communions, each with its own college of bishops, involved conflict over the efficacy of the rituals performed in other churches. Initially, the conflict focused on the ritual of penance: the laxists questioned the efficacy and necessity of the Catholic ritual of reconciliation; the Catholics restricted the intercessory power of the martyrs on which the laxists relied. The rigorists claimed that only Christ could forgive the sin of apostasy and concluded that the Catholic and laxist eucharistic fellowships had both been polluted by the participation of the lapsed. Catholics rejected the eucharistic celebrations of laxists and rigorists as violations of the unity of Christ's church. Each denied the efficacy of the others' eucharistic celebration as a pure sacrifice sanctifying the community and qualifying its members for entrance into the kingdom of Christ. The competing churches were soon questioning the efficacy of the primary ritual of purification and forgiveness, baptism. The laxist practice remains unknown but the rigorists rebaptized converts from the Catholic communion. The Catholic bishops debated the necessity of rebaptizing a convert who had originally been baptized in a competing communion.

In the period immediately following the persecution and division of the church, it may be presumed that most of the separated laxists and rigorists had been baptized originally in the Catholic communion. Some of their adherents, however, might have been baptized in the laxist and rigorist communions. Catechumens, for example, might have participated in the rebellion over the reception of the lapsed. The children born to schismatics might also have been baptized in these new communions.[1] In the following years, new members may have made their first approach and commitment to Christianity in these churches.[2] Eventually, some of the schismatics became dissatisfied with their leaders or were persuaded by the competitors' arguments; they left one communion for another, bringing their families with them. Those originally baptized as Catholics were received as penitents, just as the lapsed themselves had been.[3] The question of how to receive converts baptized in schism became the focus of debate.

Where did these converts actually come from and by whom had they originally been baptized? The laxist hierarchy was established in Africa after the petition of the dissident bishops for recognition at the council in the spring of 252.[4] A rigorist bishop had challenged Cyprian less than a year earlier.[5] The first firmly dated correspondence between Catholic bishops raising the question of rebaptizing converts from schism can be placed no later than spring 255, a maximum of four years later.[6] Would these three or four years have allowed adequate time for significant numbers of schismatic Christians to pass through the final stages of catechumenate in the laxist or rigorist communion, enter that church through baptism, become dissatisfied, then petition entrance into the Catholic church, pass a period of preparation as a Catholic penitent or catechumen, and finally be ready for admission into the church by baptism or the imposition of hands?[7] The documents of the controversy never hint that most of the subjects involved may have been children, who would be received without a probationary period.[8] The initial years of the schism, when the threat of renewed persecution loomed, moreover, seems an unlikely period for rapid expansion of newly established schismatic churches through recruitment of polytheists.[9] The Novatianists would have been likely to enforce the full time of preparation of candidates for baptism, since they rebaptized even those who had already been initiated into the Catholic communion. They would also have been hampered in making new converts by the lack of an indigenous clergy; most were missionaries sent from Italy.[10] The laxists, with their native clergy and established network, are the more likely source of the troublesome converts. In fact, the laxist church would have integrated the adherents of Privatus of Lambaesis when he established the laxist episcopal college in spring 252. Privatus had been deposed as much as a decade earlier but apparently continued to lead a local church, in which he would presumably have performed baptism on a regular basis.[11] Some of the adherents of Privatus in Lambaesis may have refused to remain in his church after he had entered into communion with sacrificer bishops, such as Jovinus, Maximus and Repostus, and with the congregations of sacrificers which made up the laxist church.[12] Thus the African laxist church must be considered the most likely source of already baptized converts to the Catholic communion, particularly in Numidia.

The inquiry addressed by the Numidian bishops to their Proconsular colleagues clearly indicated that some converts were entering their communion who had originally been baptized in schism.[13] The operating hypothesis of this investigation, therefore, will be that the laxist community in Africa provided the converts who initiated the discussion of rebaptism. The earlier conflicts over the power to forgive the sin of idolatry, moreover, made the efficacy of schismatic baptism a more pressing issue in Africa than in Italy. This would account for the unanimity and adamancy of the African bishops in upholding the necessity of rebaptizing converts from schismatic churches. Although the rigorist church actually practiced rebaptism, both in Italy and Africa, the focus of the controversy in Africa was the laxist church.[14]

Whether as a practical or theoretical issue, the question actually arose of the ritual by which those baptized in a schismatic church were to be received into the communion of the Catholic church: as reconciled penitents by the imposition of hands to restore them to membership, as baptized neophytes by the imposition of hands to confer the Holy Spirit incorporating them into the church, or as catechumens by the full ritual of baptism? Because the separation of the churches did not involve differences in belief about the Christian God, it revived an older controversy over heretical baptism within the African church, which then grew into a major conflict involving the overseas churches.

The course of the conflict

The value of baptism administered in a competing Christian communion had apparently been debated years earlier in Africa. Cyprian regularly attacked the efficacy of heretical baptism by referring to the teaching of Marcion, whose influence had peaked during the previous century. Tertullian's own judgment on heretical baptism might have been the source of Cyprian's assertion that those who do not share the same God and Christ could not share the same baptism.[15] Schismatic baptism, however, may have been an unsettled question. A council of bishops from Numidia and Proconsular Africa held when Agrippinus was bishop of Carthage established a common policy, whose application was being called into question during Cyprian's day.[16] The council may have pronounced on the inefficacy of heretical baptism alone or perhaps of that performed in schism as well.[17] No record of the meeting itself survived and the subsequent evidence is ambiguous. Some of Cyprian's letters asserted that Agrippinus' council rejected all baptism performed outside the church[18] but one specified that it dealt with heretical baptism.[19] Firmilian of Caesarea in Cappadocia, to whom Cyprian appealed for support, indicated that although his church had always rejected the baptism given by heretics, it had been required to reconsider that performed by the Montanists, who supported the Trinitarian formula and faith.[20] He also implied that the African bishops had changed their custom first on heretical and then on schismatic baptism.[21]

That a controversy over schismatic baptism arose following the laxist and rigorist schisms also suggests that only the issue of heretical baptism had been considered and determined at Agrippinus' council. A group of bishops in Numidia wrote to their colleagues in Proconsular Africa in spring 254 or 255, seeking guidance about the admission of schismatics, who shared their own faith and had originally been baptized according to the same ritual they used.[22] In responding, Cyprian tried to demonstrate that the two communities did not in fact share the same faith: denying the church's power to forgive sins was actually heresy.[23] Even at the council in September 256, only four of the eighty-seven *sententiae* mentioned schismatics, as distinct from heretics; of these only two took note of the difference between them.[24] The status of baptism performed in schism as distinguished from heresy, therefore, may have remained unresolved in the African church at the time the question was raised by the Numidian bishops.[25]

In the competition between Christian communions after the Decian persecution, moreover, the practice of accepting a rebel bishop's baptism carried new implications which changed the nature of the question itself. The dispute over the admission of those who failed during the persecution had focused on the power of the bishop to forgive sins and the conditions under which it might be exercised. Cyprian had argued that the laxists had no access to such authority; he had also defended against the rigorist charge that he and his colleagues lacked such power. Those, and only those, bishops in proper succession from the apostles had received the power which Christ had handed over to them, he asserted. When the controversy over rebaptism arose, therefore, Cyprian was astonished by his fellow bishops' failure to defend their exclusive authority to baptize and sanctify. He insisted that baptism could be given only by a bishop who had received the power to forgive sins.

To recognize a rival bishop's authority to baptize was either to legit-imate his succession to office in an established church and thereby to abandon one's own claim to that office, or to acknowledge a source of authority to forgive – such as the patronage of the martyrs – which was different from Christ's grant of the Holy Spirit to the apostles. By implication, the bishop accepting a baptism performed by his rival would surrender his church's claim to provide the only access to salvation, thereby contradicting the convert's very motive for abandoning the schismatic in favor of the Catholic commu-nion.[26] The question facing Cyprian and his colleagues, therefore, had not been settled by Agrippinus' council. A similar issue had arisen but its new context made the earlier decree appear unrelated and therefore not determinative.

Two stages in the development of the controversy over the rebap-tism of heretics and schismatics might be distinguished: the first involved a clarification of the practice and the reasons for applying it; the second brought sharp conflict over requiring or even allowing it. The first remained largely within Africa and must have focused primarily on the reception of laxists. The second introduced a debate over Novatian and entailed a bitter dispute with the bishop of Rome over the power of schismatics to perform sacred functions.

The first part of the controversy opened in spring 254 or 255, when a synod of thirty-one Proconsular bishops received an inquiry from eighteen of their colleagues in Numidia about the practice of admitting converts from heresy and schism by the ritual of baptism. The Numidians apparently affirmed their adherence to the policy of Agrippinus' council but questioned its appropriateness in their actual circumstances.[27] The Proconsular bishops responded that those baptized in schism should be received by a new baptism but did not specify the communion which the converts in Numidia were leaving to join their church. Sometime after this letter, Cyprian responded personally to an inquiry on the same subject from Quintus, a bishop in Mauretania.[28] Again, the schismatic group from which the converts were arriving was unspecified in the reply but Cyprian did include a copy of the letter which he and his colleagues had earlier sent to Numidia.[29] Finally, in spring 256, a council of seventy-one bishops from throughout Africa meeting in Carthage sent a letter to Stephen, bishop of Rome, informing him of the position they had taken on two issues arising from the schisms in Africa: the reception of converts by rebaptism and the admission of clergy from such communions into the Catholic laity.[30] They included copies of the two earlier letters on the subject of rebaptism.[31] This seems to have been a routine communication, similar to the letter the Africans had written to Cornelius three years earlier, to inform him of their decision to admit the penitent sacrificers to communion in anticipation of renewed persecution.[32] While recommending their own policy of rebaptizing, the Africans recognized that within the unity of the church others followed different practices; they intended to apply no pressure for conformity.[33] In this letter as well, no mention was made of particular heretics or schismatics. The bishops did not anticipate the reaction which their letter would provoke in Rome.[34]

In contrast to these polite exchanges, the controversy's second stage focused sharp debate on the practice of Novatian. A letter belonging to this conflict can be securely dated shortly after the council held in spring 256. A bishop Jubianus sent Cyprian an extensive list of questions about the practice of rebaptizing converts – which Novatian was following and Cyprian was promoting – as well as a copy of a letter defending the admission of converts from heresy or schism by the imposition of hands alone. In response, Cyprian asserted that Novatian was following the proper procedure for defending his claim to possess the gifts of the true church;[35] he then attacked those among his fellow bishops who refused to reject the baptism of their rivals and thus failed to protect the powers which God had bestowed upon them.[36] Jubianus' response signaled that he had been convinced by Cyprian's arguments.[37]

During the summer of 256, Cyprian received Stephen's startling response to the packet of letters sent by the springtime council. Not only did Stephen insist on receiving converts from heresy and schism by the imposition of hands alone – the policy of his own church which, he claimed, even heretics followed – but he threatened to break communion with any bishop who insisted on rebaptizing.[38] He insulted Cyprian himself, moreover, and forbade the customary hospitality to the representatives of the African episcopate. As news of Stephen's action spread through Africa, Cyprian sent his colleagues more specific information, copies of Stephen's letter, and arguments solidifying the position they had themselves taken. One of these letters, addressed to a Bishop Pompeius, has survived;[39] a response from Bishop Firmilian of Caesarea in Cappadocia is also found among Cyprian's letters and reflects the documents which had been sent to secure his support.[40]

Cyprian's exchange with Magnus, who cannot be otherwise identified, seems to belong to this period as well. This letter focused on

Novatian's power to baptize, though it did not mention his practice of rebaptizing, and shared a number of arguments with the other letters Cyprian wrote during the summer of 256.[41] Like the letter to Jubianus and unlike the one to Pompeius, the response to Magnus gave no evidence of open conflict with Stephen; thus it may have preceded the news of his rejection of the African envoys. This letter must be dated on the basis of internal evidence, whose consideration is delayed until later in this chapter.[42]

On 1 September 256, some eighty-five bishops from throughout Africa met in Carthage to take action on what had become a dispute with Stephen.[43] After listening to a reading of the full correspondence between Cyprian and Jubianus – the original inquiry, Cyprian's exposition of the earlier council's position, and Jubianus' agreement – they individually expressed their judgments on the status of baptism performed outside the church. The bishops unanimously insisted on the rebaptism of converts who originally had been baptized in heresy or schism.[44]

The conflict between the African bishops and their Roman colleague, Stephen, seems to have remained unresolved at his death. His successor, Sixtus, did restore cordial relations, perhaps by accepting the plurality of practices within the unity of the one church which the Africans had repeatedly proposed.

The opponents in the controversy over rebaptism

The preceding division of the controversy into two stages is based in part on the supposition that the African bishops were competing against two different schismatic communions: the laxists and the rigorists. The focus on baptism performed by the rigorists is made evident in what is here interpreted as a second stage in the controversy by the frequent references to Novatian in the two letters of Cyprian which can be securely dated after the council in spring 256.[45] None of the three letters which deal explicitly with Novatian, however, clearly indicated that the rigorist opponents were in Africa, although a rigorist bishop had been sent from Rome to establish a competing church in Carthage.[46] The question of rebaptism seems to have originally arisen in Africa in response to the laxists.

The laxist movement had begun during the Decian persecution as a rebellion of presbyters and deacons against the authority of their bishops, under the patronage of confessors and martyrs. By the middle of 252, however, a college of bishops led by Privatus of

Lambaesis had been established and a laxist bishop had been consecrated for Carthage.[47] At the same time, Cyprian noted that former
members of his communion who had followed the laxists into
schism had begun to return to his communion, where they were
being received as penitents.[48] He never provided specific information, however, on the reception or method of incorporation of
converts who had originally been baptized by a laxist bishop.

The first synodal action in the controversy over rebaptism was
the inquiry from a regional meeting of Numidian bishops to a
council of Proconsular bishops meeting in Carthage. The question
raised was whether the established policy on heretical and schismatic baptism was appropriately applied in their controversy.[49] The
letter of inquiry itself has not survived but because the response
from Cyprian and his colleagues argued from belief in the powers of
the church rather than from faith in the identity of the Creator or
Christ, it may be presumed that the opponents in question were
schismatic rather than heretical.[50] Furthermore, the inquiry seems
to have been sent from Lambaesis, the capital of Numidia: the lead
bishop among those addressed in the reply was Januarius, who can
be identified as bishop of that city, though only two of his seventeen
colleagues can be confidently located in the immediate geographic
area.[51] The instigator and head of the laxist episcopal college was
Privatus of Lambaesis, Januarius' deposed predecessor and current
opponent. Although the rigorist schism might have been operative
in the capital of Numidia, the laxist schism would have been the
more likely problem because it relied on indigenous clergy.[52] Thus
the first letter, which served as the foundation for the next two, may
have been directed against the laxist schismatics.

The second letter in this sequence was in response to an inquiry
addressed to Cyprian from Mauretania, though its author, Quintus,
cannot be securely identified.[53] With his reply, Cyprian sent a copy
of the response of the Proconsular bishops to their Numidian
colleagues; these two were in turn sent with the letter to Stephen
from the African council meeting in spring 256. That synodal letter
dealt with both baptism outside the church and the reception of
schismatic clerics as laymen. The renegade clergy were charged with
having turned against the church the very arms with which it had
originally equipped them. In an African context, such an accusation
fits the laxists, whose extensive clergy were drawn from among the
African Christians, rather than the rigorists, whose officers were
sent over from Italy.[54] Thus the circumstances indicate that the
initial problem may have been with the African laxist church.

The two letters composed for the African councils and Cyprian's intervening letter to Quintus share several internal characteristics which also indicate that they were directed against the laxists in Africa. First, Novatian's rebellion against Cornelius and his being ordained out of succession were never mentioned as an impediment to the opposing communion's power to baptize.[55] Second, the Apostle Peter was regularly used as a foundation for the unity of the local church, as he had been in the original version of *On Unity* and in subsequent correspondence.[56] The careful balance of Peter and the other apostles which characterized the revision of *On Unity* is found, however, in the letters which belong to the second stage of the controversy.[57] Third, each of the three early letters described the opposing bishops as sinful or unclean: their foul washing and sinful anointing polluted and stained those whom they baptized and sealed.[58] Such accusations would have been more appropriately directed against the laxist bishops, many of whom had been accused of idolatry during the persecution,[59] than against the Novatianists, who maintained the freedom of their communion from idolatry.[60] Fourth, the followers of these unholy bishops were treated as deceived and defrauded victims, who had been led astray in their sincere quest for God.[61] This fits the laxists better than the adherents of Novatian who, in contrast, were later characterized as active rebels who fully deserved the damnation they would consequently suffer.[62] Finally, these three letters all ignored the actual practice of the opposing party, an issue prominent in those letters which dealt explicitly with Novatian's rebellion against Cornelius and his practice of rebaptizing. None of the letters assigned to this first phase of the controversy indicated that the unnamed opponents were rebaptizing anyone coming to them from the Catholic church.[63] If these two synodal letters and one private letter were concerned with the laxists, then the omission of any reference to opposing practice could be explained in a number of ways. As has been suggested above, the converts in question might have been those baptized by Privatus during the decade-long schism following his deposition from office in Lambaesis. Second, the laxists themselves might not have won additional converts after the initial success following the persecution, since Catholic losses had apparently been stemmed by admitting the certified and promising eventual reconciliation to the penitent sacrificers, as well as the subsequent granting of peace to all penitents. Third, if the laxists were not rebaptizing converts from the Catholic communion because they did not consider the Catholics – whose communion they had sought at two consecutive councils – heretics, they might have been following the letter of the decree of Agrippinus' council. They might have been receiving these converts – many of them lapsed – by the imposition of hands characteristic of the rite of reconciliation and thus did not directly challenge the efficacy of baptism given by Cyprian's colleagues.[64] Only converts from polytheism would have been baptized in the laxist schism. Such new Christians would have given rise to the question of the Numidian bishops:[65] should they also recognize the baptism given by schismatic bishops – all former colleagues – who recognized their own.

On the basis of this constellation of indicators – no one of them probative in isolation – the first phase of the controversy over rebaptism will be interpreted as a conflict over the proper mode of receiving converts from the dominant opposition group in Africa, the laxists. This phase began in 254 or 255, with the letter of the Numidian bishops to their Proconsular colleagues, and ended with the report to Stephen by the council held in Carthage in spring 256.

Almost immediately after the synod of spring 256, however, Cyprian and his colleagues were faced with a barrage of questions about Novatian and the crisis of Stephen's reaction in Rome. These defined the second stage of the controversy. Three of the four letters belonging to this phase are securely dated. Bishop Jubianus wrote to Cyprian with some observations of his own and included another letter[66] which defended the practice of admitting heretics and schismatics without rebaptism. Cyprian's reply must have been sent shortly after the spring 256 meeting of African bishops in Carthage.[67] The letter Cyprian sent to Magnus is usually assigned to the first phase of the controversy but belongs more properly in the period after the synod but before the receipt of Stephen's reply to its communication. Once Stephen's response to the conciliar decision had been received, Cyprian prepared a full refutation of his arguments. Cyprian's letter to Pompeius, itself part of this effort, can be dated to the summer of that same year.[68] Firmilian of Caesarea in Cappadocia responded to a letter Cyprian had sent by the deacon Rogatianus. Cyprian's letter was sent after Stephen's rebuke but before the African bishops' meeting in September 256, though Firmilian's reply must have arrived in Carthage later, perhaps just before the end of the shipping season in 256.[69]

Jubianus suggested and Stephen charged that Cyprian and his colleagues were following Novatian's innovative practice of rebaptizing schismatics rather than the established tradition of both the church and most heretics: receiving baptized converts by the imposition of hands.[70] Cyprian returned the compliment, charging that his opponents were themselves siding with heretics by defending the efficacy of their faith and rituals.[71] More significantly, he elaborated the argument which had been developing in the African context: no salvific action may be performed outside the church. He culled the scriptures for passages which would justify a firm and high wall dividing insiders from outsiders, a boundary enclosing the efficacious rituals within the one church.

Cyprian's response to the inquiry of Magnus dealt explicitly with Novatian.[72] Although the letter to Cyprian and his response cannot be securely dated nor can Magnus be identified and located on the basis of references to or from other letters, the preponderance of evidence indicates that this exchange belonged to the second phase of the controversy.[73] First, Cyprian did not include this letter with the other letters which he sent to Quintus, Stephen and Jubianus. The letter to Magnus does, however, seem to have been forwarded to Firmilian in late summer 256; but the letters to the Numidian bishops and Quintus, which are assigned to the first phase of the controversy, do not seem to have been included.[74] Thus Cyprian grouped this letter with others of the second phase of the controversy. Second, unlike his letters to Jubianus and Pompeius, this letter to Magnus did not mention the Novatianist practice of rebaptizing.[75] Third, like his letter to Jubianus, Cyprian's reply to Magnus carried none of the personal animosity sparked by Stephen's response to the African council, which was markedly evident in the correspondence with Pompeius and Firmilian. Thus this letter might be dated after the synod of spring 256 but before Cyprian received either the letter from Jubianus in support of Novatian or Stephen's reply to the synodal letter of spring 256. The dating is complex and important enough, however, to merit fuller investigation.

Internal evidence also seems to place the composition of the letter to Magnus in the summer of 256. The arguments Cyprian used in it are characteristic of the second stage of the controversy. The images and biblical precedents which he marshaled to convince Magnus that those outside the unity of the church cannot share its power to sanctify closely parallel those used in the letters to Jubianus and Pompeius but differ from those employed in the letters sent to Numidia, Quintus and Stephen, which can be dated earlier. First, figures and images which sharply differentiate the boundary of the church and exclude those outside from its gifts are common to these later letters but absent in the earlier ones: the enclosed garden, the bride, the sealed fountain, the well of living water,[76] and the ark of Noah riding above the flood.[77] Second, the characterization of the church as the bride washed and cleansed by Christ is found only in the letters to Magnus and Pompeius.[78] Third, in addressing Magnus, Cyprian used the rebellion of Core, Dathan and Abiron against Aaron to show that their sharing true faith did not make the rebels' sacrifice efficacious; in writing to Jubianus, he cited this incident to defend the divine establishment of priests.[79] Fourth, the text of Jn. 20.22–3 was employed to connect the gift of the Holy Spirit and the power to forgive sins first to one another and then to the apostles and their legitimate successors. This argument appeared in the letters to Magnus and Jubianus, and in Cyprian's revision of *On Unity*, which was itself tied to the conflict with Stephen.[80] Fifth, the letter to Magnus used the inspiration of John the Baptist in his mother's womb to demonstrate that only those who have received the Holy Spirit can baptize; the letter to Jubianus noted the inspiration but argued that John's baptism still had to be repeated by the apostles because it had been conferred outside the unity of the church.[81] Sixth, the letters to Magnus and Jubianus both judged the supporters of Novatian deserving of their impending condemnation by Christ while the letters belonging to the first phase of the controversy treated the adherents of the unnamed schismatic church as innocent victims who had been deceived and defrauded by false clerics.[82]

The letter to Magnus alone addressed a question which might have been relevant to the controversy in Rome rather than the problems in Africa: the efficacy of a baptism performed for the gravely ill by pouring water rather than immersion and unaccompanied by the episcopal sealing.[83] In his letter to Fabius of Antioch, Cornelius had charged that Novatian had not been properly received into the church because he had been baptized on his sickbed by pouring and never anointed by the bishop.[84] In his letter to Cyprian, however, Magnus drew a parallel between reception of schismatics by the imposition of hands and the established two-step reception of the sick by deaconal or presbyteral baptism and later episcopal sealing. The bishops, he apparently argued, could therefore recognize schismatic baptism without compromising their proper role in the ritual: they alone could complete the ritual initiated by their own assistants or even by a schismatic. Cyprian, however, would allow no parallel between the efficacy of baptism performed within the church by a deacon or presbyter and the ritual performed outside by a pretender bishop. Even prior to the episcopal sealing, he insisted, the entire divine gift was conferred by baptism within the church, regardless of the rank of the minister.[85] This argument was not fully compatible with his response to Jubianus, however, where Cyprian allowed the standard distinction between the forgiveness of sins in baptism and the subsequent conferring of the Holy Spirit by the bishop's sealing.[86] Cyprian, of course, might not have perceived a conflict in the two positions because the presbyter or deacon acting within the church could not be compared to the schismatic bishop acting outside it.[87]

Thus in outlook and argument, the letters to Magnus, Jubianus and Pompeius appear closely related to one another. The letter to Jubianus, in particular, repeated and revised many of the arguments used in the response to Magnus, which might have been the first in this series. Even in their variations, however, all three were clearly distinct from the two conciliar letters and Cyprian's reply to Quintus which have been firmly dated in the first stage of the controversy.[88] As has been indicated in passing, these letters were also closely related to the revision of *On Unity*. They will, therefore, be treated as a group dealing with the Novatianist problem which became the focus of the second phase of the rebaptism controversy, during the summer and fall of 256.[89] Firmilian's letter of response to Cyprian can also be used as a mirror of the arguments which were made in the documents sent to him, so closely does it appear to have followed points which are found in Cyprian's surviving letters. The discussion shall proceed, therefore, on the working hypothesis that the first three letters[90] dealt with the reception of laxists schismatics and the other four letters[91] focused on the rigorists through the lens of African experience with the laxists.

The initial stage of the controversy

During the part of the controversy which is represented by the post-Easter councils of 254 or 255 and that of 256, as well as by Cyprian's letter to Quintus, the defining issue was the appropriateness of applying the African policy of rebaptism to converts from schism, as distinct from heresy. Unlike heretics who dissented from true doctrine, the questioners observed, schismatics shared the ritual and profession of faith through which the one Christian baptism was performed.[92] Cyprian and his colleagues, however, focused not on the similarity of doctrine and ceremony but on the exclusive unity of the church. They asserted that the one baptism could be found only within the one church and concluded that those who opposed that unity were separated from its unicity and could share none of its powers. The arguments offered in these three letters interpreted the baptismal question as an extension of the original controversy over the readmission of the lapsed into the communion of the church. In both cases, the bishops denied the power to forgive sins to their opponents and asserted the efficacy of their own rituals of purification.

One set of arguments pointed to the inseparable link between the Spirit, the unique church, and the one baptism. The church, Cyprian recalled from the first versions of *On Unity*, was built by Christ upon each local bishop, represented by Peter. Those who separated from their bishop's communion thereby lost all the endowments which Christ bestowed upon the church.[93] Cyprian insisted, moreover, that in rebelling against the church, the leaders of the schism had made themselves enemies of Christ and thus incapable of acting for him.[94] As dead men, they could give no life to others;[95] polluted by their crime of dividing the church, they could perform no sacred functions.[96] The same point was made by citing the baptismal interrogation, in which the candidate was asked to affirm that everlasting life and the forgiveness of sins came through the holy church: to grant the efficacy of baptism to schismatics would be to concede the church itself to them.[97] The Catholic bishops, Cyprian concluded, must themselves uphold and defend the unity of the church in practice by rejecting the pretensions of the schismatics and offering the one Christian baptism to converts from competing communions.[98]

A second set of arguments focused on the ritual of baptism itself. How could a bishop who was himself loaded with sins and deprived of the Holy Spirit sanctify the waters of baptism; how celebrate the sacrifice through which the oil of anointing was hallowed; how offer the solemn prayer for the neophytes; how confer the Holy Spirit?[99] Because the gift of the Holy Spirit was essential for any sanctifying action, the ritual of baptism could not be divided into parts, some of which even the schismatics might effect while others were beyond their power. A minister could effect all or nothing. Thus the African bishops reasoned that if the imposition of hands must be repeated by a Catholic bishop in order to confer the Holy Spirit upon a convert baptized and sealed in schism, then the water baptism itself must also be performed again for the forgiveness of sins.[100] Peter himself, the bishops observed in writing to Stephen, demonstrated the inseparability of the two stages of baptism: even though Cornelius and his friends had clearly received the outpouring of the Holy Spirit, Peter still ordered that they be baptized in water.[101] Cyprian and his colleagues did, of course, recognize that schismatics who had been baptized originally in the true church could be received back into it like other penitents, by the imposition of hands alone and without the repetition of baptism. Only those truly baptized, however, could be received as penitents. Hence, in receiving schismatic converts by the imposition of hands alone, a Catholic bishop would actually be performing the second half of the initiation ritual rather than reconciling a penitent, and thus would be recognizing the efficacy of schismatic baptism.[102] Such practice, Cyprian then concluded, was inconsistent with both the documented practice of the apostles and a sound understanding of the operation of the Spirit.[103]

As they had during the conflict over the purification of idolaters, Cyprian and his colleagues evinced that strong sense of ritual efficacy which characterizes tightly bounded communities. They insisted that the baptism and anointing performed in schism were not empty and meaningless rituals but actually had harmful effects on their recipients. The baptismal water and oil of anointing had become polluted by contact with the sinful ministers; they then soiled those to whom they were applied. Through the ritual, converts to schismatic Christianity contracted the sin of the ministers, even though they might have unwittingly wandered in their quest for salvation and been deceived by the schismatic clergy.[104]

Throughout this part of the debate, the ire of the Catholic bishops was directed against the leaders of the opposing communions, whom they characterized as having been adversaries of Christ even before they had gone forth in schism.[105] In contrast, the bishops remained sympathetic and welcoming to the followers of the rebels and to those whom they subsequently led astray.[106] Though these unfortunates would be deprived of salvation by dying outside the true church, Christ would require an account for their souls from the authors of their perdition.[107]

In this first stage of the controversy over rebaptism, then, the arguments were focused on the unity and unicity of the church and on the exclusiveness of its bishops' power to forgive and sanctify through the rituals of baptism and the eucharist. In the second part of the conflict, new arguments were introduced by the Catholic opponents of rebaptism which questioned this close connection between the church and the power of Christian rituals.

The second stage of the controversy

After the council of African bishops in spring 256 had affirmed a common policy on the reception of converts baptized outside the church and clerics who returned from schism, Cyprian received a series of pointed inquiries objecting to the baptismal policy. Two of these, from Magnus and Jubianus, were apparently answered before the Roman bishop rejected the decisions made by his African colleagues. A third letter was sent later in the summer to Pompeius. Unlike the two earlier letters of the councils and that of Cyprian himself to Quintus, these three letters specified Novatian as the cause of concern and discussed his baptismal practice in detail. Cyprian's responses were initially gracious but became increasingly impatient as he faced the arguments advanced for the salvific efficacy of Christian rituals performed in opposition to the church of Christ, in rebellion against its bishops. The letter to Magnus, as has been seen, appears to be the earliest of the three and thus will be considered first; then the letters to Jubianus and Pompeius will be reviewed together. Finally, the views of Cyprian which were reflected in the letter of Firmilian of Caesarea in Cappadocia will be considered.

The letter to Magnus

Cyprian's response to Magnus shared the perspectives and many of the arguments of the conciliar letters; it regularly elaborated their themes, however, and introduced new considerations. The first set of reasons which Cyprian offered for the inefficacy of the rivals' baptism was its being performed outside and in opposition to the church. The texts of Lk. 11.23 and 1 Jn. 2.18–19 which were used in the first conciliar letter to brand the schismatics as enemies and antichrists were here joined by that of Mt. 18.17, in which the community was instructed to treat those who refused to heed its warning as heathen.[108] Cyprian next introduced an array of related images which portrayed the church as the bride of Christ, a beloved only daughter, an enclosed garden, a sealed fountain, a well of living water, the ark of Noah riding above the flood. All showed that the church's treasures were fully protected from the outsider, who could not share them.[109] Finally, the unity of the church was compared to the house in which the passover meal was eaten and the home of Rahab in Jericho where her family found refuge: those who voluntarily deserted its safety were personally responsible for their own destruction.[110]

From these images of its separateness and exclusivity, Cyprian moved to the cosmic foundation of the unity of the church, in the harmony of wills shared by Christ and the Father. In discord from the unanimity of the church, a person could be neither a shepherd nor a member of the one flock.[111] The unity of many grains and grapes in the one loaf and cup of the eucharist also expressed the cohesiveness of the flock of Christ. Because Novatian rebelled against the ordinance of the gospel and the tradition coming from the apostles, he and his supporters could not share the effects of the church's one and only baptism;[112] instead, they would share the fate of the heathen.[113]

As in the earlier letters, the discussion of the unity of the church led Cyprian to the examination of the ritual of baptism itself. In response to Magnus' observation that Novatian used the same ritual and profession of faith as the Catholic bishops, Cyprian focused on the link between the church, the Holy Spirit and the efficacy of the rituals. Modifying an earlier argument, Cyprian asserted that Novatian, who had abandoned the unity of the church, should omit that section of the baptismal interrogation in which the candidate was asked to confess that sins were forgiven only through the holy church.[114] Nor, he observed, had sharing belief in the one God turned the divine wrath aside from those Israelites who rebelled against the authority of Aaron.[115] Even the ritual of imposing hands, which Magnus proposed for the reception of schismatics, demonstrated to Cyprian that no one could receive or confer the Holy Spirit outside the church.[116] Yet Christ clearly indicated that only those who shared the Holy Spirit could exercise the power of forgiving sins and could thus perform baptism.[117] The text of Jn. 20.22–3,[118] which was here employed, would play a prominent role in the revision of *On Unity*, where it demonstrated the equality of all the bishops who received their common power directly from Christ. In the letter to Magnus, the text confirmed the link between the possession of the Spirit and the power to purify from sin through baptism.[119] Finally, Cyprian observed that even John the Baptist had received the Holy Spirit in his mother's womb, thereby demonstrating that only those who shared the gift of the Holy Spirit could baptize.[120]

Nor could the efficacy of the ritual be partitioned, Cyprian argued, in response to Magnus' suggestion of a parallel between schismatic baptism and that performed by a deacon or presbyter for the sick, when the bishop did not immediately add the anointing and sealing. The implication would have been that the schismatic baptism might have a lesser though real effect which was subsequently completed by the imposition of a true bishop's hands. Cyprian insisted that the washing ritual alone had a full salvific effect when performed within the unity of the church.[121] He admonished Magnus not to belittle the baptism of the church in a vain attempt to assign some value to the rituals of schismatics.[122]

Since Magnus had focused attention on Novatian, Cyprian moved beyond his earlier arguments based on the unity of the church and the structure of its baptismal ritual to attack the attempted usurpation of the episcopate. In violating the procedure established by Christ for selecting bishops, he asserted, Novatian had made himself not only an outsider to the unity of the church but an object of divine wrath. When the ten tribes rebelled against the Davidic kingship, God had destroyed the northern kingdom which they set up. Even the prophet sent to warn the rebels was killed by a lion on the return journey because he disobeyed the prohibition of eating or drinking with schismatics. During his own ministry to Israel, Christ forbade his disciples to preach to or help the Samaritans who continued that division of Israel's worship.[123] Even within a community of faith, Cyprian observed, those who challenged the priesthood of Aaron – along with all their followers – were immediately destroyed by God and their ritual instruments were ordered to be set up as a warning to future generations.[124] Cyprian professed amazement that any of his colleagues could defend Novatian's right to share their efficacious rituals.[125]

In many of these arguments, it will have been noted, Cyprian assumed a more severe stance toward the followers of Novatian than he had taken toward the adherents of that schism treated in the earlier letters. Those who left the sanctuary established by God in the unity of the church were responsible for their own destruction, he asserted, since unlike the lapsed, they were not cast out by the bishops but had departed of their own accord.[126] Even the supporters of those who challenged Aaron's office were ordered to be shunned by Israel and summarily punished by God.[127] Thus Cyprian concluded that all who intentionally joined themselves to the Novatianists had been defiled by their sin and would justly share their fate.[128] In the earlier letters, it will be recalled, the schismatic laity had been regarded as unintentionally stained by impure rituals. All these rigorist schismatics, in contrast, were fully responsible, since they deliberately participated in the sin of their leaders.[129]

In tone and argument, Cyprian's letter to Magnus seems to

belong to the intense conflict which arose in the summer of 256, a conflict clearly focused on the Novatianist schism. As such, it serves to distinguish the earlier stage of the controversy, which was apparently confined to the laxists in Africa. Close examination of the two letters which can be more firmly dated during this later period will confirm this hypothesis.

The letters to Jubianus and Pompeius

The letter of Jubianus to Cyprian and the unidentified letter he sent along introduced new theological elements into the controversy and, in particular, appeal to the efficacy of both the divine name and the faith of the person baptized. The letter to Pompeius indicated that the bishop of Rome had strongly defended an apostolic tradition of accepting the baptism performed by heretics. Cyprian responded to these theological and historical arguments by appeals to scripture and practice but he regularly returned to what had always been, for him, the defining issue in the debate – the exclusive unity of the church and the boundary effectively dividing insiders from outsiders.

In response to the claim that baptism could be effective because of its invocation of the name of Jesus, Cyprian cited instances in which Christ himself warned that calling on his name might be inefficacious or even deceitful; he added other texts in which Christ required recognition of the Father and baptism in the name of the Trinity.[130] He then observed that the name of Jesus could not win the forgiveness of sins outside the unity of the church.[131] Would Christ, after threatening to deny anyone who denied him, then support someone who had denied his Father instead? Or, Cyprian added, the church, the very mother claimed by the false Christian?[132]

To the argument that the faith of the recipient of baptism won the forgiveness of sins, independently of the heretical beliefs of the minister, Cyprian replied that the appeal to saving belief proved too much. If the recipient's faith could win the forgiveness of sins, it would also earn the gift of the Holy Spirit. Yet even the objector required that such a convert receive the imposition of hands for the giving of the Holy Spirit.[133] Returning to familiar ground, he argued that not even martyrdom, the most perfect of baptisms and professions of faith, could save when it was suffered in opposition to the unity of the church.[134]

A third set of objections appealed to a tradition deriving from the apostles themselves which recognized the efficacy of baptism, even when performed in heresy or schism. Had not the same apostles clearly handed down the teaching of a single church and one baptism within that church, Cyprian asked.[135] His own analysis, moreover, showed that apostolic practice supported the exclusive unity of the church. Certainly Paul recognized the preaching of envious brothers, but within the church.[136] Peter and John received the Samaritans by the imposition of hands alone but they had been baptized by Philip within the church.[137] Paul, in contrast, rebaptized the disciples of John the Baptist, even though he had been filled with the spirit (of Elijah), because John's baptism was performed outside the unity of the church.[138] Thus Cyprian met Stephen's appeal to an apostolic tradition maintained in the Roman Church by demonstrating that according to the clear evidence of scripture, the apostles had always defended the unity of the church and its exclusive claim to both the Holy Spirit and baptism. The objectors, he asserted, were preferring human custom to divine law.[139]

A fourth group of arguments was based upon established practices of the church. In insisting on rebaptism, Jubianus implied, the Africans were following an innovation introduced by Novatian. Cyprian retorted that Novatian was absolutely right in principle: because he recognized that the one baptism could be held and conferred only by the one church, he claimed both of them for himself alone by refusing to recognize the baptism given by bishops outside his communion. Novatian was inconsistent, Cyprian wryly observed, only in failing to rebaptize himself and all who joined him in founding his church.[140] Thus Cyprian reversed the charge: because some Catholic bishops could not grasp a principle obvious to Novatian, they ignored their own identifying boundaries and allowed the treasures of the church to be carried off by renegades.[141] Cyprian found this same failure to appreciate the unity of the church evident in other objections raised against the practice of rebaptism. A catechumen who died a martyr before formal baptism not only achieved the more perfect baptism, he explained, but owed its efficacy to confessing Christ within the unity of the church. Even the communicants who might be admitted by erring bishops through the imposition of hands but without rebaptism could be saved through the divine mercy, because they belonged to the unity of the church.[142]

Although new arguments, specific to the practice of Novatian and the traditions of the church, had been introduced by his correspondents, Cyprian continued to define the status of heretics and schismatics primarily if not exclusively on the basis of their relation to the unity of the church and the authority of its bishops. He repeated and augmented the images by which he had earlier asserted and illustrated the significance of the containing boundary of the church: its waters could not flow outside of paradise; the water from the belly of Christ was given only in the church founded on Peter; the church was like an enclosed garden with a sealed fountain or like the ark of Noah.[143] How, he demanded, could a person be born a child of God apart from the one bride whom Christ washed and sanctified; how could one who had not yet been born of God be sanctified by the imposition of hands; how could the offspring of an adulteress or prostitute be acknowledged by the Father?[144] Could the Holy Spirit be divided and parceled out between two opposed and conflicting communities, so that baptism might be performed in both?[145] The issue, he insisted, would be easily settled by defining and defending the boundaries which separated insiders from outsiders.[146]

Cyprian also appealed to the differentiation of roles within the one church, specifically the divinely established procedures for selecting and empowering its ministers. The power of forgiveness had been given first to Peter and then to the other disciples; thus only their legitimate successors within the unity of the church received the power to baptize and forgive sins. God's annihilating those who usurped the authority and power conferred upon Aaron clearly demonstrated that no one attacking the divine ordinances could exercise the church's power or escape the divine wrath.[147]

Over the summer of 256, as this review indicates, Cyprian became increasingly impatient with bishops who did not share the African understanding of the church and its powers. After repeatedly attempting to explain and demonstrate the basis for this position, he began to denounce his opponents. As he charged heretics and schismatics with practicing fraud and deceit by offering a baptism which polluted rather than cleansed, with preventing rather than conferring the grace of faith,[148] so he warned his Catholic colleagues that they were contributing to that deception. Converts to the true church knew that the baptism they had earlier received in schism was empty and vain. When they came seeking the gifts of the true church, however, some bishops denied them.[149] By refusing to rebaptize these converts, moreover, the Catholic bishops sent a false signal to those remaining in schism: that the schismatics possessed and conferred true baptism, and thereby forgiveness of sins and the other saving blessings of the church. Reviving an argument he had originally directed against the laxist clergy after the persecution, Cyprian charged them with making the schismatics complacent in their error and thereby cruelly preventing their salvation. Receiving schismatics by baptism rather than the imposition of hands alone was, Cyprian urged, the only responsible course of action.[150]

Finally, Cyprian had become exasperated at the objections raised by his correspondents who were obstinately defending erroneous custom even after the Holy Spirit had made the truth clear.[151] Indeed, he suggested that the defenders of the efficacy of heretical and schismatic baptism were participating in the evil of their clients by dismissing their blasphemy against the Father and Holy Spirit as harmless, as well as by sharing communion with sinners whom they refused to cleanse in the waters of baptism.[152] Not only had such bishops failed to protect the gifts which had been bestowed on the church by God,[153] they now threatened to split the unity of the episcopal college by quarreling with their fellow bishops in order to defend heretics.[154] Although Cyprian ended by granting each bishop freedom to follow the direction he considered best,[155] the rhetoric of these letters clearly marked out the one path of sanity and sanctity.

The letter from Firmilian of Caesarea

The letter which Firmilian addressed to Cyprian certainly reflected the viewpoint of the dossier of letters which had been sent to him and the additional information which the courier, the deacon Rogatianus, was able to provide.[156] Although Firmilian professed that he was adopting Cyprian's reasoning and even his words, he also indicated his intention to add his own thoughts.[157] In a few areas, Firmilian's arguments were more elaborate than they appeared in Cyprian's surviving correspondence. In recalling the image of the ark of Noah, for example, he observed that everyone outside the ark had been drowned, specifying the fate of the schismatics which Cyprian had implied.[158] Additional scriptural citations supported Cyprian's thesis that the church was the only bride of Christ and sole mother of the children of God.[159] Schismatics admitted to the communion without the prior cleansing of baptism, he warned, were placed in grave danger by coming into contact with the body of Christ.[160]

Firmilian provided information about the policy of the church in

Cappadocia which paralleled and confirmed the position adopted by the African bishops. In particular, he attacked Stephen's assertion that apostolic tradition required all bishops to accept baptism performed by heretics. He insisted that such practice could hardly be traced back to the founding of the church, because heresy had arisen only after the establishment of true faith by the apostles.[161] The Romans had not always preserved customs accurately, he observed, as instanced by their deviation from the authentic practice of the earliest Christian church – the one in Jerusalem – on the proper date of the Easter observance.[162] Having thus prepared the ground, Firmilian asserted that the Cappadocian church had always followed the practice of rebaptizing converts from heresy. When the policy was questioned because of the activities of Montanus, an episcopal council had confirmed the original practice even in the case of schism. He congratulated the African church for giving up the erroneous custom of accepting converts by the imposition of hands and embracing the truth once it had been recognized. The Cappadocians, he boasted, had always united truth and custom.[163] Firmilian also attacked the appeal to the similarity of the schismatic to the Catholic ritual by citing an instance in which a woman who turned out to be possessed by a demon had baptized and offered the eucharist in the customary manner but with a different effect.[164]

Firmilian did not, however, share Cyprian's appreciation of the salvific efficacy of participation in the unity of the church. In response to the objection that in the past heretics and schismatics had been admitted to the communion without baptism, Firmilian suggested as a parallel the case of a catechumen who died before receiving baptism.[165] Both the convert and the catechumen received some unspecified but real advantage by abandoning idolatry or heresy to accept the true faith but neither qualified for the fullness of grace and the remission of sins.[166] Unlike Firmilian, Cyprian had steadfastly refused to divide the efficacy of divine grace, so that a person might receive only a partial measure.[167] The implications of his distinction were clarified, moreover, when Firmilian warned that on the day of judgment Christ would hold bishops responsible for the deaths of the converts from heresy and schism from whom they had withheld the waters of life.[168] Cyprian, in contrast, believed that the divine mercy could reach those who shared the unity of the church even though they had not been properly baptized, and consequently, he allowed each bishop to follow the procedure he considered best in admitting converts to communion.[169] Relying on the indivisibility of the divine grace, he could trust in the efficacy of the eucharist to supply for the inadequacies of baptismal initiation.

Firmilian's response to Cyprian affirmed the African policy and the reasons which had been advanced to justify it. Even in supporting the practice of rebaptizing, however, Firmilian showed that the Africans had drawn out the implications of the unity and exclusivity of the church in ways which the Cappadocians had not yet grasped. The laxist schism had shaped the thinking of the African bishops.

The climactic council

On 1 September 256, bishops from the provinces of Proconsular Africa, Numidia and Mauretania, along with a number of priests and deacons and a great number of the laity, gathered in extraordinary session in Carthage to meet the challenge of Stephen's rejection of the decision made by the council of the previous spring. The correspondence between Jubianus and Cyprian was read out as an introduction to the expression of judgments: the original inquiry, Cyprian's response, and Jubianus' consent to the reply. Each of the bishops was then asked to give his opinion in the matter. The secretary recorded eighty-five voices, one of which carried proxies for two colleagues. All asserted that the baptism performed outside the church was not to be accepted; converts were all to be baptized upon first entrance into the Catholic communion.

Some of the arguments which Cyprian had been making were clearly reflected in the opinions of his colleagues. Twenty-four of the *sententiae* explicitly affirmed that there was only one baptism and that could be performed only within the one church.[170] Six made the point that to approve the baptism performed by the opponents was to make their own ritual vain and empty.[171] Individual bishops picked up variations of this theme: those who do not have the Father, Son and Spirit could not have the church or baptism;[172] forgiveness of sins could not be given outside the church.[173] A significant minority of the bishops affirmed the hard line that Cyprian himself had inserted into the debate, asserting that to admit the converts without baptizing them was actually to communicate in their sin.[174] Three went so far as to imply that if the converts were not baptized upon entrance into the true church, they would not be saved.[175]

The listing of episcopal judgments in the *acta* of the meeting indicated that the primary issues in the controversy were those

one bishop
one true church
confuses human institution with the "body of Christ"

which the two earlier councils and Cyprian himself had put first. The ritual of baptism could be effectively performed only by the power of the Holy Spirit within the unity of the one church. The term "church" was used to encompass a set of local gatherings of the faithful, each of whose bishops brought it into union with the others. Any local communion which stood outside or in opposition to one of those local gatherings was not a church or part of the larger church. Thus the boundary between the church and the non-church was very carefully and definitely drawn. To grant to any opposed gathering the status of church, with its power to act in the name and authority of God, would have been to deprive oneself and one's whole communion of that status. For the African bishops, this was a matter not of discipline or custom but of foundational belief: those who divided from them were heretics, whose faith did not save.[176] The church itself had become part of the dogma of the African Christians.

Opposition within Africa

The treatise *On Rebaptism*, whose authorship and exact dating cannot be precisely established, was apparently written as part of a continuing controversy within the African church. It argued against the position which had been advanced by Cyprian and supported by his colleagues but does not appear to know their correspondence on the subject which has survived.[177] In many ways, however, it relied on principles and a perspective which were remarkably similar to those the African bishops had offered for the practice it challenged.

Citing scripture to buttress its assertion of the efficacy of the ritual, the treatise argued that the name of Jesus produced results which were independent of the individuals and communities by whom it was invoked. The enemies of Jesus, according to Mt. 7.22–3[178] and 24.23–4,[179] could perform miracles and control demons by calling upon his name, even though they would thereby neither gain nor confer salvation.[180] Thence the author inferred that even Christ's opponents could baptize with water in his name. He then reasoned that by repeating the invocation in a repetition of that baptism, the church would dishonor Jesus and the power of his name.[181] The treatise did not succeed in specifying the effect which water baptism alone might have outside the unity of the church, though it insisted that it either helped or hindered, depending on the person's subsequent action.[182]

Since the effect of water baptism, at least when performed

124

outside the church, remained unspecified, this author assigned the heavenly efficacy of the church's ritual of initiation to baptism in the Holy Spirit, which was usually given by the imposition of episcopal hands within the church.[183] Again citing scriptural precedent, the author argued that this spirit baptism had the power to forgive sins and bring a person to salvation.[184] Thus the normal ritual of initiation included both water and spirit baptism, in a two-stage ceremony. Within the unity of the church, water baptism alone might be salvific – as regularly occurred in the emergency baptism of the dying by lower clergy – because Christ himself would substitute for the bishop by conferring the Holy Spirit upon the departed.[185] If the newly baptized recovered, the bishop would confer the saving baptism of the Spirit.[186] Water baptism conferred outside the church, however, must be completed through the imposition of the bishop's hands upon reception into the true church.[187] If the heretic or schismatic did not join the church before death, Christ would refuse to supplement the water baptism by conferring the Spirit himself; the outsider would be condemned as an enemy. The schismatic was condemned as an evil doer; the heretic for refusing to seek Christ himself, being satisfied with the name alone.[188]

On Rebaptism partially shared Cyprian's understanding of the cosmic significance of the boundary separating the true church from false Christians. Salvation was limited to the unity of the church: the saving spirit baptism could be received only by those within the church, either from the bishop or from Christ. Outside the true church, heretics and schismatics could neither confer nor receive the Holy Spirit.[189] Even within the church, only the bishop could give the baptism of the Spirit.[190] In order to assign some efficacy to water baptism performed outside the church, however, the treatise had to postulate a heavenly supplement performed for those who died within the church after water baptism but before receiving the imposition of episcopal hands. By implication, this requirement would have undercut the efficacy of the water baptism performed within the church, removing its power to forgive and sanctify, to carry the recipient across the cosmic boundary between heaven and hell.[191] What Cyprian, his colleagues, and their congregations celebrated as the ritual of crossing both a social and cosmic boundary became a preparatory ceremony, a step toward the saving ritual of spirit baptism through the imposition of hands. Tertullian had proposed such a distinction between the two parts of the ritual.[192] The second, saving ritual, however, might even be performed in heaven by Christ. Thus *On Rebaptism* accepted the communion of the church as a necessary condition rather than a cause of salvation.

The difference between the estimation of the heavenly significance of the church in *On Rebaptism* and that of Cyprian was also evident in its consideration of the status of heretics. Like the first bishops who wrote to Cyprian about the problem of schism, the treatise focused Christian dogma on the Creator and the Christ.[193] Cyprian and his colleagues, it will be recalled, agreed that the schismatics were actually heretics not because they dissented on the identity of the Creator or the status of Christ but because they did not profess faith in the one church as the sole agent of forgiveness, sanctification and salvation.[194]

The significance of social structures

The controversy over rebaptism among the bishops of Africa and against the bishop of Rome can be analyzed in terms of the coherence of the social groups and the differentiation of roles within them. In this instance, moreover, the belief in the efficacy of ritual requires particular attention.

During the conflict over the power to forgive sins, Cyprian and his colleagues had been uncertain of their ability to forgive the sin of idolatry, because Christ had asserted that anyone who denied him on earth would be denied by him in heaven. As was proposed in the analysis of that controversy, the bishops solved the problem of readmitting the idolaters to the church by relying on the parallel element in Christ's statement: those who confessed him on earth would be acknowledged in heaven.[195] With the persecution over, of course, there was no longer an opportunity for the kind of public confession of Christ which would reverse the equally public denial. The laxist schism, however, did provide just the sort of opportunity for confession of Christ which the lapsed needed.

The laxists asserted that submission to the penitential ritual of the church and the authority vested in the bishop was not necessary for receiving forgiveness of the sin of idolatry. Instead, the lapsed could attain direct access to Christ through the martyrs and their delegated agents among the surviving confessors. Cyprian interpreted this as a revolt against the church and a second form of persecution. He identified the schismatics as agents of the devil. Thence he suggested that to resist the temptation by remaining within the unity of the church and submitting to its penitential discipline was to confess Christ by recognizing the assemblies and their bishops as God's designated agents. Those who gave up the letters of peace received from the martyrs and submitted to the discipline of penance thereby confessed before the community that Christ had made the church the sole means of access to the kingdom. Moreover, when Cyprian asserted that the sin of schism, of attempting to divide the church, was equivalent to idolatry, he implied that to resist this sin was itself a rejection of false gods and a confession of Christ. While they judged that confessing the unity and holiness of the church was more ambiguous and its heavenly result less certain than martyrdom, Cyprian and his colleagues asserted that it did sufficiently rehabilitate and cleanse the penitents, so that their idolatry was rendered non-contagious and the penitents would win a hearing before the tribunal of Christ.

The admission of the certified was begun in spring 251. Two years later, in April 253, the penitent sacrificers were reconciled to the church in anticipation of renewed persecution. The surviving records of the controversy over rebaptism indicate that this question arose in spring 254 or 255, one or two years after the admission of the last of the lapsed. Apparently, some of Cyprian's colleagues were confused because the schismatics were using the same ritual and confession of faith as they were. Cyprian, however, immediately focused attention on the well-established role of the church as the agent of Christ in the forgiveness of sins. As enemies of the church, he insisted, the schismatics could not forgive sins by calling on the name of Christ in baptism any more than they had been able to forgive the sin of idolatry by appeal to the martyrs. Instead, their rituals would spread the guilt of schism, just as they had the pollution of idolatry. Only the one church built by Christ upon the bishops had been given the authority to purify and sanctify. Observing that the role of the church as the agent of forgiveness was included in the baptismal confession of faith, he concluded that no one could profess faith and win forgiveness in opposition to the church.

Because the African episcopate had made acceptance of the church's power to forgive sins in the face of the laxist schism a form of public confession of faith in Christ, Cyprian argued that it could not recognize the efficacy of schismatic baptism. As a result, the gift of the Holy Spirit which endowed the one church with the authority to forgive sins was made a dogma of the African church. This advance in its turn eliminated the distinction between heretics and schismatics: no one could confess the forgiveness of sins through the church while acting in opposition to the unity of the church.

Thus the foundational issue in the African stand on the efficacy of baptism performed outside the church was the significance of the boundary which defined the communion of the church. In the view of Cyprian and his colleagues, this was a clearly delineated social boundary which marked off insiders from outsiders, those who were allowed to participate in the eucharist from those who were not. This social boundary was assigned a heavenly as well as an earthly significance: because it specified the limits of the presence and operation of the Holy Spirit, it also determined who might gain access to the kingdom of heaven. Within the church, water and oil could be sanctified, the divine name could be invoked, saving faith could be professed; outside the church, water and oil were polluted by idolatry or schism, appeals to Christ were in vain, the baptismal profession contradicted its very interrogation. Cyprian asserted that the rituals and prayers of the church were efficacious not because their formulae were properly invoked or their actions correctly performed but primarily because they were operations of the church.

The significance of the bounded community itself in the thinking of the African church can be grasped in the two points at which Firmilian of Caesarea differed from Cyprian. The Asians allowed some positive standing to the catechumen who had renounced idolatry but died without baptism and to the schismatic admitted to the church by the imposition of hands but without baptism. The Africans refused salvation to both the unbaptized catechumen and the unreconciled penitent because they died outside the unity of the communion. By relying on the efficacy of the eucharistic ritual, however, the Africans could regularize the status of schismatics who had been admitted to the unity of the church without being rebaptized in the past and could even tolerate such future admissions without jeopardizing the salvation of the converts. The Asians, in contrast, feared the unbaptized as polluters of the eucharistic fellowship. Unlike the Asians, the Africans made the bounded community itself the agent of salvation.

The African treatise *On Rebaptism* shared this positive view of the unity of the church. Because it acknowledged the efficacy of the name of Jesus, even when it was invoked outside the church, its author identified the imposing of hands within the church as the ritual necessary for crossing the boundary into the kingdom of heaven. Christ himself would confer spirit baptism upon those who died after water baptism in the unity of the church but not upon those who died in opposition to it. Outside the church, the name of

Jesus was effective but inadequate; inside the church it was actually a sufficient condition for salvation.

The differentiation of roles within the church also played a part in the African understanding of the efficacy of baptism. In the conflict with the laxists and rigorists over penance, Cyprian had focused on the bishop, symbolized by Peter, as the basis for the unity in the local church. In the controversy over rebaptism, he relied more heavily on the role of the apostolic college as the recipient and transmitter of the gift of the Holy Spirit and the consequent power to forgive sins. The succession of legitimate bishops guaranteed the efficacy of the baptismal ritual. Both the laxist and rigorist bishops lacked this power not only because they stood in opposition to the church but also because they had not qualified for the episcopal role by legitimate succession. To admit that a rival bishop had the power to forgive sins through baptism or to advance salvation in any other way was to abandon one's own claim to be the one legitimate bishop in the one church authorized by Christ. For Cyprian, moreover, it was to undercut the interpretation of schism upon which he had built the purification and admission of the lapsed who submitted to the authority of the church.

The Africans' understanding of the significance of the episcopal office appeared as well in their map of the unity of the church. To Cyprian and his colleagues, the church was first and foremost the specific local assembly whose unity was established by Christ upon the one bishop symbolized by Peter. These local churches were built into the full flock of Christ through equally concrete alliances of their episcopal leaders, all of them in succession to the original apostolic community, all meeting to deliberate on the good of the whole. The Holy Spirit had been conferred upon Peter and the other apostles and passed to their successors, who in turn shared the Spirit within their local communions. That someone could quit the unity of this assembly, rebel against the authority of its bishop, establish a competing community within the same town, and there exercise the power to forgive and sanctify, was unimaginable and inconceivable to Cyprian. In his view, the Holy Spirit and thus the power to purify simply could not be found on both sides of such a division between churches. His African colleagues, who had shared the struggle to maintain the coherence of the local communities under the twin attacks of the Decian persecution and the laxist schism, came to think, and more importantly to imagine, in the same way. Cyprian articulated a world view, sketched a map of the union of heaven and earth; once his colleagues grasped it, they defended it adamantly.

Cyprian and his colleagues also believed in that system of ritual efficacy which is characteristic of tightly bounded communities. All rituals were effective: those performed within the church cleansed and sanctified; those performed in opposition polluted and condemned. Within the unity of the church, the ritual of water baptism accomplished the initiation of the Christian, even if it was not supplemented by the imposition of episcopal hands. If a Catholic bishop failed to rebaptize a schismatic or heretical convert, the eucharistic ritual could effect the initiatory cleansing. Outside the church, the rituals of idolaters, heretics and schismatics were not empty and harmless; they would contaminate and condemn those who shared them. *On Rebaptism* even recognized an efficacy in the invocation of the name of Jesus which transcended the church itself, though it asserted the necessity of spirit baptism, even if it had to be performed in heaven by Christ himself. The Africans agreed in believing that the rituals were both necessary and effective in gaining access to the kingdom of heaven.

Finally, the African Catholic insistence on control over the boundary of the church by the rituals of baptism and reconciliation must be understood within the context of active struggle against the imperial culture and the schismatic churches. The social boundary of their church had been severely challenged. The Christians lived under recurring threat of persecution; they suffered repeated internal conflict and division. In the debate over rebaptism, the schismatics were former colleagues and the conflict was personal. Thus the sympathy which Cyprian extended to those who had first become Christian in the laxist and rigorist communions was not extended to those who had perpetrated the rebellion. This legacy of partisan conflict would continue to trouble the African church for centuries to come.

Conclusion

The analysis of the controversy over the rebaptism of schismatics which is here proposed rests upon two foundational hypotheses. First, the controversy was a continuation of the conflict between the three communions in Africa over the power to forgive sins rather than being driven by a demand to coordinate the procedures for accepting significant numbers of converts baptized in schism. Second, the controversy began over relations with the laxist communion and only later involved the rigorist schism, which was much less significant in Africa than in Italy. The thesis here advanced states that the African bishops responded to the question of rebaptism as they had to that of the forgiveness of the sin of idolatry; they were guided by their assumptions about the social boundary of the church and the role differentiation within it. Thus they concluded that the unity of the church and its exclusive power to sanctify were integral to the Christian confession of faith. Schism, therefore, became a form of heresy.

7

PURITY OF THE CHURCH

Cyprian might seem to have inaugurated a mediating position for preserving the holiness of the church by restricting to the clergy the purity requirement which had extended to the whole assembly: he argued that penitent apostates could be admitted to communion without polluting the entire congregation accepting them; yet he insisted that the sanctifying power of the church depended upon the holiness of the clergy, particularly their freedom from all taint of idolatry, apostasy or schism. The outcome of Cyprian's actions in response to the ecclesiastical consequences of the Decian persecution might be so summarized but his stance was actually less innovative and more nuanced. Cyprian's primary concern at the time he considered the admission of the penitent lapsed was not the danger of pollution which would jeopardize the church's holiness and power to sanctify but a fear of inciting divine wrath by contravening the corrective function of the persecution itself. When he dealt with failed clergy within the unity of the church, he judged that they posed a threat of contamination only to clergy and laity who actually consented to their sins. In neither of these cases was the holiness of the church itself necessarily in jeopardy. When Christian rituals of baptism and eucharist were performed outside and in opposition to the unity of the church, however, they not only failed to sanctify but polluted their participants in the same way as the idolatrous ceremonies of Roman polytheism.

In fact, Cyprian did not introduce an entirely new policy for dealing with either lapsed laity or unworthy clergy. The custom of the Roman church and at least some parts of the African church had allowed penitents – even those who had accused themselves of apostasy – to be reconciled and readmitted to communion at the time of death. This position was announced by the presbyters of the church in Rome[1] and Cyprian himself adopted it under pressure from the community in Carthage even during the persecution.[2] Penitents admitted at the last moment of life only for the purpose of dying in the communion would still have posed a threat to the purity of the church, as Novatian later insisted; their survival in the communion, moreover, could not be precluded.[3] The true innovations were made when the bishops voted to allow first the penitent certified and then the sacrificers into communion while still in good health. Similarly, Cyprian inherited an established practice which required that clerics who had proven themselves unworthy be removed from office. Nor was apostasy the sole charge on which clerics were excluded.[4] This view was shared not only by the bishops of Africa but by Cornelius and the bishops he consulted in Rome, as well as bishops in Spain.[5] Privatus of Lambaesis, for example, had been removed from office in a council held while Cyprian's predecessor, Donatus, was bishop of Carthage, and the decision was confirmed by the Roman bishop.[6] The innovation, introduced in Rome rather than Africa, seems to have been in demoting rather than excommunicating failed clerics.[7] Thus, at least in principle, the basic scheme for preserving church purity had been established prior to the Decian persecution and was followed during and after it.

The first task of the present chapter is to specify the concerns which faced Cyprian and his community on the admission of fallen laity and the exclusion of unworthy clergy. Then the specific positions which he and his episcopal colleagues took on the dangers posed by the sacrilegious rites of idolatry and schism will be explored.

The danger of divine wrath

In dealing with the lapsed laity during and immediately following the Decian persecution, Cyprian's concern was primarily the danger posed by their moral failures rather than their ritual impurity. During the early part of his exile, he wrote to the congregation in Carthage offering an interpretation of the persecution and urging the response appropriate for the community to make to it. Appealing to dream visions, Cyprian explained that God had allowed the persecution in order to demonstrate the church's negligence in its prayers and refusal to promote unity among its members. Since it was a divine call to repentance and reform, the persecution would be brought to an end once the entire church had mended its ways and prayed for the forgiveness of its sins.[8]

Cyprian argued that this divine intention to purify the church was manifest in the move from the first to the second phase of the enforcement of the Decian edict. After withstanding their interrogation by the Roman authorities, the initial set of confessors had been sent into exile. Some of them had then proven unworthy of their achievement: they violated their sentence by returning to Carthage, so that they might subsequently be punished as criminals rather than Christians; in addition, they transgressed the moral standards of the community in the celebration of their victory. Clearly, Cyprian observed, they had failed to grasp the divine intention in allowing the persecution; they returned to the community worse than when they had been dragged away from it.[9] As a consequence, Cyprian explained, God had allowed the Roman authorities to intensify the prosecution by introducing torture into the interrogation of the next set of Christian confessors, a development which produced both martyrs and reluctant apostates.[10] On this basis, Cyprian exhorted the community to repentance and united prayer, explaining that the persecution would continue a bit longer so that additional members of the church could be tested.[11] By reforming their lives and praying for one another in unity, however, Christians might voluntarily satisfy the purifying purpose for which God had brought the persecution. Divine forgiveness and imperial peace would then follow.[12] Clearly, Cyprian believed and expected his congregation to believe that God governed the universe according to moral standards; that God tested, rewarded and punished according to the merits and for the best interests, perhaps of all humans, but certainly of Christians. He asserted that the imperial prosecution was carried out by the Roman officials under both the instigation of Satan and the control of God. Thus he explained that although Christians had brought on the persecution by their negligence, God intended it for their correction and salvation. If they would heed the call to repentance and improvement, the imperial action would stop; if they continued to sin – as the first set of confessors had – it might be intensified still more. The divine intention to correct and punish would become Cyprian's guiding principle in directing the church's response to the persecution and in deliberating on the readmission of the lapsed.

By the letters of peace which they began to issue to all and sundry in the name of the martyrs, the Carthaginian confessors proposed the admission of the lapsed through the intercession of the martyrs and without requiring any penance. In three letters to the confessors, clergy and people, Cyprian then opposed this policy by signaling the danger of provoking divine anger through refusing that reform which the persecution was intended to promote.[13] The letter to the confessors did refer to the profanation of the body of the Lord which was perpetrated when the lapsed were admitted to communion without a purifying penance but Cyprian's focus was on the insult offered to God by the impenitence of the sinners rather than the pollution of the Christian offering. By cooperating in the audacity of the lapsed, he charged, the confessors would lead them to destruction rather than salvation.[14] In writing to the clergy, Cyprian again warned of the peril in which the lapsed had placed themselves by offending the Lord and recounted recent visions which confirmed his interpretation of the persecution as a correction.[15] God continued to rebuke, he warned, but the lapsed and their supporters, both oblivious to the threat, were in extreme danger. In contrast, Cyprian praised the faithful laity for the prayer and penance they were undertaking. Finally, he asked their support for the policy of delay in reconciling the lapsed until God had relented and given peace to the church as a whole, implying that additional time was necessary to allow the correction of Christians and even the purging of some.[16] In a subsequent letter to the clergy of Rome, in which he defended his voluntary exile and summarized the actions he had taken to care for the community, Cyprian emphasized the need for repentance and for imploring the mercy of God.[17] Thus his first response to the admission of the lapsed was to signal not the contamination of the communion by their participation but the danger of their flaunting the divine call to repentance given in the persecution itself. Even as God continued to rebuke and cleanse the church, some of the clergy and confessors were apparently allowing the lapsed, whom God had purged, to return unrepentant to the church's communion.

In writing to his community in Carthage, as has been seen, Cyprian did refer to the profanation of the body of Christ by the lapsed, using 1 Cor. 11.27 and 10.20–1.[18] In his first letter to the Roman clergy, he again spoke of the pollution of the hands and mouth of the lapsed through their contact with the sacrilegious sacrifices and even of their conscience by accepting the certificates of compliance from the imperial officials.[19] Once again, the context indicates that his intention was to signal not the threat which the lapsed posed to the sanctity of the communion but the clear and present danger that their readmission would provoke the anger of God.[20] Even after God had exhibited their sin to these people, they did not repent. Their very impenitence, he argued, confirmed the rightness of the divine judgment in bringing down persecution upon the church.[21]

Once he had returned to Carthage after Easter 251, Cyprian picked up the theme of persecution as reform again in his address to the community, *On the Lapsed*. After he had catalogued the sins of the Carthaginian community and the wider church which had originally made the persecution necessary,[22] he charged that the fallen had further provoked the divine anger by refusing to do penance.[23] Next he turned on the confessors and their clerical supporters: in a stupefying act of presumption, they claimed to have come to the aid of the church by securing divine mercy for the fallen. Could they truly have believed that God was in need of their assistance to forgive sins, to rescue Christians? In their blindness, the confessors and laxist clergy had failed to recognize that God was working the salvation of the church by testing, purifying and correcting. By their arrogance, they were impeding rather than aiding God's saving action.[24] The divine wrath of which he had been warning since the outbreak of persecution could now be discerned, Cyprian observed, in the very refusal of the lapsed to recognize and do penance for their sin. These fallen, he explained, were now being rejected rather than corrected by God.[25]

The understanding of persecution as divine correction and purification of the church remained an interpretative resource which could be applied to new situations. A year or so after his return to Carthage, for example, Cyprian argued that the lapsed bishop Fortunatianus must not be allowed to return to his office because God had intended to expose and remove such unworthy bishops through the persecution.[26] When a new imperial action was anticipated in spring 253, Cyprian again advanced his explanation of the divine purpose but in a modified form. Since he and his episcopal colleagues had decided to reconcile and restore to communion those who had received certificates and the penitent sacrificers who had come close to death, he would not assert that the church once again needed divine purification, and thereby suggest that God might be intent on removing those whom the bishops had readmitted. Instead, he argued that the church was being tested rather than purified, specifically that the divine mercy was providing a new opportunity for those sacrificers who were still doing penance to prove their devotion by public confession of the faith and thus regain full communion.[27] When the government in Rome struck at Cornelius but ignored Novatian, Cyprian observed that the persecution served the further function of distinguishing the true church from schisms. The sparing of the rigorists indicated not divine but demonic protection: Novatian was already serving Satan's cause by rebelling against Cornelius and need not be tempted again to abandon Christ.[28]

The persistence of this theme of divine testing and cleansing in Cyprian's interpretation of the persecution clearly demonstrates its significance for him. Though he signaled the impurity of hand, mouth and mind which the lapsed had incurred by their contact with idolatry, he did not identify this pollution as a source of danger to the church as a whole. Instead, as shall soon be seen, he believed it threatened primarily the individuals who carried it. His concern was not that admitting the lapsed would contaminate the communion and all its members but that their acceptance would further provoke divine wrath, which might then engulf even those who were still standing in the faith.

The danger of ritual pollution

Although ritual pollution from idolatry did not provide Cyprian's weapon of choice for attacking the laxists during and after the Decian persecution, he did hold and employ a concept of contamination through bodily contact, even involuntary contact, with the satanic ceremonies of idolatry. As has been noted, during the persecution he cited 1 Cor. 10.20–1, which he interpreted as forbidding contact with the table of the Lord after eating at the table of the demons.[29] He accused the lapsed of profaning the body of Christ by eating it unworthily, using 1 Cor. 11.27.[30] Similarly, in writing to the Roman clergy, he described the lapsed as having soiled their hands and mouths through contact with sacrilegious sacrifices.[31] In *On the Lapsed*, Cyprian employed the categories of ritual pollution more fully, returning over and again to the contamination which the fallen had incurred through their manual and oral contact with the sacrifices, again citing 1 Cor. 10.20–1 and 11.27. In this instance, however, he clarified the meaning of these texts by quoting Lev. 7.20: "Those who eat flesh from the Lord's sacrifice of well-being while in a state of uncleanness shall be cut off from their kin."[32] Thus Cyprian clearly indicated that the true danger was to the unclean individual touching the holy food of the Christian eucharist.[33] Similarly, he decried the foolishness of the lapsed when they assaulted the clergy who were trying to protect them from the divine wrath which would fall upon the sinners through their contact with the eucharist.[34] To illustrate the danger to anyone contaminated by idolatry, Cyprian then recounted the bodily and mental injuries which had resulted from sacrilegious contact with the eucharistic body of the Lord.[35] The Christian eucharist posed a danger to the contaminated, not the impure to the communion!

The examples of pollution which Cyprian offered to his congregation indicated that African Christians understood that idolatry contaminated not only through voluntary bodily contact but also when the touching was involuntary or even contrary to a person's explicitly manifest intention. In one striking instance, an infant who had been fed the demonic food by a nurse, without the knowledge or consent of the child's exiled parents, refused the eucharistic cup and then suffered extreme pain when the sacred blood was poured into its mouth.[36] In a similar vein, Bishop Caldonius wrote to Cyprian inquiring about the proper handling of the case of a wife who had been dragged to the place of sacrifice against her will. Her husband had actually forced her hand through the motion of the forbidden rituals, even as she maintained the purity of her conscience, Caldonius explained, screaming in protest that he rather than she was performing the deed. Caldonius asked whether the exile imposed by the governor for her steadfast confession of Christ, an exile shared with two male companions who had themselves sacrificed, was adequate to purify her from the sin.[37] In his response, Cyprian failed to distinguish the impurity of this woman who had been forced from that of the men who had willingly complied; he praised their confessions of Christ and consequent exile as a repentance for the sins.[38] Thus, Cyprian seems to have agreed with Caldonius in accepting a bodily pollution which could be incurred even contrary to a person's intention and thus required repentance and purification.

This significance of physical contact with idolatry was also evident in the distinction which the people made and the bishops accepted between the certified and the sacrificers. During the persecution, the focus of both Cyprian and the Roman confessors was on the moral failure of the lapsed. He declared that the certified were no less contaminated than the sacrificers.[39] Their successful avoidance of bodily contact with idolatry had, he implied, done nothing to lessen their guilt and protect them from divine wrath. The Roman confessors focused primarily on the defilement of the conscience which then entailed the pollution of the hands and mouth touching or tasting the sacrifices, and even the eyes which had looked upon the idols.[40] When his fellow bishops, both in

Africa and Italy, decided to admit these penitents immediately after the persecution, Cyprian had to acknowledge that the particular circumstances of each case were important in determining the individual's status.[41] He recognized that the certified had retained the purity of their hands and mouths; he allowed that many had acted with good-will, believing they were allowed to accept the certificates as long as they declared themselves unwilling to sacrifice. Still, Cyprian described their consciences as polluted and asserted that they had themselves admitted as much by repenting of an action which had actually been construed as a failure to confess Christ.[42] Thus Christians in Carthage were apparently prepared to allow the notion of bodily pollution through involuntary contact with idolatry to be extended to a pollution of conscience through misguided intentional contact.[43] Yet they insisted that the contamination of this non-bodily contact was not as serious as that brought on by touching, eating or drinking; it could be more easily purified or forgiven.

Finally, to advance his polemical purpose, Cyprian did not refrain from suggesting an even more contagious contamination. When the laxist schismatics appeared before Cornelius in Rome to accuse him of cruelty and rigorism, Cyprian recalled the readiness of these schismatic presbyters and bishops to enter into communion with the sacrificers whose hands and mouths were still reeking from the incense, the sacrificial meat and libation wine of idolatry. He sought to inspire horror at Cornelius' petitioners who had polluted themselves by embracing the lapsed and might infect him in turn.[44] In this particular instance, however, Cyprian was dealing with voluntary communication through what he regarded as a sham eucharist celebrated outside the protection of the church. In the later conflict over rebaptism, he would make a sharp distinction between the church's pure rituals and the polluting ceremonies of the schismatics.[45]

In the understanding of Cyprian, and apparently some portion of his community in Carthage, any form of contact with idolatrous sacrifices – according to intention, apart from intention, contrary to intention, or even by misguided intention – contaminated, so that the polluted person had to be purified by repentance. Within the unity of the church, however, that impurity was dangerous only to the person carrying it and not to any others who came into involuntary contact with it. The body and blood of Christ, at least when celebrated in the true church, could neither be defiled by the pollution of an unworthy recipient nor could it serve as a vehicle for involuntary contamination of others; instead, the polluted recipient would be harmed by contact with this holy reality. Outside the unity of the church, the laxist presbyters were contaminated by their contact – even if misguided – with the carriers of idolatrous impurity. Those contaminated in body or mind by their contact with idolatry were a danger to themselves and not to the holy church.

Sinful laity in the church

During and immediately after the persecution, Cyprian, his brother bishops, and his congregation did not regard the presence of penitents who had been guilty of apostasy and idolatry as a threat to the holiness of their communion. The twin dangers, from his perspective, were that the church would bring down divine wrath upon itself by rejecting the call to reform and that the impure would suffer from contact with the holy realities within the church. As the controversy between Novatian and Cornelius developed in Rome and the rigorists attempted to gain a foothold in Africa, Cyprian and his colleagues were drawn into the debate over the communication of impurity through the communion of the church. He consistently argued that admitting the lapsed into communion as lay persons would not jeopardize the holiness of the church, its relationship to God, or its power to sanctify.[46]

In a letter to the confessors in Rome who had joined Novatian's communion upon their release from prison, he referred to the parable of the wheat and tares, observing that the presence of some who were unworthy was no reason to leave the communion of the church. At this time, the tares would have been understood as symbolizing the certified whom Cornelius had elected to admit and the sacrificers who were in the congregation of Bishop Trofimus.[47] Shortly thereafter, in defending the African preference for Cornelius over Novatian, Cyprian explicitly repudiated the principle that one person can infect another with sin through their sharing communion in the church. Had this been the case, he observed, Novatian himself should not have followed the already established practice of accepting repentant adulterers into communion.[48] While he recognized the danger of condoning or approving of sin within the unity of the true church, he argued to the Roman confessors that sharing communion did not of itself imply consent to another's sin.[49] To an African colleague, he observed that the innovative practice of admitting repentant adulterers had not harmed the practice of continence and marital chastity within the community.[50] As has already been seen, however, in his attack on the laxist clergy, Cyprian did allude to the danger of contamination through communion with the polluted outside the unity of the church.[51]

Thus Cyprian explicitly rejected the thesis that ritual pollution or even voluntary sin could be transmitted through the communion of the true church. Instead, he did recognize – as has been discussed in considering the necessity of penance – that accepting sinners into communion without the process of public repentance jeopardized the identity of this voluntary community and its relationship to God. Intentionally disregarding the cosmic significance of apostasy, as the laxists had done, could bring down divine rejection on the church. Unlike the satanic rituals practiced in idolatry or schism, however, the unity and rituals of the church did not transmit impurity and sin among the participants.

Sinful bishops in the unity of the church

Cyprian insisted that clerics who had failed by sacrifice, certificate or similar crime must be removed from office and could be readmitted to communion only among the laity. In particular, any church which knowingly allowed lapsed bishops to perform the functions of sanctifying and praying for the community not only failed to receive the benefits of these ministries but stood in danger of sharing the sin of the leader. Apart from the controversy over the efficacy of baptism performed by heretics or schismatics, Cyprian dealt with six instances of unworthy bishops within the church. His position was remarkably consistent and his explanations provided a rationale for the established practice of removing unworthy bishops once they have been discovered.

In rehearsing the evils which God had used the persecution to punish and correct, in *On the Lapsed*, Cyprian did not hesitate to describe the greed and negligence of some of his episcopal colleagues. They shared the evils which had afflicted the people. Yet he did not speak of their sinfulness as posing a threat to the efficacy of their ministry. It had rather contributed to the sufferings of the persecution.[52]

In defending Cornelius against charges reported by his African colleague Antonianus, Cyprian implied that two of the counts might have justified Novatian's call for the deposition and replacement of his rival in Rome. The Roman bishop, he asserted, had not himself fallen during the persecution.[53] Nor had he allowed the sacrificer bishop Trofimus to enter his communion as a bishop but only as a layman.[54] Such accusations could be defended only on the basis of fact; proven true either would have disqualified Cornelius, as is evident in subsequent instances.

In his insistence that the African bishop Fortunatianus must be removed because he had been guilty of sacrifice during the persecution, Cyprian presented a full consideration of the dangers associated with unworthy bishops. As a stained priest, the bishop was himself in danger of incurring the wrath of God by approaching the altar to sacrifice, as certified by Lev. 21.17, Ex. 19.22 and Ex. 28.43.[55] Secondly, the bishop's sin had deprived him of the power to exercise the priestly role for the community: having lost the Holy Spirit, he could not sanctify; by Jn. 9.31, the sinner's prayer could not gain a hearing before God.[56] Thus the community which tolerated him would lose its intercessor before God and its rituals would have no power to sanctify. Accepting the ministry of such a sinful priest, moreover, would lead the laity to assume that penance was superfluous and that God would ignore sin.[57] Cyprian adapted his earlier interpretation of the persecution as a divine cleansing of the church to apply it specifically to unworthy bishops: God had acted to expose them, so that they could be removed and further contact between the clean and the unclean would be thereby prevented.[58] He warned that returning such a sinful bishop to office would result in his polluting the altar and infecting the community.[59] If the bishop refused to step down, the community must desert him: by supporting or even tolerating a known sinner as its representative, it would identify itself with his failure.[60] In this instance, Cyprian implied that the bishop might communicate his contagion to the entire community through the eucharistic sacrifice. The danger began, however, only once the minister's unworthiness had been made manifest by God's testing. Though Cyprian's language described a pollution by bodily contact, the community's voluntary acquiescence played an essential role in the contamination.[61]

Attacking the appeal for recognition made by the laxist college of bishops to Cornelius, Cyprian noted that its leader, Privatus of Lambaesis, and three of his colleagues had all been removed from office by their colleagues, the three followers for sacrificing during the persecution.[62] Cornelius should recoil in horror, Cyprian implied, from the emissaries of such polluted bishops.[63]

Cyprian repeated many of the arguments he had developed for the case of Fortunatianus when he responded in the name of an episcopal synod to an appeal from colleagues in Spain for assistance in preventing the two bishops, Basilides and Martialis, deposed for apostasy, from regaining their offices. The assertion that such priests were incapable of praying and offering was again supported by Jn. 9.31, "God does not hear sinners."[64] He then cited Hosea 9.4, "Such sacrifices shall be like the bread of mourning; all who eat of it shall be defiled," to indicate that sinful clergy would defile those who accepted their communion and consented to their ministry.[65] In a similar vein, the immediate divine punishment of all who had supported the revolt of Core, Dathan and Abiron against the priesthood of Aaron, in Num. 16.1–26, was invoked to show that anyone who supported the ministry of an apostate priest would thereby participate in the sacrilege of his sacrifice.[66] The unity of the church would not protect Christians who knowingly consented to polluted priests presenting their prayers, petitions and offerings to God. In a move aimed at the Roman bishop Stephen, who was apparently supporting the claims of the failed bishops to be restored to their offices, Cyprian charged that any bishop who recognized and entered into communion with such colleagues would become a willing partner in their sin and punishment.[67] This assertion might reflect the stance developed in the struggle against the laxist schism in Africa, whose episcopal college included at least three bishops condemned and deposed by their Catholic colleagues as sacrificers.[68]

In defending himself against the attack of a rigorist, Cyprian argued through a *reductio ad absurdum* by spelling out the full implications of the charges which were being brought against him.[69] Were he a failed priest, then all whom he had baptized, reconciled and communicated would have lost their salvation.[70] Were he polluted by communion with idolaters, as his opponent Puppianus claimed, then all who had communicated with him shared his contagion and thereby lost the hope of eternal life.[71] The sarcastic and even ridiculing tone of this riposte makes Cyprian's commitment to the principles of his argument uncertain; the premises might have been those of his adversary. In this instance alone, for example, he implied that Christians who acted within the unity of the church might lose their salvation through the hidden defects of the priest from whom they received baptism, eucharist and reconciliation.[72] The rhetoric employed, therefore, prevents this letter supporting the conclusion that Cyprian believed pollution could be transmitted unwittingly through the communion and rituals within the unity of the church.

In four of these six instances, Cyprian clearly affirmed that fallen bishops were capable of polluting the altars and infecting the congregations which accepted their ministry and even the other bishops who recognized them as colleagues. In all but Cyprian's self-defense, the leader's sin was public and widely known, however, so that those who communicated with the failed bishop could be construed as tolerating or approving his sin. In dealing with the Spanish apostates, for example, Cyprian built his argument on the people's role in choosing a bishop whom they knew to be worthy, and thus their responsibility for rejecting one they had come to recognize as unworthy.[73] He allowed that the Spanish bishop Basilides' deception might have protected the Roman bishop Stephen but warned that such an excuse could not endure once the blasphemy and apostasy were known.[74] Although he used the language of ritual contamination, the evidence seems to focus Cyprian's concern on intentional acquiescence and wilful participation in a leader's sin. He appears to have held to the principle articulated in dealing with the acceptance of the laity into communion: within the church's unity, contamination was not transmitted through unwitting or unintentional contact. Still, he signaled a clear difference between the intentions operative in tolerating a penitent as a lay person and allowing a failed priest to represent the community before God. The repentance of bishops such as Trofimus, Fortunatianus, Martialis and Basilides did not mitigate the danger which they posed to their churches. Once they had sinned and their sin was known, their acceptance as bishops by the laity or other bishops would jeopardize the church's relationship to God and the saving power of its rituals. To tolerate a penitent apostate as a communicant was only to preserve a sinner for the mercy or judgment of God; to tolerate an idolater or blasphemer as priest was to mock the holiness of the Spirit, to violate the baptismal oath of fidelity to Christ, to insult the holiness of God.

The sacrilege of schism

The controversy over the rebaptism of converts who had originally been baptized outside the unity of the true church focused the question on the role of the bishop in the holiness and sanctifying power of the church. Like the problem of unworthy bishops within the unity of the church, this issue involved the inability of the sinful minister to sanctify and the people's voluntary participation in a sin instituted by their bishop. According to the analysis presented earlier, the controversy in Africa over the power to baptize focused on the laxist communion, some of whose bishops were guilty of apostasy as well as schism.[75] In Italy, the primary opponent was Novatian, who did not carry the pollution of idolatry but only the sin of schism. To clarify the focus of Cyprian's concern, therefore, the two stages of the controversy over rebaptism will again be distinguished and treated separately.

The laxists

The laxist organization built in Africa by Privatus of Lambaesis included bishops who had been accepted into its fellowship although they had performed no penance after being guilty of sacrifice during the persecution.[76] Nor did this church require penitential purification of any of its lapsed members. Thus Cyprian and his correspondents could have attacked this entire group, unlike the Novatianists, as having been polluted by voluntary contact with idolatry.[77] The correspondence reporting synodal decisions and Cyprian's own letters, however, focused not on the impurity of idolatry but on the contamination arising from rebellion against Christ and the church. As the persecution in Africa was dying down, it will be recalled, Cyprian had already begun to characterize the rebellion of the laxists as a second form of persecution and the laxist clergy as taking over the demonic duties of the imperial commissioners.[78] Similarly, in noting the imperial government's neglect of Novatian at the time of Cornelius' arrest, he implied that the rigorists had already entered into the service of Satan by their rebellion against the church.[79] He did not hesitate to adopt the categories of sacrilege and ritual impurity which were proper to idolatry as weapons for attacking the rituals performed by the schismatics.[80] Later he asserted not only that the outsiders could not sanctify the converts they received but that their schismatic rituals contaminated the participants in much the same way as the idolatrous rituals of Roman religion had and would. A second, opposing altar was necessarily sacrilegious.

In the initial stage of the controversy over rebaptism, which appears to have been focused on the laxists in Africa, Cyprian clearly asserted that any minister who acted outside the unity of the church lacked the power to sanctify and thus could not cleanse from sin, purify the water of baptism, consecrate the oil of anointing, forgive sins or sanctify the recipients of his baptism.[81] Going further, he quoted texts of scripture which implied that the schismatic ritual polluted those who received it: Num. 19.22, "And

everything which the unclean touches shall be unclean," Ps. 140.5;
"Let not the oil of a sinner anoint my head."[82] The synod writing to
Stephen in spring of 256 asserted that the profane water of the
heretics and schismatics stained those they washed.[83] Even a person
erroneously seeking the church among the outsiders incurred the
sin of sacrilege through contact with their ministry and need not
have been guilty of their formal rebellion against the bishops and
the unity of the church to be blemished by it.[84] Cyprian and his
colleagues made similar arguments about inefficacy and contagion
to support the policy of deposing unworthy bishops within the
unity of the church.[85] There, however, the contagion of idolatry
could spread from a failed minister only to a knowing and
consenting recipient. In contrast, the contamination from schismatic rituals was described as independent of intention, like that of
direct contact with idolatry. Despite the language of the scriptural
citations, which focused on the sin and uncleanness of the priest,
the bishops' argument was that the schismatic rituals themselves
were polluting, like those of idolatry.

This law of impurity through contact also applied to any
minister who had left the true church or been ordained in schism:
he was permanently stained with the contagion of rebellion against
Christ and the sacrilegious sacrifices which he had offered in
schism. The African synod pronounced schismatic clerics subject to
the same pollution as the bishops who had offered sacrifice to the
demons during the persecution. Because such a priest was blemished and impure, the Lord would desert him; because he was
sinful, he would be injured through contact with the holy altar.[86]
The bishops asserted that schism caused an uncleanness as disabling
and contagious as that of idolatry. As a result, such a cleric might be
returned and admitted to the unity of the church only as a
layman.[87] Because of the shortness of time between the original
schism and this controversy, no more than four years, all the clerics
under consideration in this letter would have been baptized in the
unity of the church before going into schism and thus could be
purified from their contamination only through penance. They were
to be treated exactly as a cleric who had failed during the persecution; they could be accepted only among the laity.

Although the laxist communion, which is here identified as the
focus of the first stage of the controversy over rebaptism, contained
at least three sacrificers among its bishops, Cyprian and his
colleagues did not rely on this defect as the basis for their arguments. Instead, they charged that the rituals of their opponents

were sacrilegious and contaminating because they were performed in rebellion against the unity of the church. Moreover, they regarded the pollution of schismatic rituals as equivalent to that of idolatrous ones: it could be contracted even in error or unintentionally; it created a disability which could not be removed by repentance.

The Novatianists

In the second phase of the rebaptism controversy, this charge of contaminating sacrilege was extended to the Novatianists, who had been careful to keep their communicants, both clerical and lay, free of all stain of idolatry. In writing to Stephen in Rome about Marcianus, the rigorist bishop of Arles, Cyprian accused Novatian of setting up a profane altar, establishing an adulterous episcopal throne, and performing sacrilegious sacrifices. He then repeated the charge in writing to Magnus.[88] The assertion of using impure and contagious water, which had been implied in attacking the laxists, was boldly applied against the rigorists.[89] Instead of appealing to the purity code of Exodus and Leviticus, however, Cyprian adapted the scriptural support which had been used to warn the Spanish congregations against accepting their apostate bishops back as priests.[90] The rebellion against the priesthood of Aaron mounted by Core, Dathan and Abiron had brought summary punishment on leaders and followers alike.[91] Hosea's characterization of intentionally participating in an irregular sacrifice as eating the bread of mourning was transferred from idolatry to schism.[92] In a third appeal to precedent, Cyprian recalled the rebellion of the sons of Aaron in bringing their own fire to the altar.[93] Schism had become an act of sacrilege equivalent to idolatry.

In the controversy over rebaptism, Cyprian concluded that the rituals of the schismatics polluted those who received them in the same way that the rites of idolatry contaminated those who participated in them, even involuntarily. The original charge that the laxist clergy were continuing the work of the devil by preventing the repentance of the lapsed had been extended to the college of bishops they established in Africa. The rituals they performed to deceive failed Christians and incautious converts were not only ineffective because of the absence of the Holy Spirit outside the church but demonic: they polluted anyone who participated in them.[94] Once the schismatic rituals of the laxists had been characterized as sacrilegious, that judgment was extended to the rigorists as well.

147

The significance of social structures

The failures in unity and morality within the Christian community required the persecution as a means of correcting and purifying. The first and greatest danger which the lapsed posed was not, therefore, the contamination of the church through their contact with idolatry but the provoking of divine wrath by readmitting to communion those whom God had purged, without their having demonstrated repentance and a sincere commitment to the standards of Christ. The risk of ritual pollution through contact with idolatry was a secondary, though real, consideration. Cyprian and his community clearly manifested a fear of the contagion which had been contracted by voluntary or involuntary bodily contact with idolatrous rituals. They distinguished the certified who had avoided bodily contact with idolatry, but still required purification of their conscience. Cyprian later identified schismatic rituals as demonic and equally polluting.

The Christian who had been contaminated by idolatry, particularly voluntarily, was not so much a threat to, as a sinner threatened by the holiness of the church. Although Cyprian occasionally referred to the profaning of the body of Christ, the polluting of the holy altar and the infecting of the community, the injuries which he actually described were all suffered by the impure themselves rather than by the holy realities with which they came into contact. A Christian who had participated in the rituals of idolatry or schism after baptism could be readmitted to the communion of the church so that its priest and people could serve as advocates before God for winning forgiveness and salvation. Such a person could not, however, serve as an advocate for others. Thus the lapsed or schismatic clergy were removed from office and reconciled penitents were permanently disbarred from presenting prayer, petition or sacrifice to God for the community.

The rituals of baptism and eucharist celebrated within the unity of the church could not communicate impurity among the people independently of the intention of the participants. Because the holiness of the eucharist was stronger than the impurity of idolatry, Christians sharing the eucharist within the unity of the church were protected from any contagion carried by their fellow communicants. Thus, if an initiant had not been properly baptized, a penitent had not been purified, or a bishop was hiding infidelity from his congregation, then the endowments of the church itself supplied for their defects and protected their colleagues from harm. A behavioral standard was applied to the differentiation of roles just as it was to the protection of the boundary: an evil intention had to be addressed when it was acted upon and manifest to other members of the community; the hidden or secret sin was to be judged by Christ alone. Once impurity became public, however, the community could not tolerate or acquiesce in its presence within the communion. If sharing in the ritual indicated approval of the known sin of a fellow, then the guilt would also be shared. That union of consent was broken, however, by the ritual of public penance in which both the sinner and the community repudiated the sin. Through the rites of reconciliation, the community was protected from any contagion which might exist among the people. The church's ritual, itself pure and holy, would not transmit evil or pollution from one participant to another.

Bishops and other clergy, even within the communion of the church, posed a greater danger. They were public persons chosen or approved by the congregation, who represented it before God, to other congregations and even before the enemies of Christ. They held their positions by the continuing consent and approval of the community. Pastoral necessity provided no excuse because their salvation depended upon their standing among the people, not upon their holding office. To tolerate their sin, therefore, was to approve and thus to share it. Unworthy bishops apparently posed the same danger to any episcopal colleagues who welcomed them into communion: if their sin was known it would contaminate but apparently not if it was unrecognized. Thus within the unity of the church, contamination seems to have been communicated primarily voluntarily. Still, Cyprian did employ the language of involuntary contamination by ritual contact or consensual communion with a bishop who was unrecognized as a sinner. In his self-defense against Puppianus, however, the implication that his flock could have been polluted and destroyed by his own failings was mockingly repudiated. In practice, Cyprian applied a behavioral standard to the clergy as well as the laity: sin which was unknown could be neither approved nor repudiated and thus could not contaminate another within the unity of the church.

The rituals celebrated by heretics and schismatics, in contrast to those of the true church, would infect those who participated in them in the same way as idolatrous rites, even without knowledge of and consent to the demonic evil they symbolized. Cyprian had insisted that schism was a form of idolatry and he equated the contaminating power of the two sets of rituals. Only the power of baptism, not a ritual of penance following baptism, could so cleanse from the stain of idolatry or schism that a person could be entrusted with the priestly and mediatory role of the church. Moreover, outside the unity of the church, no minister shared the episcopate's gift of the Holy Spirit, which conferred the power to sanctify. The absence of the Spirit's power to sanctify, the sacrilege of the rituals themselves, and even the unacknowledged crimes of unworthy ministers resulted in the pollution of all who shared in schismatic rituals.

The logic of Cyprian's identification of the power to sanctify with the reception and retention of the Holy Spirit and his belief in the contaminating power of idolatry could have rendered the ministry of failed clerics within the church not only void but even polluting. Their congregations could have been left unprotected against the holiness of God and stained by the impurity of their leaders. The power of the scriptural texts he quoted against the schismatics could have made the sinful minister within the Catholic communion no less dangerous to his community than to himself. Yet Cyprian consistently refused to draw these conclusions and held back from these implications. He was no less assured that those outside the true communion of the church, both idolaters and schismatics were not only deprived of all power to sanctify but afflicted with no less effective a power to pollute and contaminate. Such assurance of the cosmic power of its own rituals, as well as the contrary power of the rituals of its opponents, is characteristic of a community which assigns cosmic significance to its boundaries, its internal differentiation of roles and offices, and the behavioral standards of conduct by which it defines them. Thus his firm sense of the unity of the Catholic church was inseparable from Cyprian's belief in the sanctifying and contaminating power of ritual.

8

UNITY OF THE EPISCOPATE

The issue of church unity has been an element throughout this study of the episcopacy of Cyprian. In the schisms which challenged the Carthaginian church at the end of the Decian persecution, he found a way for the lapsed to confess the unity of the church and thereby to be released from their sin, at least on earth. In commissioning Peter, he insisted, Christ had established the bishop as the foundation of unity for the local church. That unity, though reflected in the charity and harmony of the eucharistic fellowship, was grounded in the unity of God and the bond between Christ and the Father. The church was indivisible in principle; schismatics could leave but not divide it. All this Cyprian taught about the local church, gathered under the leadership of its bishop. Though he made similar assertions about the solidarity of the episcopate and the harmony of the world-wide church, his understanding of its unity was significantly different. Though Christ's great flock was indeed one, it had many shepherds. Each of them had been assigned a portion of the flock to govern and would answer to the Lord for his stewardship. Though none was to intrude on the work of another, all were jointly responsible for the whole and even for each of its parts. Thus the theory of the unity of the world-wide church contained conflicting elements whose balance was achieved by negotiation. It is better understood by examination of actual practices and their justification than by making any one of its components the guiding principle of a systematic whole.

Attention will first be directed to the practice of unity, to the structures of collaboration developed by the bishops. Only then will Cyprian's justification of these structures be examined. The final revision of *On the Unity of the Catholic Church*, which was undertaken during the conflict over the practice of rebaptism, will be investigated and interpreted in the light of contemporary developments.

On this basis, an attempt will then be made to sketch Cyprian's understanding of the unity of the world-wide church.

Structures of collaboration

Many of the responsibilities facing the bishops could be discharged successfully only through collaborative action. As has already been noted, the election, consecration and recognition of a new bishop required the cooperation of neighboring bishops. When a succession was disputed, consultation and a unified response were essential.[1] A bishop who had proven unworthy could be deposed and replaced only by a judgment made and enforced by his colleagues.[2] The breakdown of consensus, such as that which occurred in the case of the Spanish bishops Basilides and Martialis, could paralyze or divide local churches.[3] Similarly, the discipline of penance required the adoption of common policies which could be enforced at least regionally. The travel of Christians between Rome and Carthage had required the coordination of practice between these churches, even during the persecution; movement of people within Africa must have required even closer collaboration.[4] The Africans adopted the changes recommended by the Roman presbyters[5] and worked to prevent the circumvention of the Roman policy of withholding reconciliation from all but dying penitents until the end of the persecution.[6] The proclamation of a general forgiveness by the Carthaginian confessors required the immediate coordination of practice by the African bishops.[7] After the persecution, all African policies were formed in councils of bishops and the Romans were immediately informed of their decisions.[8] Common action was taken on the bishops who had failed in Africa[9] and on the presbyters who had extended peace to the lapsed without requiring penance.[10] When conflict arose over the practice of rebaptism of converts originally initiated into schismatic or heretical communities, they used extensive correspondence and consultation to develop a common policy.[11]

In their disciplinary decisions, the African bishops seem to have experienced no difficulty in making judgments once they had acquired the relevant facts – thus the preference for Cornelius over Novatian,[12] the confirmation of Cyprian's exclusion of the rebel clergy of Carthage,[13] the depositions of Fortunatianus of Assuras and Marcianus of Arles.[14] Making policy decisions was more complex. In considering the reconciling of the lapsed, the bishops claimed to have consulted scripture, weighed the pastoral consequences of particular options, and even read the signs and warnings of the times.[15] The attempt to mediate between such texts as Mt. 10.33, in which Christ threatened to disown those who had denied him, and Mt. 16.18–19, in which Peter was given authority to bind and loosen on earth and in heaven, can be discerned in the decrees of the councils.[16] In the case of the rebaptism controversy, Cyprian built his arguments from scripture and pastoral practice but claimed that the truth which required the displacement of prior custom had actually been revealed.[17] The bishops seem to have realized that their situation could be different from that of the apostolic times and therefore that they needed to go beyond what had been handed down from the apostles – even if it were accurately transmitted in the practice of some single church – or what was reflected in the scripture.[18]

In most instances, the bishops of Africa and Italy agreed on the proper practice. In cases of conflict, however, the Africans both argued that theirs was the right policy and defended their right to regional autonomy within the unity of the universal church. When the laxists appealed to Cornelius for the recognition of their episcopal college, Cyprian insisted that the African bishops were adequately equipped and authorized to judge the merits of the case.[19] They reversed Stephen's judgment on the deposition of the Spanish bishops and Cyprian insisted that Stephen cooperate in the removal of Marcianus of Arles.[20] The Africans defiantly refused to bow to the jurisdiction of the Roman bishop in the matter of rebaptizing schismatics.[21] Rather than simply claiming autonomy, they sought the support of other regional groups of bishops in overcoming the threat of isolation from the other churches.[22]

The authority of the collective and the autonomy of the individual were delicately balanced in the cooperative action of the African bishops. Although Cyprian and his colleagues regularly insisted that individual bishops retained the right to dissent from common decisions, they did not hesitate to reprimand deviants, particularly where common discipline was jeopardized. The plan adopted in spring 251 allowed individual bishops to withhold the allowed reconciliation from the penitent lapsed.[23] They were not, however, authorized to liberalize the policy by admission of any sinners without public penance or of sacrificers who were not in danger of death.[24] When Bishop Therapius gave the peace of the church to a former presbyter who was in good health without first consulting his congregation, he was threatened with sanctions by a synod of his colleagues.[25] A bishop who wanted to advance the giving of peace to a group of sacrificers who had finally fallen after an extended confession under torture took the precaution of seeking the advice and approval of his colleagues gathered for the consecration of a new bishop. Cyprian, to whom the matter was then referred, professed his sympathy for the proposal but also refused to recommend action on his own authority and promised to place the question before a provincial synod which would soon meet in Carthage.[26] At a subsequent council, the bishops again deliberated and together decided to liberalize their policy by admitting sacrificers who had persevered in penance up to that time. They allowed individual bishops to restrict the liberation but this time warned that anyone who did not follow the common decision would answer to the Lord on judgment day for his severity and cruelty.[27] The adherence to these policies seems to have been general, which it had not been in the earlier decision to allow reconciliation of adulterers.[28] The unanimity and cooperation of the bishops of Africa in facing the problem of the lapsed allowed Cyprian to argue later that in following a practice contrary to the one which had become universal among his colleagues, Marcianus of Arles demonstrated that he did not share the common gift of the episcopate.[29] Still, the council of seventy-one which pronounced on the rebaptism of schismatics in spring 256 allowed individuals to follow other practices, within the peace and harmony of the episcopal college.[30]

The agreement of the bishops did not preclude sharp and extended debate on the questions before them. The sustained epistolary exchange over the practice of rebaptism lends credence to Cyprian's assertion that the deliberations in spring 251 had been lengthy, with scriptural arguments advanced for both sides of the issue.[31] His own positions on the church's power to reconcile apostates and on distinguishing the certified from the sacrificers were changed by the council, whose decisions he later defended.[32] The unanimous vote recorded in the meeting of September 256 may itself have been the result of a sustained campaign of persuasion which preceded it rather than being an indication of normal practice.[33] In these debates, Cyprian did not hesitate to urge compliance in the strongest terms, threatening the wrath of God in the final judgment upon those who took a different stance than had been recommended.[34] Despite their willingness to tolerate differing practice in other regions of the world, the Africans expected to reach and follow common decisions.[35]

The bishops also mediated cooperation between local churches in the sharing of financial resources. Cyprian offered to accept and support a member of another community who had given up his theatrical profession to become Christian.[36] He and his community provided significant funds for the ransom of Christians who had been taken captive by raiders, recognizing them as fellow members of the one body of Christ.[37] During the Valerian persecution, he also sent funds to support the Christians condemned to the mines.[38] This sharing of goods between local communities reflected the practice within them.

Coordinated episcopal action required structures of collaboration. Bishops met and consulted with one another on the occasion of the election of a new colleague.[39] Synods were held regularly after Easter in Numidia and Proconsular Africa, as is evidenced by their consultations with one another.[40] Other meetings drew bishops from these two provinces and even Mauretania to Carthage,[41] one of which seems to have been an extraordinary, September 256 session called to address the challenge of the Roman bishop in the rebaptism controversy.[42] Although the bishop of Carthage or Rome might consult with his colleagues in Cappadocia, Syria or Egypt, no general meeting of bishops from across the empire seems to have been conceivable before Christian emperors provided the necessary logistical support.[43] Even a meeting of eighty or ninety African bishops with their deacons, some presbyters, and other assistants, must have taxed the resources of the communities in Carthage and Lambaesis.[44]

The bishops of the imperial administrative centers, Carthage and Lambaesis, had particular responsibilities for maintaining the flow of communication between their colleagues and with overseas bishops. Questions were addressed to Cyprian on which he was expected to advise or which he was to place before the next council. Individual bishops and groups wrote for direction in reconciling the lapsed, handling a local financial crisis, regulating the behavior of converts and dedicated virgins, disciplining an obstinate deacon, and receiving converts from schism.[45] Cyprian briefed all the Africans traveling to Rome individually during the period of uncertainty over its proper bishop.[46] He informed the Roman bishop of the decisions of the African synods and sought the support of the bishop of Caesarea in Cappadocia in the dispute with Rome over rebaptism.[47] Letters were addressed to him from Spain and Gaul seeking his support in local disciplinary actions and he responded in his own name or that of a council.[48] As the proceedings of the council in September 256 made clear, the bishop of Carthage functioned as the coordinator of an episcopal college.[49] Indeed, some of his correspondence suggests that Cyprian may have been in the habit of making the rounds of the churches in his province, much as the Roman proconsul did.[50] Though the force of his own social standing, education and personality must certainly have contributed to the status which his colleagues ceded to Cyprian, the location of his see in Carthage must certainly have been a significant factor.[51]

In practice, the African bishops maintained a balance between the autonomy of each bishop in his own church and the authority of the body of bishops acting as a group. Though they were jealous of their regional independence, they enforced strict limits on local variation when a common policy had been adopted. The desire for agreement does not seem to have hampered Cyprian's colleagues in questioning and objecting to his proposals, nor he in explaining and defending them.

The unity of the episcopate

While the commissioning of Peter to judge and govern in the name of Christ seems to have provided a clear and effective justification for the authority of the bishop within the unity of his local church, the theories which legitimated the regional structures and expressed the unity of the episcopal college as a whole were developed gradually and piecemeal.

The role of the neighboring bishops in supervising elections and in consecrating new bishops lent credibility to Cyprian's assertion that the members of the episcopal college shared a single power among them which had first been bestowed upon Peter and passed down from the apostles, the original episcopal college.[52] The regular deliberations on policy also provided an experience of bishops exercising the episcopate in unison with their fellows.[53] These successes may have been more influential than scriptural or theoretical justifications for the unity of the episcopate.

Cyprian had originally appealed to the foundation of the church upon Peter as a justification for the bishop's claim, against those of the martyrs and confessors, of possession of the power of binding and loosening within the local church. During the schisms and formation of competing episcopal colleges in Italy and Africa, he asserted that in commissioning Peter, Christ had established the indissoluble unity of the episcopate itself.[54] He cited the Petrine primacy against the division of the Roman church[55] and later noted with outrage that the laxist pretender in Carthage had lodged an appeal in Rome, the chair of Peter, whose success would have divided the African church.[56] Even when he added the giving of power to all the disciples in Jn. 20.22–3 to the bestowal of authority on Peter alone in Mt. 16.18–19, he did not abandon the foundation of the episcopal unity in Peter.[57]

The empowering of Peter and the other apostles first served as a basis for the authority of individual bishops in their local churches and Cyprian continued to support the autonomy of the local bishop. He introduced a second consideration: the one flock of Christ was so large that individual bishops had been assigned responsibility for different parts of it, and thus that they would answer only to Christ for their decisions in governing them.[58] Yet in practice, synods of bishops regularly acted to depose leaders whom they judged unworthy or dangerous to their communities.[59] To justify such action, Cyprian argued that the many shepherds shared a common responsibility for the one flock and must come to the assistance of those Christians whose salvation was being jeopardized by the action of a bishop who contradicted the consensus of his colleagues.[60] A bishop was neither solely responsible for his own community nor responsible for his community alone because that community was itself an integral part of the universal church. A unity of episcopal authority was thereby based on the unity of the church, for whose governance it had been given.

Cyprian understood the college of bishops as successor to the apostles as a group rather than as individuals.[61] In addressing the division of the Roman church, he moved from the commissioning in Mt. 16.18–19 to that in Jn. 21.17, in which Peter was commanded to feed Christ's sheep. Christ addressed Peter alone in order to show that he established but one church and chair, and that he has but one flock. All the apostles, however, shared that authority and responsibility, feeding the flock in common accord.[62] The episcopate was one and each bishop shared it in union with his fellows.[63] After developing the image of the church as the indivisible tunic of Christ, Cyprian returned to the metaphor of the unity of a flock by citing Jn. 10.17, "one flock and one shepherd." He attacked the schismatics in both Carthage and Rome by asking how anyone could believe that Christ had authorized more than one flock or more than one shepherd in the same place.[64] As he had originally appealed to the glue of concord which united the members of a local church,[65] he later characterized the mutual love of the bishops as the glue which bound together the universal church.[66]

During the rebaptism controversy, Cyprian broadened the

scriptural foundation for the unity of the episcopate by introducing the text of Jn. 20.22–3, in which Christ bestowed the power to forgive sins upon all the disciples simultaneously. The thesis that the bishops were successors to Peter and the apostles as a college had already been functioning in the exercise of episcopal office.[67] It justified individual bishops ceding their own judgment to the collective decision of their colleagues, as Cyprian had in agreeing that the bishops had the authority to reconcile first the certified and then the sacrificers.[68] It legitimated collective action against individuals who dissented from common accord, such as the warning of Therapius not to grant peace without penance and the removal of Marcianus for refusing pardon to dying penitents.[69] It had also been used to protest Cornelius' review of the disciplinary decisions of the bishops of Africa,[70] and to remind Stephen that he too was bound by the decisions of his predecessors and colleagues.[71] Although the text of Jn. 20.22–3 was introduced late in Cyprian's writing, the structure it supported had been functioning for years.

The thesis that the individual bishop's succession to Peter guaranteed his authority to forgive and sanctify had to be argued over and again in the face of challenges from the martyrs and schismatics. In contrast, the idea of an episcopal college was so well established in church practice that it required and received minimal justification. Even the schismatics sought recognition from the established bishops and formed competing colleges when they were rejected.[72] Only when disagreements arose among bishops did Cyprian advance arguments to legitimate the regular practice of consultation and common action.

Cyprian did not offer a justification for the authority which the bishops of imperial administrative cities, such as Carthage and Lambaesis, actually exercised within the episcopal college. When Stephen asserted such a right, by virtue of being the successor of Peter and the bishop of a church which preserved authentic apostolic practice, Cyprian explicitly rejected the claim.[73] Firmilian of Caesarea ridiculed Stephen's assertion and gave priority to the church of Jerusalem, particularly in the matter of remembering when to celebrate Easter.[74] Stephen's decree of excommunication against the bishops who opposed his practice of accepting schismatic baptism was greeted by Cyprian with outrage and by Firmilian with sarcastic incredulity. Neither could conceive of such authority being wielded legitimately by a single bishop over his colleagues.[75] Such action could be taken only by a community of bishops large enough to address and resolve the issue. The primatial sees which have been identified – Rome, Carthage, Lambaesis, and Caesarea in Cappadocia – must have emerged because they were necessary for effective collaboration of the bishops. In the African understanding of the church, however, their status was simply functional and not based upon any divine ordinance or cosmic foundation, as was the unity of the episcopal college itself. Thus the idea of a council of bishops from all over the empire may have been inconceivable not only because it was logistically impossible but because these African bishops could not imagine who might preside over a universal council in the way that the bishops of Carthage and Lambaesis regularly did over provincial and regional synods.[76]

The baptismal controversy and the revision of *On Unity*

The issue which occupied the last of Cyprian's polemics was the exclusivity of the church's power to forgive sins. In his conflict with the confessors and laxist presbyters, he had asserted that within the church only the bishop – and not the martyr – has been granted the power to loosen and hold bound. This issue arose again in the controversy over the rebaptism of converts who had originally been baptized in schism. This time Cyprian insisted that the power to forgive was held and exercised only by bishops who were established within the unity of the church in legitimate succession from the apostles upon whom the authority had originally been conferred by Christ himself. In the letters of this controversy and in a final revision of his treatise *On Unity*, he explained that a single power was held in common by all and only those bishops joined in the unity of the episcopal college. Thus he linked the authority of the bishops, the unity of the episcopate and the unity of the church.

In the baptismal controversy, Cyprian's interest was the church's exclusive authority to forgive sins. He insisted that those outside the unity of the church had no access to this power and thus could not perform the ritual of baptism. For the most part, his arguments were derived from scripture, though they built upon the experiential foundation of the unity of the episcopate. In two instances, Cyprian began to use texts in new ways. The commissioning of Peter in Mt. 16.18–19 had been the standard for establishing the bishop's exclusive power to forgive sins since the lapsed advanced the claims of the martyrs. To this, he began to add the bestowal of power on all the apostles in Jn. 20.22–3 because it associated the authority to forgive with the gift of the Holy Spirit to the apostles,

"Receive the Holy Spirit. If you forgive the sins of any, they are forgiven them; if you retain the sins of any, they are retained." In his letter to Magnus, Cyprian used the latter text alone, arguing that only those who had received the Holy Spirit could baptize and forgive sins. He immediately observed that John the Baptist had also been filled with the Holy Spirit in his mother's womb because he was to baptize Jesus.[77] In writing to Jubianus shortly afterward, Cyprian's objective was to show that only those established within the church could baptize and forgive sins. He began with the anticipated allusion to the power conferred on Peter and continued with the citation of Jn. 20.22–3, concluding that only those within the church could bind and loosen.[78] This point was then amplified in responding to an objection regarding the baptism of the Samaritans by Philip. Peter and John imposed hands to confer the Holy Spirit, not to forgive sins, because the Samaritans had been baptized in true faith and within the unity of the church by a deacon sent out by the apostles.[79] Later in this letter, he cited the account of Paul rebaptizing those who had already been baptized by John the Baptist to show that baptism was effective only within the church.[80] He then described John as filled with the divine grace while in his mother's womb and supported by the spirit and power of Elijah,[81] carefully avoiding the earlier assertion that John had been given the Holy Spirit: that gift now belonged exclusively to the apostles and the church.[82] John could baptize Christ, through whom everyone else would be baptized, but he could no longer be recognized as filled with the Holy Spirit because he had been the precursor and not the follower of Christ and thus had not been established within the church itself. Cyprian continued to argue that the foundation of the church's unity was laid upon Peter, linking the two commissions in the letter of Jubianus and the final revision of *On Unity*.[83] The objective in adding the text of Jn. 20.22–3 was not to lessen the importance assigned to Peter but to expand the meaning of Mt. 16.18–19 by identifying the authority to forgive sins with the gift of the Holy Spirit to the first bishops.

Similarly, the text of Eph. 4.4–6, "There is one body and one Spirit, just as you were called to the one hope of your calling, one Lord, one faith, one baptism, one God and Father," had been used at the time of the schisms to affirm the unity of the church.[84] During the baptismal controversy, however, this text was consistently employed in the letters and in the revision of *On Unity* to affirm the connection between the unity of the church, the power to baptize,[85] and the presence of the Holy Spirit.[86] By these two texts, Cyprian was able to introduce a new argument which limited the authority to forgive sins to the unity of episcopal college.[87]

Cyprian also introduced other incidents, all connected with the privileges of Aaron to function as priest, to bolster the connection between membership in the episcopal college and the authority to sanctify. Core, Dathan and Abiron, along with all their followers, were incinerated by divine fire and then swallowed by the earth for challenging the exclusive authority of Aaron.[88] Even the sons of Aaron who appeared with strange fire for the altar were destroyed.[89] Finally, King Uzziah's usurpation of the priestly role was punished with leprosy.[90] The danger threatening anyone who attempted to usurp the role of the bishops was thus illustrated by the fate of rebels against the Israelite priests. All three texts were employed in the revision of *On Unity*.

In the letters of the second, Novatianist phase of the baptismal controversy and the contemporary revision of *On Unity*, Cyprian also introduced a new set of scriptural images to illustrate the restriction of sanctifying power to the unity of the church. In writing to Magnus, he linked the injunction which forbade taking any of the passover lamb outside the house in which it was being eaten to the warning given the family of Rahab that they would be safe during Joshua's assault on Jericho only by staying within the confines of her house.[91] In *On Unity*, he interrupted the reflection on concord and the Holy Spirit to insert these two texts, insisting that the sacred flesh of Christ cannot be eaten outside the one church.[92] He also began to use texts from the Canticle of Canticles to characterize the church first as dove and chosen daughter.[93] To these images he then added those of the bride, the enclosed garden, the sealed fountain and the well of living water.[94] In a third instance, he joined to these the figure of a paradise filled with fruit-bearing trees, all drawn from the Canticle of Canticles.[95] The exclusiveness of the church as the source of salvation was also reinforced by linking the images of the enclosed garden and sealed fountain to that of the ark of Noah, the sole vehicle of safety in the flood.[96] In introducing all these new images, Cyprian's objective was to illustrate and establish that the sanctifying power of the church could be held and exercised only within its clearly defined boundary. These images were juxtaposed and intermingled with those texts which linked the sanctifying power itself to the Holy Spirit conferred upon the apostles.

These scriptural images and arguments, which are peculiar to the baptismal controversy and in particular to its second or Novatianist phase, appeared together in Cyprian's treatise *On Unity* and indicate a final revision of that text during the conflict. Two of the most important texts, Jn. 20.22–3 and Eph. 4.4–6, were introduced in the alternate, *Textus Receptus* version of chapter 4, thus indicating a replacement of either the original version, or of the *Primacy Text* revision prepared for dealing with the Novatianist schism in Rome.[97] The text of the Canticle of Canticles introduced in this chapter was also cited in one of the letters.[98] Some of the most striking images drawn from the Canticle of Canticles, such as the enclosed garden, the paradise, and the sealed fountain, focused on baptism and thus appeared not in this text but only in the letters of the controversy.[99] Thus the *Textus Receptus* version of chapter 4 seems to belong to the period of conflict with Stephen and concern with the Novatianist practice of baptism.[100]

The rewriting of *On Unity* was not, however, confined to the replacement of chapter 4 and part of chapter 5. Other scriptural references which were peculiar to the baptismal controversy are found throughout the common version of the treatise. The texts which defended the prerogatives of Aaron were common to the second stage of the controversy and the treatise,[101] as were the references to the passover meal and the house of Rahab.[102] The discussion of the usurpation of the power to baptize, the assertion that schismatic washing polluted rather than purified, and the reference to crumbling cisterns from Jer. 2.13 all reflected the arguments peculiar to the baptismal controversy.[103] They indicate that the treatise was extensively revised during the baptismal controversy.

Cyprian's objectives in this final revision of *On Unity* do not seem to have been exhausted by the elimination of unfortunate language about the primacy of Peter among the apostles. Except for the insertion of Jn. 20.22–3 and the excision of the term *primatus*, the relations between Peter and the other apostles are remarkably similar in the two surviving versions of chapter 4. Even if Stephen's claims were the precipitating cause, Cyprian took the opportunity to link the unity of the church, the unity of the episcopate, and the power to forgive sins. Peter remained the foundation and symbol of unity but the authority conferred upon him was actually the gift of the Holy Spirit bestowed upon the apostles in their role as the apostolic college, after Jesus had been glorified.

The unity of church and episcopate

The argument of this chapter is that Cyprian built his theory of the unity of the world-wide church up from the collaborative practice of the African bishops. Local churches were never autonomous units but always part of a whole, since they were dependent upon the leaders of neighboring churches for the establishment and removal of their bishops. Individual bishops actually held and exercised their power to judge and sanctify in union with their colleagues. Thus the commissioning of Peter by Christ, which was the foundation of the unity of the local church in its bishop was in practice also the foundation of the unity of the church as a whole.

The foundational text, then, for the unity of the church, was the commissioning of Peter in Mt. 16.18–19. Cyprian introduced this during the conflict with the confessors and rebel presbyters but he was still using it during the baptismal controversy and the final revision of *On Unity*. It had been modified only to restrict the loosening power to earth, as a necessary condition for being loosened in heaven. This first commissioning of Peter was developed through two post-resurrection commissionings. The first was in one or both of the versions of *On Unity* (chapter 4 *PT*) prepared during the summer 251, in which Jn. 21.17 authorized Peter to feed the sheep of Christ. Thence Cyprian argued that Christ has one flock and all the apostles together were called to feed that one flock. In this reading, the unity of episcopal power was justified and balanced by the unity of the church, the purpose for which it was given. The multitude of pastors was seen as a function of the greatness of the flock, as was laid out in the first version of *On Unity* and repeated in other contexts.[104] The second was in the final version of *On Unity* (chapter 4 *TR*) in 256, in which Jn. 20.22–3 placed the emphasis, as was appropriate in the baptismal controversy, upon the one sanctifying power which was held by the many pastors. They and they alone had the authority and power to pastor the flock of Christ. Anyone not in the union of the college which succeeded to them had no part in this power.

In practice and chronologically in the development of Cyprian's theory, the unity of the church as a whole preceded and justified the unity of the episcopate. The richness and fecundity of the church made it too large for any individual to rule, so the shepherds were multiplied and assigned parts of the flock. The autonomy of each leader was strictly limited, however, because the unity of the flock and the bishops' shared responsibility for it required the unity of coordinated and collaborative action. As the persecution ended, Cyprian had already asserted the power of the local bishop in his church; the local bishop was not a delegate of the college but a constituent member. As the schisms developed, Cyprian recognized

that the individual bishop's autonomy was limited by his membership in the college: he had responsibility not only for his own part
of the flock but together with his colleagues for the whole of the
flock; each of his colleagues had a corresponding responsibility for
his part of the flock within the whole. The collaboration which had
become absolutely essential for the good of the whole and of its
individual parts was justified by the theory of the one flock and its
many pastors.

As the schisms developed and controversy continued, however,
the unity of the episcopate itself became the necessary means for
maintaining the unity of the church. Churches were understood as
linked to one another through the mutual recognition of their
bishops. Some of the laxist Christians in Carthage abandoned a
bishop isolated in a small, Numidian college for Cyprian, who held
his place in a large college linked to those across Africa and beyond
the sea. Thus the second set of texts comes into play: the unity of
the episcopate and its indivisible authority to judge and sanctify
became the foundation of the unity and unicity of the church. Only
those communities whose leaders were recognized members of the
world-wide college could be parts of the true and universal church,
benefiting from its power to sanctify on earth and intercede in
heaven. The one power shared by their pastors made many local
communities into a unified church.

In Cyprian's theory, the unity of the church and the unity of the
episcopate were dialectically related. The episcopate existed for the
sake of the church and must be one because the church was one. The
church functioned as one because the episcopate was one; its structures of unity beyond the local level were those of episcopal
collegiality.

The local church and the episcopal college had radically
different social structures. At the local level, the community had a
variety of differentiated roles which were assigned by the group as
a whole. Some had authority over others, though all were responsible to the community. In the episcopal college, each member
was the equal of every other and no one had authority over
another, though the group as a whole had authority over each. In
actual practice, of course, some bishops had greater influence over
their peers but their power was based on the location or size of
the city, the wealth of the congregation, or the talents of the individual; it was not based upon any cosmic or religious foundation,
as was the differentiation of roles in the local church.

Placed in the context of the development of the practice of the

North African church and the theory through which Cyprian and his colleagues justified their actions, the primacy language used in the early version of *On Unity* could have had a very limited range of meanings. It could have referred to authority and power over others only within the local church, which must surely have been the author's intention in the summer 251. It could have referred to the symbolism of the single power which was given to one person to demonstrate its singularity and indivisibility, which must surely have been the author's meaning in summer 256. The primacy of one bishop over others which developed into the patriarchal system in the fourth and fifth centuries might have been practically conceivable by Cyprian and his colleagues. Such a regional primacy of the patriarch, however, would have been contradicted by their shared belief that bishops are equally and communally successors to the apostles. Furthermore, they consistently rejected the Roman bishops' claims to authority on the basis of apostolic foundation. They may have welcomed the possibility of an ecumenical council as an expression of the unity of the episcopate, though like Firmilian of Caesarea they may have expected the bishop of Jerusalem, as custodian of apostolic tradition, to preside. The primacy of the papal system which emerged in the medieval period would have been puzzling to the African bishops of the third century: they firmly grasped Peter as a symbol of unity but understood the Petrine office only at the local level. They found the reality of their shared episcopate, first conferred upon Peter, in the gift of the Holy Spirit bestowed upon all the apostles once Christ had been glorified.

Both locally and universally, the church was in the bishop and the bishop in the church.

9

CYPRIAN'S AFRICAN
HERITAGE

Investigation of the correlation between the social structures of
Cyprian's church and its theology depends upon the unusual historical evidence, Cyprian's letters and treatises, which permit modern
scholars to specify many aspects of church life in the third century
in Roman Africa. For the life of this church during the 140 years
which separated the death of Cyprian from the ordination of
Augustine, the historical record is much less full. Only with the
surviving letters, controversial writings and preaching of
Augustine, as well as the decrees of the African councils which
carried forward the reform program of Bishop Aurelius of Carthage,
does the historical record once again reflect the life of Christian
communities in any detail. By that time, however, the situation of
Christianity within the Roman world and the social structures of
the churches had changed significantly. The thesis of this study can
be confirmed by a sampling of these social changes and the corresponding shifts in the appropriation of the Cyprianic theology.

At the end of the Diocletian persecution, the situation of the
African church changed dramatically. The Constantianian toleration
and support of Christianity brought to the fore a conflict over the
episcopal succession at Carthage, which was cast in Cyprianic terms.
The elected candidate, Caecilian, was charged with cooperation
with the government and one of his consecrators, Felix of Aptunga,
was charged with denying Christ by turning over the scriptures to
the imperial authorities. A schism resulted in which commissions of
bishops appointed by the emperor and the bishop of Rome chose
between the rival candidates. They recognized Caecilian as the
rightful bishop but as a condition for communion required that he
adopt the Roman practice of receiving schismatics and heretics
without rebaptism. Having made the concession, this Catholic
party enjoyed the support of the imperial government and the
universal church. The opposing Donatist party claimed freedom

166

from idolatry and identified itself through resistance to imperial oppression. It ostentatiously continued Cyprian's practice of rebaptism, especially of converts from the Catholic communion. Both parties developed their claims to the heritage of Cyprian, the one appealing to universal unity and being charged with contamination by idolatry; the other claiming purity and being charged with schism.

The Donatists

In their theology the Donatists held to Cyprian's understanding of the purity of the church as the necessary condition for its power to sanctify. They focused the purity of the church on the freedom of the clergy from all taint of idolatry and apostasy. Any Christians who had been contaminated by these sins after baptism were permanently banned from functioning among the clergy, though the sinner might presumably be admitted to communion among the laity. The sin of schism does not seem to have been regarded with the same horror: Augustine pointed out that Parminian and his colleagues had accepted the supporters of Maximinian's schism back into communion and even into episcopal offices.[1]

The Donatists also insisted that the Christian rituals transmit contamination, within the church or outside it, from a bishop to the participants in his communion and among the members of the episcopal college. Cyprian, as has been seen, had focused this danger within the unity of the church on situations in which the acceptance of the minister had been with knowledge and approval of his sin, though his language and his citations from the Hebrew scriptures had not so limited his thesis. The Donatists claimed that Caecilian's apostasy had spread from his consecrator to the new bishop and thence to those bishops in Africa who recognized him, and finally to the whole episcopal college which maintained communion with the polluted African episcopate. Donatus' charges of apostasy were rejected at the time of the schism and contested continuously thereafter. Thus the operative question quickly became whether a bishop's sin could contaminate his church and colleagues rather than whether it actually had done so. The debate focused on Cyprian's understanding of the constitution of the episcopal college and particularly on the recognition and approval by which a bishop became and remained a member. The consecrators' acceptance of the candidate elected by the people and the letters through which other bishops welcomed a newly elected bishop into their communion seemed to indicate a judgment of his standing before God and worthiness for ministry. Thus a bishop's colleagues might be construed as supporting his sin and thereby sharing his guilt. Over the longer term, therefore, the debate focused not only on the transmission of guilt without informed consent but on the role of mutual recognition in the establishment of a bishop and constitution of the episcopal college. A college built, as Cyprian had conceived it, on mutual acceptance seemed necessarily an instrument for transmitting sin and sharing guilt. On the basis of this theory, the Donatists accused the Catholic bishops of a complicity in apostasy which disqualified them for office and voided their sacramental ministry.

The Donatists maintained Cyprian's understanding of the defined social boundary of the Christian church and the episcopate. In their practice, the local church seems to have retained a large measure of voluntary adherence because it involved active opposition to the government and the suffering of certain civil disabilities. The episcopal college was also a voluntary community, in which each of the bishops consented to the initiation of a new member and thereby became responsible for any guilt he was carrying. These closely bounded groups retained the social structure which supports both a belief in efficacious rituals which could purify or contaminate and a behavioral standard of conduct for determining purity. The retention of a hierarchal differentiation of offices and roles within the local church allowed the Donatists to develop Cyprian's system and to assign responsibility for the purity of the church to the bishop and clergy.[2] Cyprian's understanding of the episcopal college, however, allowed no differentiation of roles within it, through which sin and impurity could be isolated and thereby tolerated. Because each bishop was a full member, the sin of any one could pollute the whole. In order to maintain the plausibility and functioning of their system, therefore, the Donatists narrowed the behavioral standard to the sin of apostasy or idolatry. The principal danger of such pollution in the fourth and fifth centuries arose not from the practices of the imperial cult but from contact with the Catholics, who were judged to be burdened with the guilt of Caecilian and his consecrator. To protect the purity which identified and justified their separate church, the Donatist bishops had to maintain the assertion that the Catholic communion had been contaminated.[3] As they became increasingly isolated from the church outside Africa, they also had to overlook Cyprian's warning to the Roman confessors that schism, even schism undertaken in protection of the gospel and the holiness of the church, was as sacrilegious and polluting as idolatry.

The Donatists adapted the theology of Cyprian to a new social circumstance, in which their church found itself isolated from the universal Christian church. They maintained the dependence of sanctifying power on purity from apostasy while ignoring its restriction to the unity of the universal episcopate and church. As a clearly bounded and role-differentiated community, the Donatists maintained Cyprian's trust in the efficacy of rituals for sanctification or contamination.

The Catholics

The Catholic position after the Constantinian toleration and the Theodosian establishment of Christianity was significantly different from that of the Donatists. Though the Catholic communion in Africa was in the minority, it enjoyed communion with the universal Christian church and thus could claim continuity with the apostolic foundations throughout the empire. The Catholics had the support of the imperial government and were preferred to the Donatists and the traditional polytheists. Catholic bishops, for example, were civil magistrates and had access to various forms of imperial assistance and support. This recognition carried a price. To gain the approval of the bishops appointed to judge between the rival candidates in the schism, Caecilian and his supporters had to commit themselves to the Roman practice of accepting converts from schism and heresy by imposition of hands rather than baptism. The subsequent imperial preference for Catholics meant that many of those who associated themselves with the church made no significant commitment to its standards of conduct; their objective was economic and political advancement. The result was a lowering of the voluntary cohesion and a blurring of the boundary which defined the Catholic communities.

In accepting the Roman practice of receiving converts from schism, the African Catholics had to face a major problem in the definition of the boundary of their church. In Cyprian's theology, baptism was identified as the sacrament of initiation by which a candidate was purified and transferred across the border separating the holy realm of Christ's church from the demonic realm of idolatry and schism. If baptism could be effectively performed in an opposing Christian community, it could no longer define and negotiate the boundary of the Catholic church. The Roman practice of accepting baptism performed in schism or heresy came without a theoretical justification; it was based upon customary practice alone. In Africa, however, the Catholics had to explain how they could recognize the baptism of the Donatists without, as Cyprian had warned, giving up their own claims to be the true church and to exercise the single power to sanctify conferred upon it by Christ. The Catholics had available a combination of theoretical positions: they could redefine their boundary so that it included the schismatic communities as still part of the one church;[4] they could divide the efficacy of baptism so that it might be performed without purifying;[5] they could assign some other ritual, such as the imposition of hands or the eucharist, as the purifying and boundary-crossing action.[6] Could the Donatists be recognized as a true Christian church, though they lived in active schism from the universal communion? Could the Christian ritual of baptism fail to purify? Could the imposition of hands, either as the second part of the baptismal ritual or as the culmination of the ritual of reconciliation, become the actual boundary-crossing ceremony? To accommodate the new practice required of them, the bishops had to make some adjustment in Cyprian's understanding of the necessary link between the power to purify and adherence to the unity of the church and its episcopate.

In accepting citizens who joined the Catholic church in order to secure their status and fortune in the empire as much as their standing before God, the bishops had to expand the marginal classes at the boundary of the church — inside and just outside — and redefine the efficacy of baptism and the eucharistic fellowship in the economy of salvation. Many converts enrolled as catechumens but sought baptism late in life or at the time of death. Others accepted baptism but withdrew from communion after serious sin — often under episcopal threat of exposure — and sought reconciliation only on their deathbeds. Some failed a second time after the one public penance and reconciliation allowed by the church; forbidden communion even at death, they persisted in private penance and hoped to receive that forgiveness from Christ which the church could or would not mediate.[7] What had been transitional stages toward full communion in Cyprian's church became long-term forms of limited adherence in the imperially sponsored church. The baptismal, eucharistic and even reconciliation rituals were transformed into means of gaining access to the kingdom of heaven rather than ceremonies for constituting and maintaining the church as its sacrament on earth.

Faced with the continuing dispute about the idolatry of Caecilian and its implications for their power to sanctify, with the recognition of schismatic baptism as a real but inadequate means of salvation, and with the blurring of the boundary defining the church, the Catholics eventually modified and developed Cyprian's theology. Augustine put together what may be described as a four-part solution. First, instead of the purity of the episcopate, he focused on the link between the unity of the church and its sanctifying power. Second, he recognized that the church's rituals could be performed outside its social boundary, which he then redefined as the limit of the eucharistic fellowship. Third, he modified the priority which Cyprian had assigned to behavior over intention, so that performance became a condition but not an effective cause of unity and sanctity. Fourth, he abandoned the distinction which Cyprian had made between the episcopal college and the universal church, so that the church community as a whole held the power of sanctifying and guaranteed the efficacy of episcopal ministry.

First, Augustine broadened the definition of the necessary purity of the church to exclude sins other than idolatry and apostasy. Cyprian had accused Novatian of inconsistency in accepting adulterers but not idolaters. Augustine accused the founding generation of Donatist bishops and their successors of murder, fraud and civil strife. The objective was to show that maintaining the standard of purity set by Cyprian was beyond the capacity, or at least the achievement, of the Donatists. More importantly, he seized on the significance of the sin of schism, which Cyprian had treated as equivalent to idolatry. The gift of the Holy Spirit, which Cyprian had identified through Jn. 20.22–3 as the power to forgive sins, was also the foundation of unity within the church. To violate the unity of the church, therefore, was to lose the power both to sanctify and to be sanctified. As a result, he asserted, none of the Christian rituals performed in opposition to the unity of the church had any sanctifying effect.

According to Cyprian, schismatics who had originally been baptized within the church retained that sacrament and could be readmitted through the ritual of reconciliation. Similarly, he charged that the clergy who revolted against the church had turned the arms and endowments which the church had bestowed upon them against it. Thus Augustine proposed a second point: that the Donatists had retained baptism, eucharist and the priesthood in schism, as well as the power to transmit them to their adherents and successors. Hence, the schismatic rituals were true Christian

171

sacraments and need not be repeated or replaced upon their return to the church. The African bishops not only accepted schismatic converts without rebaptism but offered to install returning Donatist bishops as successors to Catholics without a new ordination.

Thus the sharing of the eucharistic fellowship, rather than the acceptance of baptism, became the behavior which indicated and effected membership in the unity of the church. Using Cyprian's identification of Christ and the community in the eucharistic elements, Augustine expanded the symbol from the local to the universal church. Thus the bread and wine in the celebration actually united the participant to Christ and to all true Christians. In this way, the eucharist not only symbolized but actually effected the unity of Christians in Christ. Participation in the eucharist, therefore, was the appropriate ritual of adherence to the unity of the church. Those who refused to accept the behavioral obligations which accompanied eucharistic fellowship were outside the church and would be excluded from the kingdom of heaven.

Cyprian had recognized a limited efficacy in the ritual of reconciliation because the people and bishop could not accurately judge the interior dispositions of the penitent. He asserted, however, that the performance of the ritual was necessary to qualify the sinner for appearing before the judgment of Christ and winning his approval. Augustine, in a third development, expanded this distinction and applied it to the other Christian rituals, even those celebrated within the unity of the church. Baptism could be performed, inside or outside the unity of the church, but it sanctified only a recipient who was truly converted and adhered to the unity of the church. Thus both the schismatic and the Catholic seeking temporal gain remained in their sin, having added to it the abuse of the sacrament. The same principle was applied to participation in the eucharist: the schismatic and the false Catholic received only the sacrament, and that to their harm; the true Christian was joined to Christ and the church. Augustine even allowed that good intention alone could save a Christian unjustly excluded from the unity of the church or a penitent who was refused a second opportunity for reconciliation. Thus all performances of the rituals were recognized as effective but the purifying or polluting effect followed upon the intention of the recipient rather than the community in which it was performed or status of its minister.

More generally, Augustine defined the unity of the Catholic church primarily by intention rather than bodily inclusion. Many persons might be found within the visible, social unity of the church who did not adhere to its true reality, the union of wills in love of God and neighbor. Schismatics were presumed to dissent from this unity and thus to be separated from the true church. Within the church, the union of wills in love rather than joint participation in the eucharist defined the true church. Thus Augustine distinguished within the social unity of the church between the society of saints and the sinners whom they supported and tolerated in the hope that they might be converted and saved. The cohesion and unity of the visible church spread throughout the world was the visible manifestation and effect of the mutual love of the saints, through the sharing of the gift of the Holy Spirit. A union constituted by love of God and forgiveness of neighbor could not transmit sin and guilt. Thus the true church remained pure and holy, though indistinguishable from the visible communion.

Finally, Augustine explained that the gift of the Holy Spirit which Christ bestowed upon his disciples in Jn. 20.22–3 was given to the whole church, or more specifically to the true church formed by the society of saints within the visible church, and not to the episcopal college alone. Christ had empowered his true disciples to forgive sins and the saints performed this service by their prayer and intercession. The bishops acted as the agents of the true church, exercising a power which individual leaders may or may not have shared.[8] Thus the standards of purity which Cyprian had applied to the bishops were more appropriately applied to the society of saints which constituted the true church than to either the entire assembly of the faithful or the episcopal college. The purity of the saints was itself maintained by the sharing of the Spirit's gift of charity, which covers and wins forgiveness for their sins.[9]

As a corollary of these positions, Augustine redefined the episcopal college so that it was constituted by the same means as the communion of the church, the sharing of charity. An unworthy bishop might hold a place in the visible assembly of his colleagues, just as he did in his local church. He was not, however, joined to them in charity and they tolerated rather than approved him as an office holder. The episcopal college, like the local church communion, could not serve as the instrument for transmitting guilt because the evil were not members of its true inner reality.

The Catholics, no less than the Donatists, had to modify the theology of Cyprian to make it fit the structures of their church. Some of Augustine's transformations of Cyprian's thought, such as the understanding of the unity of the local and universal church as the invisible society of saints constituted by the charity which inspires love of God and neighbor, and the distinction between the performance of a ritual and its sanctifying effect, were shifts from a behavioral to an intentional standard which followed upon the loss of the sharply defined boundary of the community. Others were necessary to deal with problems arising from the application of Cyprian's theory, such as the transfer of the sanctifying power from the bishops to the invisible society of saints and the redefinition of the episcopal college itself, which avoided the unresolved problems of the ministry of unworthy bishops, whether known or hidden. Much of Cyprian's heritage remained well established, particularly the belief that salvation must be mediated through a social institution which acts through its rituals.

The theology of Cyprian was not only transformed by the changed social circumstances of Christianity in Roman Africa during the fourth and fifth centuries; it also shaped those churches. The Donatist church was inconceivable outside Africa and won no support elsewhere. The theology of Augustine – not only his understanding of the church and its sacraments but of grace and divine election – was immediately accepted in the African Catholic church shaped by Cyprian but only gradually and with continuing resistance elsewhere, even in the Latin church.

Uniquely Cyprian

Theologies, particularly theologies which are well rooted in practice, have a hard time leaving home and settling elsewhere. Yet Cyprian's writings, like the relics of his body, were precious to North African Christians, who were more avid disciples of his than he had been of Tertullian. As has just been seen, Cyprian's understanding of the church and its sacraments set the terms of debate between Catholics and Donatists and laid the foundation upon which Augustine was to build much of Latin Christian theology. Some of Cyprian's more important ideas and practices, however, seem to have remained behind in the third century, or at least not to have been so widely taken up in other times and places.

This study has revealed, for example, the degree to which Cyprian not only insisted that the church is in the bishop and cannot be separated from him but also that the bishop is in the church and cannot act independently. Although his people accepted a hierarchy of offices and roles within the church, theirs was a voluntary adhesion to the community and consequently a face-to-face form of government in which the leaders were the subject of immediate and effective pressure from their people and colleagues. Cyprian steadfastly resisted the privileges of the martyrs and their laxist supporters but he accommodated his own judgments to his people and colleagues on many issues. His biographer explained that his people forced him to serve as their bishop. During the persecution, he agreed to the reconciliation of dying penitents; afterwards he accepted the distinction between certified and sacrificers; two years later he affirmed the church's power to forgive, at least on earth, the sin of apostasy. He recognized that the lapsed and their supporters were attracted to the laxist communion, so he cultivated and rewarded their loyalty to the one church. He observed that the bishop must be prepared to learn as well as to teach and he followed that principle.[10]

Cyprian recognized implicitly in facing the deliberations on the lapsed and explicitly in the conflict over schismatic baptism that he and his colleagues were dealing with questions and situations which were truly new and for which, consequently, the scripture provided inadequate or ambiguous precedents and principles. He followed a well-established African tradition in seeking the divine guidance of new revelations. These came in dreams setting forth the reasons for the persecution, in reading the actions of the Roman government when it instituted torture during the Decian persecution and threatened renewed prosecution of Christians, in deliberations with his fellow bishops in council, and in changing established custom to respond to a new challenge to the unique authority of the church to baptize and sanctify. When the martyrs urged the reconciliation of all the lapsed, for example, Cyprian responded that he could find no scriptural foundation for such action and would need some other sign of divine approval of the proposal.[11] Thus he did not oppose the prophetic charism within the church but balanced it with the established structures of office.

In opposition to the laxists, both Cyprian and Novatian recognized that the judgment of Christ and the standards of the kingdom of heaven might be significantly different from those of the earthly church. The laxists claimed that the advisory and intercessory role promised the martyr at the judgment of Christ should be exercised in the decisions made by the people and bishop. Cyprian clearly distinguished the earthly deliberations of the church from the final judgment of Christ and refused to accept any role for the martyr. Moreover, in making his decisions, Cyprian recognized that the earthly church could judge a person's dispositions only on the basis of conduct and behavior; reading the intentions of the heart belonged to Christ alone. Hence he was prepared to loosen sins on earth while recognizing that Christ might not loosen them in heaven. Yet he insisted that the judgment of the church, and particularly its binding of sinners on earth, would be binding in heaven. Christ might reject some whom the bishop had accepted but Christ would not reverse the rejection pronounced by the bishop; instead he would require from the hands of the bishop those to whom he had refused the peace of the church on earth. Novatian seems to have taken a contrary stand, that Christ might loosen and forgive sins which the church had been denied the authority to loosen. While Cyprian and his community seem to have believed firmly that the communion of the church was the earthly sign and the only way to gain access to the kingdom of heaven, they had already recognized that some in the church might not be admitted to the kingdom. Yet they were content to act with the resources at their disposal for judging individuals, for binding and loosening.

Finally, following Tertullian before him, Cyprian asserted that the church itself was an integral part of Christian faith and the necessary means of salvation. To submit to the rituals and invoke the intercessory role of the church was, he would explain, to confess Christ and thus to reverse the sin of apostasy. His episcopal colleagues should, he suggested, reflect upon the creed in which the forgiveness of sins was professed as given through the church. Most tellingly, Cyprian insisted upon the necessity and the efficacy of the church's rituals for establishing and maintaining the heavenly standing of the Christian. Sins must be repented, confessed and forgiven in the church because there was no such ritual in the grave after death. The eucharist joined the community and each of its members to Christ, empowering them to offer their bodies and shed their blood for him. The Holy Spirit who would give the Christians words to speak before the proconsul was conferred by the imposition of the bishop's hands. He believed and led others to believe that the local communion of the Christian church was actually, though not exclusively, the enclosed garden, the fruitful paradise, the bride of Christ, the earthly reality of the kingdom of heaven.

The Christian church in Africa would grow, in divergent and opposed ways, and be nourished by the life of Cyprian's church. His disciples would change and adapt much of what he defended and held dear. The Christians of Africa – Catholic and Donatists alike – held him their father in faith and celebrated his triumph each year, with singing and dancing.

NOTES

PREFACE

1 Mary Douglas, "Cultural Bias," in *The Active Voice*, Boston, Routledge & Kegan Paul, 1982, pp. 183–254.

2 Mary Douglas, *Natural Symbols*, 2nd edn, Barrie and Jenkins, 1973, and with a new introduction, London, Routledge, 1996.

3 E.W. Benson, *Cyprian: His Life, His Times, His Work*, London, Macmillan, 1897.

4 Michael M. Sage, *Cyprian*, Cambridge, MA., Philadelphia Patristic Foundation, 1975.

5 Clarke, *Letters* 1–4.

6 In addition to the introduction to the *CCL* edition and the extensive bibliography listed therein, see *The Tradition of Manuscripts: A Study in the Transmission of St. Cyprian's Treatises*, Oxford, Clarendon Press, 1961.

7 Michael A. Fahey, SJ, *Cyprian and the Bible: a Study of Third-Century Exegisis*, Tübingen, J.C.B. Mohr, 1971.

8 "On Rebaptism: Social Organization in the Third Century Church," *Journal of Early Christian Studies*, 1 (1993):367–403.

9 "Confessing the Church: Cyprian on Penance," *Studia Patristica*, ed. Edward Yarnold, S.J. and Maurice Wiles, Leuven, Peeters, 2001, 36:338–48.

1 HISTORY OF CYPRIAN'S CONTROVERSIES

1 Pontius, *uita Cyp.* 5; *ep.* 43.1.2.

2 The edict itself has not survived. See Clarke, *Letters* 1:27–8 for evidence that the requirements may have extended to those who were not citizens as well.

3 For the current state of scholarship on the *libelli*, see Clarke, *Letters* 1:26–7,134, n.135. Striking witness to the process of compliance is provided in *epp.* 8.2.3, 21.3.2. In *ep.* 43.3, Cyprian made an oblique reference to the five commissioners who supervised the procedures in Carthage.

4 The certificate provided to those who complied with the edict does not mention the renunciation of any other religious loyalty. The central statement in the surviving Egyptian copies of *libelli* runs, "I have always and without interruption sacrificed to the gods, and now in

your presence in accordance with the edict's decree I have made sacrifice, and poured a libation, and partaken of the sacred victims." See J.R. Knipfing, "The Libelli of the Decian Persecution," *Harvard Theological Review*, 16 (1923):345–90. In the two accounts of the martyrdoms of bishops during the subsequent persecution of Valerian, they were not required to disavow Christianity but only to participate in the Roman cult. Of course, even an apostate Christian would have committed perjury by swearing the required statement. See the *acta proc.* 3–4 for the interrogation and sentencing of Cyprian and Eusebius, *h.e.* 7.11, for Dionysius of Alexandria.

5 The clergy had full access to the imprisoned confessors, including the holding of services in the prison, *epp.* 5.2.1, 12.1.1–2.2. Christians were apparently witnesses to the death under torture of some of the confessors, *ep.* 10.2.2. For the full evidence, see Clarke, *Letters* 1:132, n.118.

6 G.W. Clarke, "Some Observations on the Persecution of Decius," *Antichthon*, 3 (1969):63–76. On the Jewish exemption from the edict, see Clarke, *Letters* 1:131, n.117. Christians were disliked as a separatist group which did not participate in common rituals, see *ep.* 7.1. This resentment was the principal danger to the presbyters visiting the confessors in prison and to the Christians in the city, *epp.* 5.2.1, 6.4, 40.1.

7 Eusebius, *h.e.* 6.40. He was subsequently rescued by other Christians.

8 The death of Fabian was first noted in Cyprian's *ep.* 9.1.1, in response to him receiving a copy of a eulogy from the Roman clergy.

9 Cyprian defended his conduct to the Roman clergy in *ep.* 20.1.2. This letter gave a summary of the progress of the persecution and the Christian response to it through the summer of 250. Throughout his exile, Cyprian insisted that he had withdrawn because of the danger which his presence, as both a notable person in the city and the leader of the Christian community, posed for the community itself. See *epp.* 7.1, 14.1.2–2.1, 43.4.2.

10 Cyprian later charged that many Christians in Carthage eagerly complied with the edict as soon as it was promulgated, *ep.* 11.8; *lap.* 7–9. *Epp.* 15.4, 24.1 imply that some involved their dependants as well. For evidence of compliance at Rome, see *ep.* 8.2.3.

11 Those who obtained certificates either did so in person or through an agent by a payment. Some later asserted that they had explained to the imperial commissioners that they were Christians and could not comply with the edict. They regarded the payment as a fine or bribe. By this means, some Christians were able to exempt and to protect their families and dependants. Similarly, some of the sacrificers also seem to have protected other Christians by their compliance. On the different attitudes, see *epp.* 21.3.2, 55.13.2–14.2,26.1. Precedents for the use of subterfuge are detailed in note 58 below.

12 See *epp.* 14.1.1, 11.8. Cyprian later indicated that the majority of the Christians at Carthage had failed to honor their commitment to Christ, *lap.* 4,7. In addition, some of the bishops in Africa and Italy complied and even led their whole congregations into idolatry, *epp.* 55.11.2, 59.10.3.

13 Cyprian expected their torture and deaths, *ep.* 6.1–2. The problems addressed in *ep.* 13 made it clear that many of the confessors had been released and rejoined the community; see also *ep.* 14.2.2. The punishment of exile was also indicated in *ep.* 13.4.1. *Ep.* 19.2.3 showed that some of the exiles had suffered confiscation of their property.

14 *Epp.* 10.1.1–2.3, 12.1.2, 20.2.2, 21.4.1, 22.2.1. When the Roman confessor been held for eight months already, apparently without formal trial, *epp.* 31.1.1,5.1, 37.1.3. The experience of Celerinus in Rome was recounted in *ep.* 39.2.2. For the dating, see Clarke, *Letters* 1:226.

15 For death under torture in Carthage, see *epp.* 11.1.3, 10.1.2–2.3, 12.1.3, 22.2.2. In Rome, the presbyter Moyses seems to have died under these conditions; in *ep.* 55.5.2, Cyprian referred to him as a martyr.

16 *Lap.* 13; *epp.* 24, 25, 55.13.2, 56.1.

17 The letter of the Roman clergy to Cyprian, written by Novatian, rejected any distinction between those who sacrificed and those who acquired certificates by other means, *ep.* 30.3.1.

18 *Ep.* 21.3.2.

19 This policy is enunciated in *ep.* 8.2.3–3.1 and repeated in *ep.* 30.8. In *ep.* 30.8 it is identified as the common practice of the bishops in the area. In a similar way, the comfort of baptism was to be extended to a catechumen in danger of death, *ep.* 8.3.1.

20 The Roman confessors urged restraint on their counterparts in Carthage, *ep.* 28.2.3. Their following of the policy of delay was also indicated in the letter of the Roman clergy, *ep.* 30.4, and in the confessors' own letter to Cyprian, *ep.* 31.6.2–7.1. Celerinus' appeal from Rome to the confessors in Carthage attempted to evade this policy, *ep.* 21.3.2.

21 Cyprian became aware of this problem before mid-April 250, if *ep.* 14.4 indicated this practice. He treated it in *epp.* 15–17, which date from May of that year. See Clarke, *Letters* 1:254–5, 261, 269–70 for dating. *Ep.* 16.3.2 indicated that the death of the martyr was necessary for the validation of the letter of peace. See Tertullian, *pud.* 22, for an earlier witness.

22 *Ep.* 16.2.3. The letters may have specified that the lapsed were to be admitted to communion only after peace had been restored to the church as a whole, *epp.* 15.1.1, 16.3.2.

23 Cyprian charged that favors were extended to certain individuals and that some persons were actually selling the letters, *ep.* 15.3–4.

24 *Epp.* 22.2.1, 27.1.1. See also *ep.* 21 which requested such a letter of peace. One of the martyrs, Paulus, authorized another of the confessors, Lucianus, to grant peace in his name after his death to whoever asked, *ep.* 22.2.1.

25 *Ep.* 16.2.3 specified the procedures which must be followed in the reconciliation of a penitent. Cyprian reminded his clergy and people of the seriousness of the sin of apostasy, *epp.* 16.2.2, 17.2.1. Still, he seems to have been assuming that forgiveness could be given, though perhaps only by Christ after death, *epp.* 17.3.1–2, 18.2.1.

26 Cyprian seems to have regarded the persecution as God's chastisement of the church for its sinfulness. He insisted that granting peace to

those who had fallen would incur the divine wrath and place the entire church in danger. See *epp.* 13.6, 11.3–7, 15.2.1, 16.1.2, 17.1.2.

27 He referred explicitly to the intercessory power of the martyrs, *ep.* 18.1.2. Earlier, he cited the precedents of the African church to restrain the confessors in the distribution of letters, *ep.* 15.3.1. At the same time, he instructed that catechumens were also to be allowed the peace of the church through baptism, if they were in danger of death, *ep.* 18.2.2. See Clarke, *Letters* 1:295.

28 His policy had caused conflict in Carthage between those who had letters of peace and those who did not, *ep.* 19.2.1–3. In *ep.* 20.3.2, he broadened the dispensation to include all dying penitents. This might not have seemed a significant concession to Cyprian at the time he made it, since he seemed then to have shared Novatian's belief that penitents would appear before the tribunal of Christ even if they had not been admitted to the communion of the church. For the Roman practice, see notes 19–20 above.

29 *Ep.* 19.2.1. Elsewhere in Africa some of the lapsed were tried a second time and refused to comply. Some suffered torture, *ep.* 56.1, and others were exiled with loss of goods, thereby restoring themselves to the peace of the church, *epp.* 24.1–2, 25.1–2. See Clarke, *Letters* 1:346 for the location of Caldonius' see, where these events took place. The Roman clergy envisaged an involuntary second arrest following repentance, *ep.* 8.3.1.

30 *Ep.* 17.3.2, the Romans agreed to this procedure in *ep.* 30.5.3.

31 The consensus is reported in *ep.* 26.2, written in late summer 250.

32 *Epp.* 15.1.2, 16.3.2, 23.

33 *Ep.* 22.2.1 of Lucianus to the confessor Celerinus in Rome, announced that the martyr Paulus had authorized him to grant peace to anyone who asked. The confessors as a group had then decided to grant peace to everyone. *Ep.* 23 announced this decision to Cyprian and instructed him to communicate it to the other bishops.

34 *Ep.* 26, to which he appended his correspondence with Caldonius on the reconciliation of those who had confessed the faith after an initial failure, *epp.* 24, 25. He also sent an urgent letter to the Roman clergy, which had not yet corresponded directly with him, *ep.* 27. In addition, it seems that the Roman confessors had written to their counterparts in Carthage, attempting to restrain them, *ep.* 28.2.1.

35 *Ep.* 33.2.1, they did have certificates from the martyrs.

36 Cyprian's *ep.* 33 responded to these letters. His letter to the Roman clergy recorded the claim that the martyrs had already given peace, *ep.* 35.1, and the response of the Roman clergy reported the claim that peace had been already given in heaven, *ep.* 36.1.2.

37 The rebels seem to have written anonymously, in the name of the church. Cyprian responded that the church was built upon the bishop, the clergy and the faithful who had remained standing. He demanded that the correspondents identify themselves, *ep.* 33.1.1–2,2.2.

38 *Ep.* 31.6.2. *Ep.* 30 from the clergy and *ep.* 31 from the confessors were sent in response to Cyprian's report of the general amnesty granted by the confessors in Carthage. *Ep.* 35, from the clergy, followed the receipt of a copy of the subsequent letter in which the lapsed claimed immediate peace.

39 *Ep.* 31.7.2–8.1. Celerinus' appeal to the confessors in Carthage indicated that the Roman confessors actually followed this policy, *ep.* 21.3.2.

40 *Ep.* 32.1–2.

41 Cyprian commented on the difficult position of the loyal clergy in *epp.* 26.1,4, 27.2.2, and reported that some had been forced to grant the peace in *ep.* 27.3.1. There is no reason to believe that such pressure would have been stopped by the distribution of the letters from Rome.

42 *Epp.* 34.1, 38.2.2, 39.1.1 mentioned these collaborators.

43 Two clerics, one a confessor, had been appointed during the summer of 250, to serve as couriers in the extensive correspondence of that period, *ep.* 29. The new readers, Aurelius and Celerinus, were famous confessors, and were marked out to become presbyters in the future, *epp.* 38.1.2–3, 39.4.1–5.2. Numidicus, also a martyr and already a presbyter, was enrolled among the clergy of Carthage and destined for the episcopate, *ep.* 40.3.

44 The bishop Caldonius and the presbyters Rogatianus and Numidicus can be identified as confessors; the status of the bishop Herculanus cannot be confirmed. See *ep.* 41 for the identity of the commission and *epp.* 24.1.1, 40, 43.1.1 for the status of the confessors.

45 The status of the identified leader, Felicissimus, is somewhat uncertain, though he seems to have been a deacon, see Clarke, *Letters* 2:204–5. The role of the five presbyters is asserted in *ep.* 43.1–3. The laity who supported the movement may have feared the loss of financial support, since Cyprian had specified that it should be given only to those who had been faithful, *epp.* 5.1.2, 12.2.2, 14.2.1.

46 *Ep.* 41.2.1–2. The sentence against Felicissimus and some of his lay supporters was reported by the commission in *ep.* 42, an action joined by the bishop Victor. Cyprian pronounced sentence on the presbyters in *ep.* 43.1.2. The refugee presbyter Gaius may have been excommunicated earlier, *ep.* 34.1.

47 *Ep.* 43.4.2; *unit.* 12,20–23, and Clarke, *Letters* 2:214, n.2.

48 *Ep.* 43.3.1,6.1–7.2.

49 Decius himself was not killed until June of that year. The imperial action had apparently ceased earlier but Cyprian remained in exile because of the fear of popular action upon his return. See *ep.* 43.4.2.

50 The characterizations were apparently derived from the position taken by the group during the assembly. Tertullian described the penitents as prone, begging for the intercession of their standing colleagues. See *paen.* 10.6.

51 This division of the community grouped the fugitives, such as Cyprian, and all those who had escaped detection in Carthage with the public heroes, *lap.* 2,3. Any who had lacked this firm intention to confess (should it have been required by the imperial commissioners) were invited to repent privately of their failure, *lap.* 28; *ep.* 55.13.2–14.1.

52 *Lap.* 7–9,27–28,36. Cyprian upheld the Roman position that no distinction was to be made between the certified and the sacrificers, *ep.* 30.3.1.

53 *Lap.* 15–16,34. The same charge had been made in *ep.* 43.2.2–3.2, and would be repeated in *unit.* 1–3 and *ep.* 59.12.2–13.2.

54 *Vnit.* 19,23. Bévenot indicates that chapter 19, like chapter 4, of this treatise underwent a subsequent revision. Both versions survived. See his "Hi qui sacrificaverunt," *Journal of Theological Studies*, 5 (1954):68–72. This issue will be revisited in chapters 5 and 8.

55 In one early version, the primacy of Peter provided an argument for the unity of the local church under its bishop, *lap.* 4.

56 Probably in late April, about a month after Easter, according to Clarke, *Letters* 2:222.

57 *Ep.* 55.6.1.

58 *Ep.* 55.13.2–14.2. Tertullian indicated that the practice of paying bribes in order to avoid prosecution was widespread among the wealthy Christians of Carthage and even institutionalized in the case of one church. Christians regularly signed or accepted business contracts which were sworn before the Roman deities, though they avoided actually pronouncing the oaths. See *idol.* 23 and *fuga* 5.3,12–14.

59 *Ep.* 55.17.3, a decision which Cyprian defended by noting the confusion and even compulsion under which the certified acted, *ep.* 55.14.1,26.1.

60 *Ep.* 55.17.3. Some of them, of course, would recover from the illness and would remain in the peace of the church, *ep.* 55.13.1.

61 *Ep.* 55.23.4.

62 *Ep.* 55.6.2. For information on this meeting, see Eusebius, *h.e.* 6.43.2 and Clarke, *Letters* 3:172.

63 *Ep.* 45.1.2,4.1. Clarke suggests that an independent commission of bishops, of which Cyprian was not a member, investigated the dispute and decided on the formal excommunication, *Letters* 2:242–3.

64 *Ep.* 59.10.1, where the action is reported to Cornelius. Fortunatianus of Assuras, who had failed in the persecution, tried to regain his see sometime during this year, *ep.* 65.1.1. For the dating, see Clarke, *Letters* 3:316–7.

65 In *epp.* 52.2.5 and 54.3.1, written after some of the confessors abandoned Novatian, Cyprian indicated that the parties divided over the policy of reconciling the lapsed. For the support of the confessors, see *epp.* 49.1.4, 54.2.2. Cornelius' account of the events is preserved in Eusebius, *h.e.* 6.43.5–20.

66 *Ep.* 45.2.1–3.1.

67 *Epp.* 44.1.2–2.2, 45.3.1

68 *Ep.* 44.1.3.

69 Cornelius reported on the events in *ep.* 49.

70 Because of miscommunication, the church at Hadrumetum initially recognized Cornelius and then withdrew its approval pending the report of the episcopal commission. Cornelius protested the withdrawal of support and Cyprian tried to explain the sequence of events, *ep.* 48. Cyprian later considered Cornelius altogether too willing to entertain the Carthaginian rebels' complaints against him, in apparent retaliation for his own questioning of Cornelius' credentials, *ep.* 59.1–2,18.

71 Cyprian recounted the agreement in *ep.* 55.6.2.

72 Cyprian argued that the Italian bishops had no real options in this case, *ep.* 55.11. He expressed horror of lapsed clergy in *epp.* 65.1–2,4, 67.3,9.

73 Cornelius provided a detailed defense of this decision to Cyprian in *ep.* 49. The confessors themselves claimed to have been deceived by Novatian, *ep.* 53. Cyprian congratulated Cornelius and the confessors on their reunion without comment on the procedures adopted, *epp.* 51, 54.

74 Novatian apparently sent letters to African bishops attacking Cornelius' practices. The charges can be reconstructed from Cyprian's responses to accusations drawn from that letter in his *ep.* 55. Cornelius was charged with entering into communion with idolaters: bishops who had sacrificed (10), Trofimus and his congregation (11), sacrificers among the laity (12), and those who received certificates (14–15). Cyprian's letter implies that Novatian denied reconciliation to all the penitent lapsed, even at the time of death (17–18,26,28).

75 *Ep.* 44.3.1.

76 *Ep.* 50.1.1–2.

77 *Ep.* 55 responding to such an attack defended Cornelius' person and policies; it also pointed up inconsistencies in Novatian's own behavior.

78 *Ep.* 59.9.2, not to be confused with the confessor presbyter who had returned to Cornelius, *epp.* 53, 51.1.1. Earlier references to this individual as a supporter of Novatian appear in *epp.* 44.1.1, 50.1.1. See Clarke, *Letters* 2:226, 278, 3:249 for his identity.

79 Cyprian detailed the background of each member of this group for Cornelius, see *ep.* 59.10.

80 *Ep.* 59.1.1–2.5.

81 During the persecution, his position on the exclusion of the lapsed had resembled the rigorist stance of the now disgraced Novatian.

82 In *ep.* 59.15.1–16.2, Cyprian defended his own practice as extremely lenient; in *ep.* 59.18.1, he referred to Novatian's threat and closed with the specific request that his own letter of defense be read out to the Roman community as a whole, *ep.* 59.19.1.

83 *Ep.* 55.13.1. The plague which Cyprian described in detail in *de mortalitate* would have influenced the decision to grant peace to those expected to die.

84 *Ep.* 59.16.1–2.

85 *Ep.* 57.1.2–2.1.

86 *Epp.* 57.1.1, 68.5.1. Pressure from the laxist church may have influenced this decision. In arguing for it, Cyprian asserted that the sacrificers needed the strength which only the bishops could provide to face the coming challenge, *ep.* 57.4.1–4. He admitted to having perceived no such need during the prior persecution when the lapsed were urged to regain the communion of the church by publicly confessing their faith, *ep.* 19.2.3. The peace was to be extended, of course, only to those who had submitted to the authority of the bishops.

87 *Ep.* 57.4.1–4. In his subsequent letter praising Cornelius' confession of faith, Cyprian pointed to the triumph of the united Roman church, including those who had failed during the earlier persecution, as a sign of the efficacy of this policy, *ep.* 60.2.1–5.

88 *Ep.* 57.5.1–2.

89 *Ep.* 60.1–2. Cyprian interpreted this public display by the penitents as a confession of faith by which they reversed their prior failure and earned the peace of the church.

90 On Cornelius' death, see *ep.* 61.3.1; on his adoption of the lenient policy, see *ep.* 68.5.1.

91 *Ep.* 68.5.1. On the exile, see *ep.* 61.1.1–2.

92 *Ep.* 68, written late in 254 or early in 255. Cyprian argued that a bishop who dissented from this common decision of his colleagues could not be participating in the same Spirit (5.2). The Novatianist in Arles apparently posed no threat to Stephen's authority in Rome.

93 *Ep.* 67, esp. 9.1–3. Cornelius had admitted Trofimus, a sacrificer, but only as a layman. Cyprian allowed that Stephen might have been deceived by the petitioner but that would neither excuse his violating established procedure by overruling the local church nor protect him from the danger of pollution by the apostate, *ep.* 67.4–5.

94 Tertullian disputed the practice in *bapt.* 15.

95 The question of custom and the change made by the Africans appears in *epp.* 70.1.2, 71.2.1, 73.13.1. Reference to the council under Agrippinus appears in *epp.* 71.4.1, 73.3.1. Though Cyprian tried to hide the fact, Firmilian of Caesarea in Cappadocia explained that, unlike the Asians, the Africans had actually changed their practice in the council, *ep.* 75.19.3. For a full discussion of the council under Agrippinus, see Clarke, *Letters* 4:196–9.

96 The identity of faith appeared as an argument for the efficacy of Novatian's baptism in *ep.* 69.7.1; the argument was pushed back to Marcion in *ep.* 73.4–5.

97 The treatise *de rebaptismo* may also have been written in Africa before Cyprian's death. See J. Quasten, *Patrology* 2:368.

98 According to Clarke, *Letters* 4:173–4. The dating of the letters of this controversy will be considered more fully in chapter 6.

99 *Ep.* 70. This meeting was held in 254 or 255; the later date is judged more likely by Clarke, *Letters* 4:192–3.

100 *Ep.* 72.1.1–3. This letter also indicated that Stephen may have been admitting schismatic clerics to office, contrary to all established policy, *ep.* 72.2.1–3. Along with it went copies of the letter sent by the council to the bishops of Numidia (*ep.* 70) and Cyprian's subsequent letter to Quintus in Mauretania (*ep.* 71).

101 The vehemence of Stephen's response might have been caused, in part, by his receipt in the same packet of a copy of the letter to the Spanish congregations (*ep.* 67), in which he was strongly criticized. For the conjectural dating, see Clarke, *Letters* 4:139–40, 142–4.

102 Stephen's letter has been lost (or discarded, since the Roman correspondence survived only in the African collection); his position was reported in Cyprian's letter to Pompeius, *ep.* 74.1–3.

103 The reference to excommunication can be found in *ep.* 74.8.2, as something well known to the addressee. Firmilian of Caesarea reported that Stephen had broken communion with the bishops of Asia as well on this same issue, *ep.* 75.24.2,25.1. He added that Stephen had characterized Cyprian as a false Christ, a false apostle and a deceiver, *ep.* 75.25.4.

104 Firmilian of Caesarea was presumably not the only bishop whose support Cyprian sought.

105 The record of the voting is to be found among the works of Cyprian, *sententiae episcoporum numero LXXXVII.*

106 Cyprian reported Sixtus' martyrdom, 6 August 258, in *ep.* 80.1.4. The *uita Cyp.* 14 characterized him as peace-loving.
107 On which, W.H.C. Frend, *The Donatist Church*, Oxford, Oxford University Press, 1952.

2 CHRISTIANS OF CARTHAGE UNDER PERSECUTION

1 Thus Cyprian urged the consecrated virgins to make their wealth available to the poor, *habitu* 10–11. After the persecution, the fallen were warned that their love for property had bound them to the world; they were urged to contribute to the common chest and thus to place their treasure in heaven, *lap.* 10–13,35.
2 The eucharistic ritual seems to have been celebrated in common on a regular basis, perhaps even daily, early in the day, *ep.* 63.15.2,16.1–2. Mention was never made of dependence upon particular individuals for assembly space. Moreover, the church had access to space which could accommodate gatherings of up to eighty-five bishops, with their assistants, see *sententiae episcoporum*.
3 *Ep.* 41.1.1–2.1 showed the conflict between the laxist party and the bishop for control of the church funds; the deacon Felicissimus was charged with embezzlement. Cyprian himself asserted that the funds belonged to the church and were dispensed by the bishop, *ep.* 41.2.1. In the support of the confessors, however, both common and private funds were used: common *ep.* 5.1.2, private *ep.* 7.2, unspecified *epp.* 12.2.2, 13.7, 14.2.2.
4 *Epp.* 1.1.2, 34.4.2, 39.5.2.
5 For support of the poor, widows and those who had given up inappropriate professions, *epp.* 2.2.2, 5.1.2, 7.2. During the persecution, this fund was used to sustain the poor and the families of the confessors, as well as the confessors themselves, *epp.* 5.1.2, 13.7. Cyprian later authorized his representatives to give aid for setting people up in trade again, *ep.* 41.1.2. The salaries of the clergy were paid, *ep.* 39.5.2; but those who had fled during the persecution were not to be paid when they returned, *ep.* 34.4.2.
6 *Ep.* 62.3.1–4.2. In this instance, a special collection was made among the laity of Carthage and Cyprian named the major contributors; he also indicated that bishops of other cities made gifts in the names of their whole communities.
7 *Epp.* 5.1.1–2, 77.3.1, 78.3.1, 79.1.1.
8 During the persecution, there were some indications that Christians used alms as bribes to win the intercession of the martyrs from their agents among the confessors, *ep.* 15.3.2. Those who had fallen undertook works of charity as a sign of their commitment, *epp.* 21.2.2,4.1, 33.2.1, 33.7.1. In *lap.* 35, Cyprian exhorted the fallen to give alms as a method of repentance.
9 Subsequent references to the reconciliation of the lapsed usually indicated the offering of the sacrifice and the giving of peace, *epp.* 15.1.2, 16.2.3, 17.2.1. In the case of the dying penitents, the reference was always to the giving of peace, *epp.* 18.1.2, 19.2.1, 20.3.1; there was no explicit reference made to offering of sacrifice and giving of the eucharist.

10 In *ep.* 63.13.5, Cyprian made the connection between the united community and the one loaf which is the body of Christ. He made a similar symbolic connection between the people and the water which is mixed into the wine in the cup. In *ep.* 63.16.2, he asserted that the true sacrament was celebrated with the whole community present, rather than a select portion. It should be noted that this letter cannot be securely dated; it might indicate attitudes which were in place prior to the persecution, Clarke, *Letters* 3:287–8. At the first sign of division, Cyprian stressed the one altar in the one church, *ep.* 43.5.2.

11 The laity overrode the objections of a number of presbyters in electing Cyprian, *epp.* 43.1.2, 59.6.1. The decision once made was reversible only for the gravest infidelity, *epp.* 65.4.1, 67.4.1,5.1.

12 The appointment of clergy was usually with the approval of the laity, *epp.* 34.4.1, 38.1.1. When Cyprian acted without the agreement of the community, he provided an explanation, *epp.* 29.1.2, 38.1.2, 39.1.1, 40.1.1. The bad performance of the clergy was to be judged by the people as a whole. The threat against rebels was made, *ep.* 16.4.2; it would be carried out for the clergy who had taken to flight, *ep.* 34.4.1; and those who rebelled, *ep.* 34.3.2.

13 The practice was reported in *ep.* 59.15.2. During the persecution, Cyprian asserted that the whole community would be involved in setting policy and judging individual cases, *epp.* 14.1.4, 17.3.2, 19.2.1, 20.3.3, 26.1.2.

14 During the persecution, the confessors were called upon to pressure their fellows, *ep.* 15.3.2, and the people were urged to bring the clergy into line, *ep.* 17.3.1–2. Afterwards, Cyprian had to persuade the people to welcome schismatics as penitents, *ep.* 59.15.3. Some of these schismatics failed to persevere, perhaps because they were being shunned, *ep.* 59.15.4.

15 Thus Cyprian spoke of breaking the *sacramentum Christi*, *lap.* 7.

16 Tertullian, *idol.* 23, *fuga* 5.3,12–14. This might have been part of the problem with having the clergy serve as guardians for minor children in wills, *ep.* 1.1.1. Cyprian castigated the fallen for both taking oaths and breaking them, *lap.* 6.

17 The Roman confessors spoke of the sin of the eyes which had looked upon heathen images, *ep.* 31.7.1; for Cyprian's own belief, see *ep.* 58.9.2 and *lap.* 28.

18 Thus for example *ep.* 2.1.2 for an actor. Interestingly, the confessor Celerinus, like his martyr uncles before him, seems to have been in the Roman army because he was tried before the emperor himself, *ep.* 39.2.1,4.

19 Evidence can be found for the presence of wealthy people in the community. Some had slaves and property to protect, and attempted to add to their patrimony, *lap.* 6. Bishops were leaving their sees and flocks to seek estates and loaning money at interest, *lap.* 6; *ep.* 65.3.1. Cyprian urged that Christians should have abandoned their patrimony, *lap.* 10,11,12; he asserted that the persecution was allowed by God because the people were seeking after property and profit, *ep.* 11.1.2. The practices of personal decoration which Cyprian described in *lap.* 30, would have required considerable wealth. The contribution which Cyprian and his community made to the ransoming of Christians

taken captive was quite large. The total gift, of which the Carthaginian Christians accounted for the greater part, would have fed 12,000 persons for a month, see *ep.* 62.3.2–4.2, with Clarke's notes in *Letters* 3:284–5. In addition, Cyprian indicated that some Christians had large numbers of dependants, both family members and farm workers, over whom they exercised control and responsibility, *ep.* 55.13.2.

20 The use of the bath, cosmetics and the concern for wealth were advanced in *lap.* 6,30. *De habitu uirginum* shows that the virgins wanted to retain control of their property and to follow the Roman practices in dress and use of the baths, *habitu* 5,7–9,14–19. *Ep.* 63.15.2 addressed the concern that participation in the morning eucharist would leave the smell of wine on the breath and thereby identify Christians, a care which Cyprian characterized as a precursor to apostasy.

21 Cyprian was concerned to replace the tools of the craftsmen, which may have been confiscated during the persecution, *ep.* 41.1.2. They needed additional financial support during the persecution to prevent them from failing, *epp.* 12.2.2, 14.2.1.

22 During the persecution, some of the poor were supported by church funds, lest their indigence provide a further temptation to apostasy, *epp.* 12.2.2, 14.2.1. This was, moreover, a form of control since those who did fall were cut off from financial support. Thus in *ep.* 7.2, Cyprian provided support for all the poor; thereafter he specified that only those who had stood fast would be given support, *epp.* 5.1.2, 12.2.2, 14.2.1. The episcopal commission which acted for Cyprian may have been charged with seeing that none of the fallen were receiving alms from the church, *ep.* 41.1.2.

23 *Lap.* 8–9 and *ep.* 55.13.2 may imply that slaves were forced to comply with the imperial edict by some Christian masters.

24 L. William Countryman, *The Rich Christian in the Church of the Early Empire*, Toronto, Edward Mellen Press, 1980, pp. 22–6.

25 The letter of the Roman clergy to their counterparts in Carthage indicated some level of resentment of the *insignis*, *ep.* 8.2.3. As shall be seen below, the Roman enforcement of the Decian edict affected the rich and poor in radically different ways. The upper classes might be subject to confiscation of property and exile but not to torture, as the lower classes were.

26 The clergy were not allowed to assume financial responsibilities which were permitted to other Christians, *ep.* 1.1.1. They were chosen by the bishop with the advice of the community as a whole, *epp.* 29.1.2, 34.4.1, 38.1.1 They were paid by the church, *epp.* 1.1.2, 34.4.2, according to rank, *ep.* 39.5.2.

27 The rights of the catechumens are mentioned in *epp.* 18.2.2, 8.3.1 (Rome). Cyprian referred to the use of excommunication in *ep.* 4.4.1–3. He also distinguished others who were in a probationary state but within the communion: the virgins who had not been defiled even though they had shared their beds with men were to do penance and be warned that they would be excommunicated if the practice were repeated, *ep.* 4.4.1; the persons who had been repeat offenders were treated more harshly, specifically the men who had slept with virgins, *ep.* 4.4.1; the clergy who had abandoned their duties during the perse-

cution were suspended from office but not communion, *ep.* 34.4.1–2. Even the persons who had lapsed were still within the church, under the care of the bishops, who had to look to their salvation, *epp.* 31.6.3, 35.1.2. If these people fell away because they were not offered the hope of reconciliation, the bishops would be held responsible by Christ, *ep.* 55.6.1,15.1,17.2. Finally, some persons were in a penitential state or subject to certain restrictions within rather than outside the communion: those who sinned only in their intention during the persecution, *lap.* 28.

28 *Epp.* 43.1.2, 55.8.4, 59.5.2–3, 64.4.1–2, 66.1.2.

29 *Epp.* 65.4.2, 66.10.1, 67.3.1–5.2, 68.2.1–4.3.

30 Cyprian complained of bishops who abandoned their pastoral responsibilities to pursue personal financial advantage, *lap.* 6. He even recommended that one be "excommunicated" after his death for financial irregularities, *ep.* 1.2.1, with Clarke, *Letters* 1:151, n. 4. Moreover, Cyprian had to explain his own voluntary exile as serving the good of all rather than his own protection, *epp.* 14.1.2, 20.2.1, 43.4.2.

31 *Epp.* 2.2.2–3, 5.1.2, 12.2.2, 14.2.1, 34.4.2, 39.5.2, 62.3.1–4.2, 77.3.1, 78.3.1, 79.1.1.

32 On appointing clergy, *epp.* 29.1.2, 38–40, 64.1–2; on their discipline, *epp.* 3.3.1–3, 16.4.2. Interestingly, a vision of the personified church convinced Celerinus to accept the ordination which Cyprian had unsuccessfully urged upon him, *ep.* 39.1.2.

33 Cyprian took the initiative in calling synods and in writing the reports of them, *epp.* 3, 4, 56, 57, 58, 62, 63, 64, 70, 72. Cyprian also had the central role in determining the African policy regarding the lapsed, *epp.* 25.1.2, 26.1.2, 56, 57.

34 Once they were satisfied that he had not abandoned his office, for example, the Roman presbyters began to deal primarily with Cyprian himself, *epp.* 30, 36. His extensive correspondence with the Roman bishops showed his role as spokesman for the whole of the African church, *epp.* 44, 45, 47–52, 59, 61. He also dealt with problems in Spain, *ep.* 67, Gaul, *ep.* 68, and Asia, *ep.* 75.

35 This claim was advanced during the controversy: the bishop's action was evident in *ep.* 59.3.3,4.2. His authority came from God, through the apostles, *unit.* 4–5, but was not independent of the community, so that decisions were made with the advice of all, *epp.* 14.4, 16.4.2, 17.3.2, 26.1.2. The presbyters and deacons could be authorized to grant reconciliation, *ep.* 18.1.2.

36 *Ep.* 63.14.3. In *ep.* 5.2.1, Cyprian indicated that the presbyters were celebrating in the prison but in *ep.* 16.4.2, he threatened to withdraw authorization to celebrate from presbyters who were abusing their position.

37 See chapters 3, 4 and 6 for fuller discussions of these roles.

38 *Vnit.* 4; *epp.* 33.1.1, 43.5.2, 59.7.3, 66.8.3.

39 In appointing Celerinus and Aurelius readers, Cyprian acknowledged that they were too young to be presbyters, but still assigned them the higher salaries appropriate to that rank, *ep.* 39.5.2.

40 Cyprian asserted that only the bishop was chosen by God, like the apostles were, *epp.* 55.9.1, 59.5.3, 66.1.2; the deacons were created by

the apostles or bishops, *ep.* 3.3.1. Deacons may have been assigned to individual presbyters, *epp.* 34.1.1, 52.2.3.

41 *Ep.* 1.1.1. Cyprian claimed that this was a conciliar decision.

42 *Ep.* 7.2. In *ep.* 5.1.2 the specification was added that only those who remained faithful should receive support. This restriction was continued in *epp.* 12.2.2, 14.2.1. The commission established by Cyprian during his exile may have had the responsibility of weeding the lapsed from the welfare rolls, see *ep.* 41.1.2.

43 *Epp.* 4, 62.2.3. The virgins retained their property, though they were exhorted to use it for the good of the church, *habitu* 7,11.

44 Thus Cyprian seems to have been particularly concerned not only for their physical integrity, *ep.* 4.1.1,3.1,4.1, but also for their separation from contact with men which might undercut their symbolic value, *ep.* 4.2.1–3,4.2. *Ep.* 62.2.3 focused on the dishonoring of Christian virgins which was an attack on the church as a whole. In addition, Cyprian demanded that they serve as outstanding examples of that separation from Roman values which all Christians were to practice, particularly in regard to clothing and grooming, *habitu* 11–17.

45 *Ep.* 18.2.2, they would be rewarded if martyred, *ep.* 73.22.1–2.

46 For descriptions of the penitential ritual, see *epp.* 4, 15.1.2, 16.2.3, 17.2.1; *lap.* 16,36. The requirement of charitable works is evident in *epp.* 21.2.2, 31.7.1, and *lap.* 35. It is also evident that not all of the penitents were excluded from communion: consider the cases of the virgins whose integrity remained intact despite their improper relations with men, *ep.* 4.4.1; and the Christians who admitted that they would have lapsed had they been called before the Roman authorities, *lap.* 28. Peace was to be given to those in danger of death, *epp.* 20.3.1–2, 55.13.1. The bishops also had to be concerned that the penitents did not become discouraged and fail, *epp.* 4.5.1, 55.17.2,28.1.

47 During the persecution, Cyprian argued that the Church did not have the right to turn them away, *epp.* 18.2.1, 35.1.2 Afterwards, he learned that the community was occasionally opposed to accepting back schismatics as penitents, *ep.* 59.15.2–3.

48 *Ep.* 3.3.3. Such a provision was made for Bishop Trofimus, *ep.* 55.11.2–3, the African presbyter Victor, *ep.* 64.1.1, and the bishops in Spain, *ep.* 67.6.3. Cyprian would later put reconciled apostates in this same class.

49 Pontius, *uita Cyp.* 5.

50 *Ep.* 43.1.2. Jumping over established clergy was not totally unprecedented: Fabian of Rome had been a layman when elected bishop, though he may have been a Christian of long standing. Eusebius, *h.e.* 6.29.2–3. Novatian was unfavorably compared to Cornelius, however, who had a longer record of service in the clergy, *ep.* 55.8.2.

51 The initial report of the Carthaginian clergy to their counterparts in Rome set Cyprian's exile in a particularly bad light, if judged by the Roman response, see *ep.* 8.1.1. For the signs of conflict, see *epp.* 14.4, 15.1.2 with the explanation provided by Clarke, *Letters* 1:266, n. 32. The clergy in Carthage initially refused to respond to Cyprian's letters from exile, *ep.* 18.1.1. The disaffected presbyters were said to be the force behind the actions of the confessors as well as the revolt of the deacon Felicissimus, *ep.* 43.2.1.

52 The presbyter Novatus was awaiting discipline for fraud, causing his wife's miscarriage, and allowing his father to starve, *ep.* 52.2.5. The deacon Felicissimus, an associate of Novatus, was charged with stealing and adultery, *epp.* 41.1.1,2.1, 59.1.2. Cornelius had similar complaints about some of his clergy, *ep.* 50.1.2.

53 *Habitu* 3,22. They were the glory of the church but they were acting in ways which did not indicate the separation, *habitu* 7 and *ep.* 4.2.1. The same complaint was made with regard to the other privileged group in the community, the confessors, who were charged with defiling themselves, not providing good example, and not renouncing the world, *ep.* 13.4.1–5.3.

54 Many in the community whom Cyprian grouped as standing – with the confessors – because they had allowed the deadline to pass without complying with the edict also admitted that they would have fallen, *lap.* 2–3,28. The *honestiores*, however, were a target for the authorities; their proper course of action was voluntary confession of Christian faith by abandoning their property to imperial confiscation and withdrawing into exile, *lap.* 10. Two of the Carthaginian presbyters were among the first group of those arrested, which also included whole families, *ep.* 6. Cyprian's own station was an obstacle to his being in the city because he was a target, not only as a bishop but as a prominent person, *epp.* 12.1.1, 20.2.1; his goods were forfeited and his punishment was demanded by the mob, *ep.* 62.4.1. Many of the other presbyters were in little or no danger, *ep.* 14.2.1. The Roman clergy signaled the same problem for *honestiores*, *ep.* 8.2.3.

55 In contrast, Cyprian was later allowed house arrest and was executed by beheading, *acta proc.* 1,2,4. He was not subjected to torture, imprisonment or the imperial mines as were the *humiliores* in the same persecution, *epp.* 76–79.

56 Cyprian's particular status was noted in *epp.* 8.1.1, 12.1.1, 43.4.2, 66.4.1.

57 The clergy and a large number of the faithful were even able to visit the confessors in prison without particular danger, *ep.* 5.2.1. Some of the clergy, however, did take to flight, *ep.* 34.4.1.

58 See note 16 above for Tertullian's description of this procedure of giving an oath without really performing it. Cyprian dealt rather harshly with the certified in *lap.* 27 but more sympathetically in *ep.* 55.14.1–2. The Roman clergy indicate that some of the certified used agents to protect them from contact with idolatry, *ep.* 30.3.1.

59 A significant number seem to have chosen this route, forcing themselves upon the magistrates to secure their status, *lap.* 8.

60 Cyprian made explicit provision for the support of these exiles, who sought the anonymity of the larger cities, *ep.* 7.2. Celerinus reported the presence of a large number of Carthaginian refugees in Rome, who were being cared for by the penitents, *ep.* 21.2.2,4.1.

61 These must include many who later confessed that they would have sacrificed had they been required to do so, *lap.* 28.

62 Persons who lost their livelihood because of their Christian commitment were, it will be recalled, often supported from church funds, *ep.* 41.1.2. In *ep.* 34.4.1–2, Cyprian suspended clergy who had taken to a

flight which was perhaps not essentially different from his own voluntary exile; presumably they were not among the *honestiores*.

63 Cyprian would make allowance for those who failed under torture but not for those who faced immediate confiscation of their goods, *lap.* 10,13.

64 *Epp.* 59.6.1, 66.4.1.

65 *Epp.* 20.1.2, 34.4.1–2. The difference might also be explained, however, by Cyprian's episcopal status. Cyprian claimed that the rest of the clergy were not in the danger that he was as bishop, *ep.* 14.2.1. Caldonius had been a confessor before taking refuge in Carthage, *ep.* 24.1.1. Herculanus and Victor were bishops in good standing but were in apparently voluntary exile in Carthage, see *epp.* 41, 42.

66 *Ep.* 12.1.1.

67 *Ep.* 12.1.2,2.1.

68 Cyprian suggested, from exile, that the ministers visiting the prison should be rotated so that none became too prominent in the minds of the guards, *ep.* 5.2.1.

69 Cyprian implied this differentiation in *lap.* 13–14 as well as *ep.* 56.2.1–2.

70 They were living riotously, *ep.* 11.1.3; they refused to subject themselves to the authority of the clergy, *ep.* 13.3.2.

71 Cyprian tied this privilege to Wis. 4.8 in *ep.* 6.2.1, and acknowledged it again in *ep.* 15.3.1. The Roman confessors also indicated the judging role of the martyr in *ep.* 31.3,4.2. Cyprian readily recognized the efficacy of the prayer of the Roman confessors, who did not use their authority to challenge his own, *ep.* 37.4.2. Similarly, he asserted that God himself had chosen the confessor Celerinus for clerical appointment, *ep.* 39.1.2.

72 *Lap.* 8–9; *ep.* 55.13.2.

73 *Lap.* 27; *epp.* 30.3.1, 55.14.1.

74 *Lap.* 13.

75 *Lap.* 10.

76 *Epp.* 19.2.3, 24.1.1, 25.1.1.

77 *Ep.* 4.2.2–3.2.

78 *Epp.* 10.1.1–2.1, 11.1.3, 12.1.2, 20.2.2, 22.2.1.

79 *Epp.* 24.1.1, 25.1.1; *lap.* 13.

80 *Lap.* 28.

81 *Ep.* 20.3.2.

82 *Ep.* 57.3.1.

83 *Epp.* 11.7.3, 16.4.2, 19.2.2, 26.1.2.

84 *Ep.* 18.1.1 indicated that the clergy had been ignoring Cyprian's frequent letters. The letter of the Roman clergy criticized Cyprian for having left Carthage, *ep.* 8.1.1–2.1.

85 They might have used Mt. 10.32, along with Mt. 10.19–20 as foundation for their claim of freedom, see *epp.* 10.3, 12.1.3.

86 Cyprian called for such pressure from the clergy, the other confessors, and the faithful people, *epp.* 13, 14.

87 Cyprian first addressed this practice in *epp.* 15–17, directed to the confessors, clergy and – for the first time – to the laity. *Ep.* 31.3, of the Roman confessors, witnessed to the belief that martyrs entered immediately into heaven.

88 Mappalicus gave letters only to his mother and sister, *ep.* 27.1.1, in contrast with the practice of giving general letters, naming whole households, *ep.* 15.4.

89 Thus did Lucianus claim in the case of Paul, *ep.* 22.2.1. In *ep.* 23 the confessors granted peace to all the lapsed.

90 Especially, *ep.* 23.

91 Cyprian excused the self-interest of the fallen in *ep.* 15.2.1, directed to their patron confessors.

92 Cyprian even made excuses for the confessors and laid the burden of responsibility squarely on the clergy, *ep.* 16.3.2. This tactic might have accurately reflected the authority which the confessors enjoyed among the faithful, which placed them above direct attack. He was similarly circumspect in writing to his clergy about the general letter of amnesty issued by the confessors, *ep.* 26.1.1.

93 *Ep.* 15.2.2–4.1.

94 *Ep.* 25.1.2.

95 *Epp.* 16.3.2, 43.2.1–3.2, 59.12.1–2.

96 The difference in controlling the lapsed's access to the eucharist provided evidence of multiple gatherings or house-churches in Carthage. *Ep.* 41.2.1 referred to those "communicaturos in monte secum," which might indicate a subcommunity established on the Byrsa which had become separatist (*CCL* 3C:197.34). Cyprian's addresses to the community upon his return, however, indicated some plenary meetings of the church.

97 In contrast, the presbyters in Rome had little difficulty in maintaining control over both the confessors and the lapsed, *epp.* 8, 21, 30.

3 NECESSITY OF REPENTANCE

1 The text of Mt. 10.32–3 played a significant role in the evaluation of the behavior of the lapsed. See Cyprian's use in *epp.* 12.1.3, 58.3.2, 59.12.2, and *lap.* 20.

2 *Ep.* 55.17.2.

3 Cyprian provided examples of financial irregularity, disrespect for parents, and sexual infractions, *epp.* 1, 4, 42.2.1, 52.3. For a description of the ritual of penance itself, see Tertullian, *paen.* 9–12, and Cyprian, *epp.* 4, 15.1.2, 16.2.3, 17.2.1; *lap.* 16,36.

4 Adultery had originally been one of the excluding sins. Tertullian objected to the granting of readmission after penance in *pud.* 1.6 and Cyprian noted that some bishops had resisted the change, *ep.* 55.21.1.

5 Such, it will be recalled, was the policy which Cyprian had urged during the persecution and which the Roman presbyters supported, *epp.* 20.3.1–2, 55.13.1.

6 *Ep.* 31.3. Tertullian objected to the procedure of appeal to the martyrs for reversal of the sin of adultery in *pud.* 22.

7 *Ep.* 13.

8 To use Mary Douglas' terminology, the laxist churches shifted downward on the group scale; some members were forced upward on the grid scale by the martyrs and their allies, who moved themselves downward on that scale, toward greater autonomy. See "Cultural Bias,"

in *The Active Voice*, Boston, Routledge & Kegan Paul, 1982, pp.183–254.

9 Thus in *epp.* 7.1, 14.1.2, 20.1.2. At the end of the persecution, he delayed his return for the same reason, *ep.* 43.4.2.

10 They were to vary the persons who went to visit the confessors being held in prison, *ep.* 5.2.1.

11 Assistance was to be provided to the widows, the sick, the poor and the refugees, *ep.* 7.2, but only on condition that they remained faithful, *epp.* 5.1.2, 12.2.2, 14.2.1.

12 *Epp.* 5.1.2, 12.1.1, 13.7.

13 *Ep.* 14.2.2.

14 *Epp.* 5.1.2, 13.7, though he recognized that individuals were providing help directly to the exiled confessors, *epp.* 13.7, 14.2.2. The subsequent charges of theft of church funds which were directed against rebel clergy would seem to indicate that they had served as agents for the distribution of these monies, see *epp.* 41.1.1, 52.2.5, 59.1.2.

15 The three visions, temporally separated, were narrated in *ep.* 11.3–5. It was revealed that the community as a whole had refused to pray for certain particular members, as it had been commanded, and thereby provoked God's wrath.

16 *Ep.* 11.1.2,5.1,5.3,7.2.

17 *Ep.* 11.1.3. This also served as a warning that the community must bring them into line.

18 *Ep.* 11.1.1,5.1,5.3,6.2.

19 *Ep.* 11.7.3–8. This would have corrected the primary cause of the persecution, the disharmony in prayer specified in *ep.* 11.3.1–2.

20 *Ep.* 6.2.1.

21 *Epp.* 13.4–5, 14.3.2.

22 *Epp.* 13.2.1, 14.2.2; indeed they might expect even more savage attacks after their victory, *ep.* 14.3.1.

23 *Ep.* 10. He clarified the role itself by declaring that even those who had died as a result of deprivations in prison rather than under torture must be regarded as martyrs, *ep.* 12.1.2–3.

24 *Ep.* 12.1–2.

25 *Ep.* 11, which explained the causes of the persecution, seems to have been written in late April 250. Within a few weeks, Cyprian wrote *epp.* 15–17, dealing with the letters of peace. The reference in the earlier *ep.* 14.4 may have raised this problem already. On the dating, see Clarke, *Letters* 1:238–40.

26 *Ep.* 15.2.1–3.

27 *Ep.* 15.3.2, 16.4.1, 17.1.2. In accepting the unpurified lapsed, the presbyters were placing the whole church in danger of offending the Lord, *ep.* 16.1.2.

28 He addressed three separate letters, to the confessors, the clergy and the whole people, with instructions that all three were to be read to each group, *epp.* 15.4, 16.4.2, 17.3.2.

29 *Ep.* 15.

30 *Ep.* 16.1.2; the confessors and the people were also urged to remind the presbyters of the limits of their authority, *epp.* 15.1.2, 17.2.1.

31 *Ep.* 16.4.2.

32 *Ep.* 17, especially 3.1. In particular, the warning that the clergy would have to answer to the entire community authorized the laity to apply pressure, *ep.* 16.4.2.

33 *Ep.* 17.2.2.

34 *Ep.* 14.4. A thinly veiled rebuke to the presbyters who had opposed his election and now acted independently of both himself and the community.

35 *Ep.* 17.1.2, to the people; repeated in *ep.* 19.2.2 to the clergy.

36 Reported in *epp.* 25.1.2, 26.1.2.

37 *Epp.* 18.1.2, 19.1.1. At this point, Cyprian might have believed that the penitents could be accepted by Christ without being admitted to the peace of the church.

38 *Ep.* 20.3.2. The Roman practice, which had been announced in Carthage and may be presumed to have increased popular pressure for this concession.

39 *Ep.* 19.2.3. His subsequent recall of this command indicated that he meant it, *ep.* 55.4.1–2.

40 *Epp.* 24.1.2, 25; *lap.* 13.

41 *Ep.* 18.2.1.

42 Indeed, the concession of communion to all the dying penitents seems to have been forced by popular sentiment. The restriction announced in *ep.* 18.1.2 and reiterated in *ep.* 19.2.1 was soon removed, as reported in *ep.* 20.3.2.

43 *Ep.* 15.3.1. In the same vein, he asserted that precedent had already been established in the African church which limited their authority, *ep.* 15.1.2,3.1.

44 *Ep.* 27.3.3.

45 *Ep.* 28.2.3.

46 *Epp.* 33.2.1, 35.1.1.

47 *Ep.* 34.1, with the advice and support of refugee bishops in the city. On the identity of Gaius, see Clarke, *Letters* 2:155–6.

48 *Epp.* 41, 42. The bishop Caldonius and the presbyters Rogatianus and Numidicus can be identified as confessors; the status of the bishop Herculanus cannot be confirmed. See *epp.* 24.1.1, 40, 43.1 for the status of the confessors. On the identity of the clergy, see Clarke, *Letters* 2:202–3.

49 *Lap.* 1,5,7,21.

50 *Lap.* 2,3.

51 *Lap.* 13.

52 *Lap.* 28. This confession of a sin of intention was used to shame those lapsed who were refusing to do penance for their open, voluntary sin of action. Those admitting it may have intended to blur the sharp lines of the distinction and thus assist the fallen.

53 *Lap.* 10–14.

54 *Lap.* 16.

55 *Ep.* 43.3.1–2.

56 *Lap.* 14.

57 *Lap.* 17.

58 *Lap.* 18–19. The text of Rev. 6.9 provided the evidence against the martyrs, whose own deaths were not yet vindicated by God. For the

others, Cyprian cited Ex. 32.31–3, Jer. 11.14 (LXX) and Ezek. 14.13–18.

59 *Lap.* 20–21, recalling the themes of *ep.* 11, and the opening sections of *de lapsis*.

60 *Lap.* 20, a point which the Romans may have originated in the lost letter to which reference is made in *ep.* 27.4. Cyprian advanced the argument in his *ep.* 28.2.3 and the Romans echoed it in their *ep.* 36.1.3–2.2.

61 *Lap.* 22.

62 *Ep.* 11.3–5.

63 *Lap.* 23–26. The community's belief in the efficacy of both the Christian and the pagan rites and of the moral governance of the universe is evident in these stories. According to Mary Douglas' analysis, such a view is characteristic of tightly bounded or high-group communities.

64 *Lap.* 30. In *de habitu uirginum*, Cyprian indicated that all these were ways in which the Christian should be distinguished and separated, *habitu* 6–17.

65 *Lap.* 33,34.

66 *Lap.* 27,28. The community's morality was not limited to performance, though it did judge the sacrificers more harshly than the certified and those who failed in intention alone most leniently.

67 *Lap.* 29. These arguments were repeated in *ep.* 65, which dealt with the attempt of a sacrificer bishop to regain his office after the persecution.

68 It is interesting to compare Cyprian's explanations of the onset of the persecution as a correction of the church, of the summer plague as morally and religiously neutral, and of the threat of persecution under Galienus as an indicator of the coming end of the world; *ep.* 11; *mort.* 8; *epp.* 57.5.1, 58.1.2, 60.3.2, 61.2.3.

69 In *ep.* 55.6.1, Cyprian explained that the lapsed would return to the way of the world, pointedly ignoring the invitation of the laxists, which would not have helped his apology for the decision. The letter was written in response to the challenge of an African bishop who was under Novatianist influence.

70 *Ep.* 55.17.3. Setting aside the observation of *lap.* 27, that the certified had tried to serve two masters, Cyprian defended this decision by arguing that they had acted under compulsion and had avoided participating in the sacrifice.

71 *Ep.* 55.17.3; *ep.* 57.2.1 indicated that the penance may have been intended to last throughout the person's life.

72 *Ep.* 55.23.4.

73 *Epp.* 45.4.1, 59.1.1,9.1. Clarke suggests that a commission, of which Cyprian was not a member, was established to review and thus lend authority to his decision, *Letters* 2:242–3.

74 *Ep.* 59.14.2; thus the community which had been offended would serve as judge of the penitent. This retained a necessary face-to-face system of justice.

75 Cyprian had urged them to do penance in *lap.* 28.

76 Some colleagues requested approval for the immediate admission of sacrificers who had failed under torture, after three years of penance, *ep.* 56.2.2.

77 Thus the bishops in *ep.* 57.3.3,4.3,5.2. Cyprian expanded on these themes in subsequent letters of exhortation, *epp.* 58.2.1–3,3.1, 61.2.3,4.1.

78 *Ep.* 58.3.2; indeed Cyprian anticipated that the whole faithful body would immediately march to glory in heaven, *ep.* 58.10.1. So was Cornelius portrayed as leading the Roman church to glory, as the faithful accompanied him to arraignment at his arrest, *ep.* 60.1.2.

79 *Epp.* 57.2.1,3.3,5.1, 58.8.2. The bishops feared God's wrath if they failed to admit the penitents, *ep.* 57.4.3–5.2.

80 The bishops made provision for the reconciliation of only those who had never forsaken the church, *ep.* 57.1.2.

81 *Ep.* 57.3.1–2.

82 *Ep.* 57.1.1. There has been extensive discussion of the contrast between the effects of binding and loosening in the sentence,

> Nec enim fas erat aut permittebat paterna pietas et diuina clementia ecclesiam pulsantibus cludi et dolentibus ac deprecantibus spei salutaris subsidium denegari, ut de saeculo recedentes sine communicatione et pace ad Dominum dimitterentur, quando permiserit ipse et legem dederit ut ligata in terris et in caelis ligata *essent*, solui autem *possent* illic quae hic prius in ecclesia soluerentur.
>
> (*CCL* 3B:301.14–25.)

See Clarke, *Letters* 3:218. M. Bévenot's appeal to *de zelo* 18 for an interpretation of the grammatical form is instructive but does not remove the lexical distinction between *essent* and *possent*, "The Sacrament of Penance and St. Cyprian's *De Lapsis*," *Theological Studies*, 16 (1955):210–11. The bishops themselves made the point clear later in the letter by observing that Christ himself would soon judge those whom they had decided to admit and would himself remove any who were not truly penitent but he would require of them the souls of those who would have stood fast had they been given the peace of the church, *ep.* 57.3.3,4.3–5.2. Thus the bishops recognized that they could present the penitents to Christ but not guarantee forgiveness of their apostasy. Those whom they declined to present, however, could not be forgiven by Christ and thus he would punish their cruelty. The same point was made during the baptismal controversy when Cyprian attributed to Peter and his successors the authority to loosen on earth, omitting any reference to heaven, *ep.* 73.7.1. For an analysis of the question from a different perspective, see the discussion in chapter 4, pp. 70–1.

83 *Ep.* 57.4.2, echoed by Cyprian in *ep.* 58.5.2.

84 *Ep.* 57.2.2,4.2; echoed by Cyprian in *ep.* 58.1.2.

85 In *ep.* 57.4.3, the bishops warned of the consequences of refusing the peace of the church to penitents who might subsequently die as refugees during the persecution.

86 In *lap.* 3, Cyprian counted the returned refugees among the confessors; in *ep.* 58.4.2, he proclaimed that communicants who died even by acci-

dent in voluntary exile thereby won the crown of martyrdom. Here both were denied.

87 See *ep.* 19.2.3 and the peroration of *de lapsis*, 36.

88 *Ep.* 57.4.1. He had shared the earlier position with Novatian, who maintained it, see *epp.* 19.2.3, 55.25.1–2.

89 *Ep.* 57.3.1,5.1. The renewal of the persecution could have been viewed as a form of judgment by Christ himself, who would soon come, *epp.* 57.3.3, 58.2.1,7.1.

90 In *ep.* 60.4, written to congratulate Cornelius on his confession, Cyprian argued that by rejecting peace on earth, schismatics excluded themselves from the kingdom of God.

91 The laity was much less sympathetic to the rebels who were returning from the laxist church, *ep.* 59.15.1–4. No provision was made for reconciling those who had not been loyal to the church, *ep.* 57.1.2.

92 *Ep.* 31.3; *lap.* 20.

93 *Epp.* 10.4.1, 57.4.3, 58.5.2.

94 *Epp.* 6.2.1, 15.3.1, 31.3.

95 *Epp.* 16.3.2, 18.1.2, 19.2.1, 20.3.2, 21.2.1–2,3.2,4.1, 37.3.1,4.2, 39.3.1; *lap.* 17.

96 Even the public confession of Christ without death was efficacious, *epp.* 19.2.3, 25.1.1–2. Cyprian's own evaluation of the Roman church's massive display of faith, *ep.* 60.1.2, made the same point. See also Tertullian's concession of this point in *pud.* 22.

97 *Lap.* 18–19.

98 *Epp.* 15.3–4, 20.2.1–2. A promise to care for surviving family members might have been regarded as an act of charity by the confessor or as a bribe by the bishop. Even some of the more restrained martyrs, whom Cyprian praised, did issue a few letters, *ep.* 27.1.1.

99 *Epp.* 22.2.1, 27.1.2.

100 *Epp.* 22.2.1, 27.2.1. In *lap.* 20, Cyprian observed that the martyrs gave the appearance of having replaced God as patron or benefactor of the church.

101 For the delay, *epp.* 15.1.2, 16.3.2, 22.2.2; for the confession, *ep.* 22.2; for the examination of life, *epp.* 22.2.2, 23, 26.1.4, 27.2.2

102 *Epp.* 34.1,2.1–2, 43.2.2,3.2,7.2, 59.12.2,13.2,13.4–5,14.1; *lap.* 16,31,33–34. Cyprian argued that they regarded the invocation of the martyrs as the equivalent of the naming of the Trinity in baptism, *ep.* 27.3.3.

103 *Epp.* 15.1.2, 16.2.3,3.2, 17.2.1, 20.2.3, 34.2.1, 43.2.1–2,3.2, 59.12.2; *lap.* 15–16.

104 *Epp.* 19.2.1–3, 20.3.1, 25.1.2, 27.3.1, 35.1.1, 55.4.2.

105 *Epp.* 35.1.1, 36.1.2,3.2.

106 The action was forced by Cyprian's delegation of confessor bishops and presbyters, which excommunicated the leaders and some supporters, *epp.* 41.1.2–2.2, 42. This action was later confirmed by the bishops of Africa, *ep.* 59.9.1,14.2,15.1.

107 Cyprian claimed that Privatus of Lambaesis had been condemned before the persecution and that all his episcopal colleagues had sacrificed during the persecution, *epp.* 36.4.1–2, 59.10.1. *Ep.* 65.1.1

provided evidence of another attempt by a sacrificer bishop to regain his see.

108 In advance of their rejection at the meeting in May 252, the laxists had promised to ordain a bishop for Carthage, *ep.* 59.10–11. For their attempts to establish communion with Rome, see *ep.* 59.1.1–2.1,9.1,11.2,14.1.

109 This was Cyprian's charge, *ep.* 15.3.2.

110 Cyprian's community, in contrast, had to be persuaded to allow certain of the rebellious lapsed to be admitted to penance; indeed the lingering disapproval of the community may have ultimately driven off some of the penitents, *ep.* 59.15.2–4.

111 Cyprian later attacked the unrepentant lapsed for their unwillingness to assist their poor brethren, *lap.* 30.

112 *Ep.* 19.2.3.

113 They even threatened the faithful who were cooperating with Cyprian's delegates, *ep.* 41.1.2.

114 *Ep.* 41.1.2.

115 According to Cyprian, all of the laxist bishops had been sacrificers and as such would not have been eligible for continuing membership in the African college of bishops, *epp.* 59.10–11, 65.1.1.

116 Cyprian made the charge in *ep.* 15.3.2. It might also be noted that the Carthaginian confessors exiled in Rome recommended the two lapsed Christians who were providing them with lodgings, *ep.* 21.4.1. Cyprian himself indicated that some of the fallen provided refuge to exiled confessors, who would then intercede for them before the bishop, *ep.* 55.13.2.

117 *Ep.* 59.15.1. Cyprian reported the return; the causal connection is an interpretation of events.

118 Unlike the rigorists gathered by Novatian, the laxists soon ceased to be an effective force in the affairs of the church.

119 On the efficacy of baptism, see *habitu* 2; *epp.* 63.8.1–3, 64.2.1–5.2.

120 Cyprian also pointed out that a hasty readmission of the apostates would give non-Christians cause for despising the church, *ep.*15.3.1.

121 The distinction between sins committed against God and against humans was used in *lap.* 17. The significance of Christ's threat to deny before the Father those who had denied him (Mt. 10:33), should not be underestimated.

122 Even as the persecution itself continued, Cyprian began this process by ordaining confessors to clerical office and by appointing a commission including clerical confessors to oppose the rebels in Carthage, *epp.* 29, 38–42.

123 Thus sins of insubordination, sexual irregularity, and misuse of money were handled by the normal procedures, see *epp.* 3, 4, 41.2.1, 52.3. Tertullian provided a full description and explanation of this ritual in *paen.* 9–10, which was fully compatible with Cyprian's use of the practice, see *epp.* 4, 15.1.2, 16.2.3, 17.2.1; *lap.* 16,36.

124 This presumption was evident in the demands for reconciliation before death and in Cyprian's presentation of the judgment itself, see *epp.* 55.18.1,29.2–3, 65.5.1–2, 57.3.3.

125 *Deprecatio* was used in 1 John 2.1–2, which Cyprian cited in *ep.* 55.18.1. The term also appears in *epp.* 17.2, 34.1, 43.3, 55.11.2,29.1,

65.5, 57.1, 59.13, 67.6, *lap.* 13,16,18,19,22,28,29,30,36. *Rogare* is used in *epp.* 55.6, 59.14, *lap.* 16,29,32,35,36. *Orare* and *exorare* in *ep.* 11.1, 55.29.1; *lap.* 17,32,35,36.

126 *Epp.* 19.1,26; *lap.* 31,32.
127 *Epp.* 16.2, 55.6,23,29, 65.5; *lap.* 17,18,28,29,32,36.
128 *Epp.* 16.2, 17.2, 55.11, 65.5, 59.12,13,14; *lap.* 17,28,29,32,36. It was used independently in *ep.* 59.16 and *lap.* 15.
129 Relying on Joel 2.12–13, in *lap.* 29. For the same point, see *epp.* 19.1, 34.1, 55.23,28; *lap.* 32,35.
130 *Lap.* 30.
131 *Lap.* 33.
132 *Lap.* 35.

4 EFFICACY OF THE RECONCILIATION RITUAL

1 Cyprian argued, for example, that unless the certified were allowed to enter the communion after doing penance, they and their supporters would defect to the laxists, *ep.* 55.15.1.
2 He originally refused the church's peace to the dying penitents, *ep.* 18.2.1 and later made no distinction between the certified and the actual sacrificers, *lap.* 27.
3 *Ep.* 8 does not seem to have reached Cyprian before June 250, when it was presumably responsible for his shift in position on the reconciling of dying penitents. See Clarke, *Letters* 1:204–5.
4 *Ep.* 8.1.1,2.3.
5 *Ep.* 8.2.3–3.1. The granting of peace to penitents at the time of death, confirmed in *ep.* 30.8 from the Roman clergy, was apparently traditional practice in Rome.
6 *Ep.* 21.2.1,3.2. In *ep.* 8.3.3, the Roman clergy had claimed the support of the imprisoned confessors. Celerinus' appeal to the African martyrs indicated that at least the African immigrants within the Roman church were attempting to circumvent the clergy's policy, *ep.* 21.4.1–2.
7 *Epp.* 18.1.2, 19.2.1.
8 *Epp.* 18.2.1, 19.2.1.
9 *Ep.* 19.2.3.
10 *Ep.* 20.3.2.
11 *Ep.* 20.2.1. We might speculate that these letters had an influence on Novatian, who then took over the Roman church's correspondence with Cyprian.
12 Cyprian himself attributed *ep.* 30 to Novatian, *ep.* 55.5. The confessors named in the greetings of the accompanying *ep.* 31 subsequently supported Novatian's position. For the attribution of *epp.* 31 and 36 to Novatian, see Clarke, *Letters* 2:133–4,165. Of course, Novatian may also have been involved in writing the earlier (lost) letters which are summarized in *ep.* 30.
13 *Ep.* 8 had probably been sent in spring 250. Its language stands in sharp contrast to that of the later letters, *epp.* 30, 31, 36. See Clarke, *Letters* 1:203–5.
14 Reference was made to these lost letters in *ep.* 27.4.1 and their contents were outlined in *ep.* 30.3.1–2.

15 The letter was acknowledged in *ep.* 27.4.1 and in *ep.* 28.2.1–3, Cyprian congratulated the Roman confessors on the admonition which they had sent to their counterparts in Carthage on this point. The content of the letter was reported in *ep.* 30.4. The point was echoed by the Roman clergy in *ep.* 36.2.1, indicating that it may have originated with Novatian himself.

16 *Ep.* 30.2.1–2,3.3,7.1–2.

17 *Ep.* 30.8. Abuse of the privilege of the ill, specified in *ep.* 8.3.1, might have already begun.

18 *Ep.* 31.8.1–2. The second letter of the clergy made the same point, *ep.* 36.2.2.

19 *Ep.* 31.6.2.

20 *Ep.* 36.2.1–3.

21 *Ep.* 30.8. A similar concern for the charge of harshness is found in *ep.* 36.3.2.

22 *Epp.* 30.6.2–7.2, 31.6.3,8.2, 36.1.1–2.1. Lucianus responded to Celerinus, still in Rome, that peace had been granted to everyone by the African martyrs, *ep.* 22.2.1. This could have affected the discipline of the Roman church or at least the clergy's control of the Carthaginian exiles in Rome.

23 The second surviving letter of the clergy, attributed to Novatian, allowed the practice, *ep.* 30.8. The accompanying letter of the confessors, also drafted by Novatian, made no mention of the practice, *ep.* 31. *Ep.* 55.13.1 indicated that the practice continued to give rise to controversy. Indeed, Cornelius later accused Novatian of refusing to comfort the faithful who were in danger during the persecution, Eusebius, *h.e.* 6.43.16. The further charge that he renounced his priesthood and Christianity to preserve his personal safety is hardly compatible with the position Novatian actually occupied in the church at Rome and his ministry to the confessors in prison, who later took up his cause. The event behind Cornelius' slander may have been Novatian's refusal to bring reconciliation and the eucharist to an allegedly dying penitent.

24 The confessors included those who had corresponded with Cyprian during the persecution, see *epp.* 28, 31, 37, 46. Clarke differentiates two stages in the schism, the first focused on Cornelius' character and the second on his policy of reconciling the lapsed, see the comments on *epp.* 48.4.1, 55.8.3 in *Letters* 2:261–2, 3:174–5. The principal issue may always have been the reconciling of the lapsed and the attempted character assassination may have been an extension of the polemics, such as are found in Cornelius' letter to Fabius of Antioch, in Eusebius, *h.e.* 6.43, and in Cyprian's attacks on the rebels in Carthage, *ep.* 52.2.1–5.

25 Cyprian reported the events in defending Cornelius to an African colleague, *ep.* 55.6.2. Clarke asserts that Cyprian is accurate in claiming priority for the African decision, against Eusebius' report in *h.e.* 6.43.2, see Clarke, *Letters* 3:172.

26 *Ep.* 55.11.1–3.

27 *Ep.* 55.13.1. Novatian's letter during the persecution had apparently foreseen and attempted to forestall the abuse of this privilege by calling for delay until the last moment, *ep.* 30.8.

28 Cyprian advanced this charge in a defense of the policy of reconciliation, *ep.* 55.27.2; later he threw it up to an opponent in Africa, *ep.* 66.7.3. One of the specific charges against Cornelius was that he had entered into communion with apostate bishops. Cyprian denied the fact but not the implication of contagion which would have resulted, *ep.* 55.10.2; indeed he later charged Stephen with incurring such pollution through communion with a failed bishop, *ep.* 67.9.2.

29 *Epp.* 55.13.2–16.1,24.1, 60.3.1.

30 *Epp.* 30.6.2–7.2, 31.6.3–7.2, 36.1.2,3.3.

31 *Ep.* 55.22.1–23.3.

32 *Ad Nouatianum* 7.1, *CCL* 4:142–3. For the dating and attribution see *CCL* 4:134–5.

33 The charges are echoed in the fourth century by Eusebius, *h.e.* 6.43.1, and the Spanish bishop Pacian, *ep.* 2.4; *PL* 13:1060; see Clarke, *Letters* 3:188.

34 *Ep.* 55.22.1,28.1. The same charge was made against Marcianus of Arles, who was said to be following Novatian's policy, *ep.* 68.1.1.

35 *Ep.* 8.3.1. This letter is not attributed to Novatian himself; see notes 12–13 above.

36 *Ep.* 57.4.1.

37 *Ep.* 60.2.5.

38 The text of Mt. 10.32–3 is cited in *Ad Nouatianum* 7.1; *CCL* 4:142–3. A similar stance can be found in Cyprian's concurrence with Caldonius' reconciliation of those who stood firm in a second trial and in the peroration of *de lapsis*, where he urged that repentance might lead to the crown of martyrdom rather than to reconciliation, *ep.* 25.1.1–2; *lap.* 36.

39 The letters of neither the clergy nor the confessors in Rome asserted that the church had authority to forgive this sin of apostasy. See *epp.* 8.2.3, 21.2.2.

40 Thus Cyprian would have anticipated the objection which he had earlier raised against the laxists that granting communion prevented the true repentance and restoration of the lapsed. In response, he argued that they would have to prove their mettle during the persecution, *ep.* 57.3.2, and secure their salvation by confession of Christ, at least the passive non-compliance which he had acknowledged in *lap.* 3.

41 Their divergent responses to the threat of renewed persecution might have driven the final wedge of division between the churches and led Novatian to begin the practice of rebaptizing converts to his communion. During his conflict with Stephen, Cyprian never appealed to Cornelius' stance in regard to a Novatianist practice of rebaptism. That silence might, of course, have been based upon ignorance or the inconvenience of a view opposite to Cyprian's own. Cyprian did, however, appeal to Cornelius' practice of admitting lapsed clergy to communion only as laymen, *ep.* 67.6.3. Novatian, however, had already sent a rival bishop to Carthage a year earlier, *ep.* 59.9.

42 This charge was leveled even by Cyprian in *ep.* 55.27.1–2.

43 Mt. 10:32–3, which was used in *ep.* 30.7.1 and *ep.* 31.2.2, both of which are associated with Novatian's position.

44 *Ep.* 45.2.5.

45 This charge was reported and refuted in *ep.* 55.3.2–7.3, where Cyprian reviewed his practice.

46 See Clarke, *Letters* 1:193–4, 275–6 for evidence of the precedents. The confessors, for example, never claimed the power to give the peace without the concurrence of the bishop, see esp. *ep.* 23.

47 *Epp.* 18.1.2, 19.2.1, 20.3.1.

48 *Ep.* 15.1.2,3.1.

49 *Epp.* 18.2.1, 19.2.1.

50 *Ep.* 20.2.2.

51 *Ep.* 19.2.3.

52 *Ep.* 8.3.1.

53 *Ep.* 20.3.2.

54 *Ep.* 24.1.2, for the report of Caldonius. Cyprian agreed in *ep.* 25.1.1–2, wishing that all should repent in this way. He sent copies of both letters to exhort the congregation in Carthage and to inform the Roman clergy, *epp.* 26.1.3, 27.3.2. The same argument was advanced in *ep.* 55.4.1–2,7.1.

55 *Ep.* 27.2.1,3.3.

56 *Ep.* 28.2.3. This argument was contained in the first letter of the Roman confessors, as was reported by Novatian in *ep.* 30.4.

57 *Lap.* 20 repeated the Roman argument; *lap.* 18–19 showed the limited efficacy of the martyrs' intercession.

58 *Lap.* 35. This point was particularly important to Novatian, as evidenced in *ep.* 55.13.2. See also the charges that Novatian counted all sins equal, which may have been directed at a refusal to distinguish the certified from the sacrificers, *ep.* 55.16.1.

59 He later leveled the charge that Cyprian had slackened in his support for the church's discipline, *ep.* 55.3.2.

60 In fact, this line of argument was suggested in the letter which Novatian drafted for the Roman clergy, *ep.* 31.6.2–3.

61 *Ep.* 43.6.1–7.2. Novatian, of course, faced no such danger nor did the Roman penitents face such a temptation from a laxist camp in Rome.

62 The Roman confessors, in their lost letter to Carthage, had argued that the martyrs' request was contrary to the gospel, *ep.* 30.4. Cyprian picked up the argument in *ep.* 28.2.3.

63 *Lap.* 18.

> Mandant aliquid martyres fieri, sed si scripta non sunt in Domini lege quae mandant, ante est ut sciamus illos de Deo impetrasse quod postulant, tunc facere quod mandant; neque enim statim uideri potest diuina maiestate concessum quod fuerit humana pollicitatione promissum.
>
> *CCL* 3:231.366–71.

64 *Lap.* 5–12.

65 *Lap.* 13. Cyprian had agreed with Caldonius on a similar case during the persecution, *epp.* 24, 25.

66 *Lap.* 14–16, 22–26.

67 *Lap.* 29–32.

68 *Ep.* 43.3.1–2, 6.1–7.2. He even identified the five leaders of the schism with the commissioners who had enforced the imperial edict, *ep.* 43.3.1.

69 *Lap.* 33–35.

70 *Lap.* 36.
71 *Ep.* 44.1.1–2.1; on the discussion see *ep.* 55.6.1.
72 *Ep.* 44.2.1 and *ep.* 45.2.2. Clarke understands Cyprian to be saying, in *ep.* 45.2.1–5, that only Cornelius' own letter was read out to the bishops, *Letters* 2:238–41. Yet in *ep.* 45.3.1, Cyprian allowed that his colleagues were aware of the charges Novatian raised against Cornelius. Cornelius' subsequent behavior, in allowing laxist accusations against Cyprian to be read out in his church, would seem to indicate that he also believed the rigorist charges against him had been publicly aired in Carthage, see *ep.* 59.2.1.
73 *Ep.* 44.1.2.
74 Thus in *ep.* 55.6.1.
75 *Ep.* 55.17.2–3.
76 Repostus of Satunurca, as reported in *ep.* 59.10.3,11.2. Cornelius, it will be recalled, admitted Trofimus and his entire congregation into communion without extended penance, *ep.* 55.11.1–3. Cyprian later gave the impression that the Africans took the initiative in admitting the certified and were followed by Cornelius, *ep.* 55.6.2.
77 The phrase "euangelium Christi adserere" in *ep.* 46.2.1 may echo a watchword of the Novatianists, as Clarke suggests in *Letters* 2:249, or may recall Cyprian's praise of these same confessors in *ep.* 28 for upholding the discipline of the gospel. Once they had left to join Cornelius' communion, however, Cyprian was free to accuse Novatian of arrogating a divine privilege to himself, *ep.* 54.3.1–3. He also sent a copy of *de lapsis*, which took a more rigorous stance than had been approved at the preceding council of African bishops.
78 It is argued in chapter 5 that *de unitate* was originally prepared for the laxist schism in Carthage and revised before it was sent to Rome to help deal with the disputed election or Novatianist schism there. The sections cited here are judged to belong to the earliest version.
79 *Vnit.* 20–22.
80 *Vnit.* 3, citing 2 Cor. 11.14–15.
81 *Vnit.* 10, along with 19.
82 *Epp.* 55.17.3, 56.2.2.
83 *Ep.* 55.16.3–17.1.
84 *Ep.* 55.17.3.
85 *Ep.* 55.13.1. Even when the peace had been improperly given to the healthy, the bishops refused to withdraw it upon review, *ep.* 64.1.1–2.
86 Only later, they claimed, did they learn from the clergy that they should not even have accepted the certificate in return for their paying a fine, *ep.* 55.13.2–14.2.
87 Cyprian feared that not only the apostates but all those they had assisted would find his requirement of life-long penance implausible. They might abandon him to join the laxists. See *ep.* 55.15.1.
88 *Ep.* 57.1.2,3.1–2.
89 *Ep.* 57.2.2,4.2.
90 *Ep.* 57.4.3–5.2. The bishops feared the judgment of Christ. As has been noted earlier, they did not remark on the probability that some of the penitents might actually win the crown of martyrdom outside the church and thus be elevated to sit in judgment with Christ upon the very bishops who had excluded them from communion.

91 *Ep.* 60.2.2–5.
92 *Ep.* 55.20.3.
93 *Ep.* 55.29.2.
94 Cyprian argued that none of the lapsed would undertake penance if they were refused admission to communion before death, *ep.* 55.28.1–29.2. This assumption was also attested in Cyprian's own appeals for the replacement of Marcianus of Arles, *ep.* 68.3.1,4.2.
95 All these charges are to be found in Cyprian's response to the letter of an African colleague which argued for the Novatianist position, *ep.* 55.
96 Cyprian answered this charge in *ep.* 55.13.1.
97 *Ep.* 55.15.1,17.2,19.1–2.
98 *Ep.* 55.27.1–2. On this point, Novatian seems not to have returned to the position of the prior rigorist schismatic in Rome, Hippolytus.
99 *Ep.* 55.27.3. As shall be argued below, the difference in his perspective and Novatian's on this point can be correlated with the difference in the internal structures of their communities.
100 This provision was made for Trofimus, Basilides and Martialis in Italy and Spain, *epp.* 55.11.3, 67.6.3. It was apparently used as well for a presbyter in Africa, *ep.* 64.1.1. Other African bishops were apparently subject to full excommunication, *ep.* 59.10.1–2.
101 *Ep.* 4.1–2. Cyprian's clergy who had taken to flight during the persecution were temporarily suspended from office, *ep.* 34.4.1, but the disposition of their cases is not known. Another instance of permanent disability might be indicated in Cornelius' charge that Novatian should not have been made a presbyter because he had been baptized by sprinkling on his sickbed rather than by the full ritual, Eusebius, *h.e.* 6.43.
102 *Ep.* 57.3.2.
103 *Ep.* 55.20.3 effectively expresses the fear in which the reconciled lapsed anticipated the judgment of Christ.
104 The same restriction would be applied to schismatics, *ep.* 72.2.1–3. In contrast, the confessors were particularly well qualified for clerical positions, *epp.* 38–40.
105 The community's assumptions about the necessity of purity among the bishops and clergy become clearer in the subsequent controversy over the efficacy of baptism. See chapters 6 and 7.
106 In contrast, in the controversy over rebaptism, Cyprian argued that admitting heretics to full membership without baptism would pollute the whole communion, *ep.* 73.19.3.
107 Thus Trofimus and his congregation were partially excused as incense offerers, *ep.* 55.2.1.
108 *Ep.* 55.16.1.
109 *Ep.* 4.1.
110 See *ep.* 52.3 for Novatus.
111 The situation of those who had paid to acquire certificates and those who failed under torture was uncertain, as has been seen. Those who had fallen only in intention, however, were subject to no penalties within the church, *lap.* 13,28; *ep.* 14.1–2.
112 Cyprian seems to have presumed that even the apostates might eventually be readmitted to communion, *epp.* 16.2, 17.3, 18.2.
113 *Lap.* 17–20; *ep.* 59.16.3.

114 The surviving evidence does not permit the secure determination of the order in which Cyprian developed and introduced these ideas to his community and colleagues; the sequence in which they appear in the surviving letters and treatises may be quite different from their development.

115 *Ep.* 55.29.3. He argued that having rebelled against the peace and charity of the church, they could find no place in heaven.

116 Their very inability to recognize the horror of their sin and to turn from their evil was itself a sign of divine punishment, *lap.* 33.

117 *Ep.* 55.17.2–3,29.2.

118 *Ep.* 55.29.2.

119 *Ep.* 55.26.1–27.2,20.3.

120 *Ep.* 57.4.1–4. The rationale, however, was given in heavenly terms.

121 *Ep.* 19.2.2. See also *ep.* 17.1.2, where the entire community was promised a voice in judging individual cases.

122 *Ep.* 55.17.3. They argued that they had acted in good faith, had not actually sacrificed, and had even identified themselves as Christians. The contrast between this defense of their behavior and its denunciation in *lap.* 27 is striking and indicates the pressures to which Cyprian had been subjected.

123 *Lap.* 28; *epp.* 55.15.1, 57.1.2,3.1.

124 In *ep.* 57.4.3, the bishops argued that the exiles in particular would need the encouragement of the church because they would not have the assurance of a public confession of faith. In *ep.* 58.4.1–3, however, Cyprian himself stated the firm conviction that a refugee dying even by accident would be counted a martyr by Christ. The inconsistency may be accounted for by the exaggerations of exhortation and the personal pressure which the penitents had brought to bear.

125 If those who had enrolled as penitents were denied any hope of the church's advocacy when they stood before the judgment of God, Cyprian had earlier argued about the certified and the dying sacrificers, they would certainly be driven to seek the protection of the martyrs which was being offered by the laxists or even return in despair to their former life according to the ways of the empire. They would, moreover, have taken all their dependants and supporters with them. See *ep.* 55.6.1,15.1,17.2. In addressing the reconciliation of the sacrificers, the bishops asserted that they must respond to the endurance which the penitents had already demonstrated and the sufferings which they proclaimed themselves prepared to sustain, even as exiles, *ep.* 57.1.1,4.3.

126 *Ep.* 59.15.3. The bishops made no provision for schismatics who had not long persevered as penitents of the church, *ep.* 57.1.1.

127 *Epp.* 55.15.1,19.2,29.1, 57.4.3–4,5.2.

128 This social analysis provides an interpretation of Cyprian's assertion of the church's power to loosen sins in heaven in *ep.* 57.1.1 which is different and more literal than that which Bévenot defends in "The Sacrament of Penance and St. Cyprian's *De lapsis*," *Theological Studies*, 16 (1955):210–13. See the earlier discussion of this matter in chapter 3, at note 82, pp. 40, 196.

129 *Epp.* 55.18.1, 57.3.3.

130 *Lap.* 28.

131 *Epp.* 55.20.3, 68.1.1,4.2

132 *Ep.* 34.4.1–2 for the clergy; *lap.* 10–11, *epp.* 57.4.3, 58.4.1 for the laity.

133 *Ep.* 4.2.3.

134 *Ep.* 31.6.2.

135 *Lap.* 15,22–6. Even during the persecution, Cyprian had warned the lapsed that they were in danger if they approached the eucharist unworthily.

136 *Ep.* 57.2.2.

137 Communicating with an unworthy bishop, however, might ruin the value of the rituals, as shall be seen in chapter 7, pp. 141–4. See for example *epp.* 65.2.1–2, 67.3.1.

138 The principle of church unity ultimately moved a group of confessors back into Cornelius' church. See *epp.* 49, 53.

139 In his letter preserved in Eusebius, *h.e.* 6.43.16, Cornelius made the charge that Novatian required an oath of loyalty to himself from each of his adherents as he distributed the eucharist. The reality may have been an oath that the communicant was not guilty of apostasy or sacrilege through communicating with Cornelius.

140 *Ep.* 30.3.1.

141 *Ep.* 30.3.1–2. In responding to a letter defending Novatian, Cyprian attempted to justify these distinctions, *ep.* 55.13.1–14.2.

142 This charge seems to have been the lead-off accusation in Novatian's letter, to judge by Cyprian's *ep.* 55.2.1. His removing Trofimus from episcopal office seems to have been of no significance to the rigorists. Even the differentiation of roles, however, would not have helped explain the admission of Trofimus' entire community, each member of which apparently sacrificed. No other group of sacrificers seems to have been admitted before May 253, by which time the rigorist schism was already well established.

143 For the practice during the persecution, see *ep.* 30.8; for subsequent practice, see *epp.* 55.27.1, 59.18.1, 68.1.1,3.1,4.2.

144 *De cibis judaicis* 7, CCL 4:101. He alluded to 1 Cor. 10.21 but otherwise ignored the more liberal Pauline teaching on this subject.

145 In *ep.* 73.19.3, for example, Cyprian himself asserted that admitting the unbaptized – presumably contaminated by prior contact with Roman idolatry – would spread sin throughout the communion. This question will be further explored in chapter 7.

146 It must be remembered that Cyprian's attacks on Novatianist practice are based on his own group's assumption that no one could be saved outside the communion, a position which the rigorists might not have shared, as for example in *epp.* 55.28.1–3, 68.1.1,3.1.

147 *Epp.* 18.2.1, 19.2.3, 55.29.2.

148 *Epp.* 55.28.1–3, 68.1.1,3.1.

149 *Lap.* 36.

150 *Ep.* 57.4.1.

151 The call for consultation was in the letter of the Roman clergy, *ep.* 30.5.4. Novatian's behavior contrasted with Cyprian's acceptance of the reversal of his position on the certified by the African bishops.

152 *Ep.* 44.1.1–2.1. Cyprian, in contrast, was willing to tolerate differences in practices within the communion of bishops, as long as they did not involve support for those who divided the church.

153 *Ep.* 55.24.2.
154 *Ep.* 55.11.3, and that by the decision of some sixty bishops.
155 *De pudicitia* 3, 11, and passim, *CCL* 4:115–16,123–4.
156 *Epp.* 30.3.2, 55.16.1. Cyprian's discussion of the pollution of the conscience of the certified was an incoherent extension of the behavioral standards: the persons who acted in ignorance of the evil involved had contaminated their consciences though not their hands and mouths, *ep.* 55.14.2. The African bishops, in contrast, refused to maintain sanctions against those who had not actually sacrificed.
157 *De cibis judaicis* 3–4, *CCL* 4:93–7.

5 INDIVISIBILITY OF THE CHURCH

1 *Ep.* 11.3.1–2,7.1. The second vision recounted, in *ep.* 11.4.1–2, was received well before the persecution itself.
2 *Vita Cyp.* 5; *ep.* 43.1.2–3,5.4. The *uita* may well have taken the opportunity to exaggerate Cyprian's virtue.
3 *Ep.* 52.3.
4 *Ep.* 13.7.
5 *Ep.* 14.1.2.
6 *Ep.* 14.2.1.
7 *Ep.* 13.4.1.
8 *Ep.* 5.2 made clear they were performing this duty and *ep.* 16.4.2 included a threat of suspension of this privilege.
9 *Epp.* 34.1, 59.12.1–2.
10 They were instructed by the Roman clergy's exhortation to penance in *ep.* 8.2.3, as well as Cyprian's demands.
11 *Ep.* 16.3.2,4.2.
12 *Epp.* 15.2.2, 16.3.2.
13 *Ep.* 19.2.3.
14 *Epp.* 15.1.2, 22.2.2, 26.1.4, 27.2.2.
15 *Ep.* 33.2.1.
16 *Epp.* 14.4, 17.3.2, 26.1.2.
17 *Epp.* 17.3.2, 19.2.2, 20.3.3, 24, 25, 26.1.1–2.1, 27.3.2–3.
18 *Epp.* 21, 22.2.1.
19 *Ep.* 23.
20 *Epp.* 15.1.2, 16.1.2,2.3,3.2, 17.1.2–2.1.
21 *Ep.* 16.3.2.
22 *Epp.* 22.2.2, 23. The Roman clergy picked up on this point as well, *ep.* 36.2.3, but Cyprian argued that the provision was in fact unenforceable once forgiveness for the apostasy had been guaranteed by the martyrs, *ep.* 27.2.2–3.2.
23 *Ep.* 26.1.2.
24 *Ep.* 27.2.2–3.1.
25 *Ep.* 17.3.1.
26 *Epp.* 15.3.1,4, 18.1.2.
27 *Epp.* 16.1.2, 17.2.1, 19.2.1.
28 *Ep.* 35.1.1.
29 *Epp.* 35.1.1, 36.1.2 where the Roman clergy cited their copy of the letter which was not itself preserved in the collection of Cyprian's

correspondence. In *ep.* 27.3.1, he reported that some clergy were being forced to grant communion to the lapsed.

30 *Ep.* 33.1.1. This was his earliest surviving citation and explanation of this text.

31 *Ep.* 43.5.2–4. The text would be cited again in *unit.* 4 during the summer of 251.

32 *Ep.* 28.2.2–3. The argument which developed from this observation was based on Mt. 10.32–3: on the basis of Christ's promise to acknowledge confession, no one could presume to disregard his threat to punish denial. It is fully laid out in *lap.* 20.

33 *Epp.* 29, 38, 39, 40. Cyprian even specified that two of the readers, Celerinus and Aurelius, were to begin receiving the salaries of presbyters immediately, *ep.* 39.5.2.

34 *Epp.* 41, 42. *Ep.* 24.1.1 established the status of Caldonius and *ep.* 43.1.1 that of the two confessors.

35 In *epp.* 5.1.2, 12.2.2, 14.2.1, Cyprian had specified that assistance was to be restricted to the standing poor. None of these letters had been acknowledged by the clergy in Carthage.

36 *Ep.* 41.1.2.

37 *Ep.* 41.1.2–2.1.

38 *Epp.* 41.2.1–2, 43.1.2–3.

39 G.W. Clarke notes that at one point, only one of the presbyters actually in Carthage may have been faithful to Cyprian, see *Letters* 1:40–1.

40 When the rebels did finally create a rival bishop in 252, they began to lose adherents, *ep.* 59.15.1. This sort of pressure technique subsequently worked in Rome, where the community gathered around Trofimus was admitted to communion by Cornelius, *ep.* 55.11.1. It was steadfastly resisted in Africa, *ep.* 59.10.3,11.2.

41 *Ep.* 43.1.2.

42 *Ep.* 43.2.1–2.

43 *Ep.* 43.3.1–4.3.

44 *Ep.* 43.5.2.

45 *Ep.* 43.5.2. Cyprian characterized this action as *adulterium, impium, sacrilegium*, all terms associated with idolatry. He exhorted the people to flee the contagion.

46 *Ep.* 43.4.3–5.2. He compared them to the elders who had assaulted the chastity of Susannah.

47 *Ep.* 43.7.1.

48 *Ep.* 43.5.2.

49 *Lap.* 2–3. Those who had actually died in defense of the faith were, of course, in a different category but they were no longer in the earthly community.

50 In *epp.* 13, 14, he had already insisted that confessors remain subject to the same standards and the same temptations as their fellow Christians.

51 *Lap.* 5–14,27.

52 *Lap.* 29–30.

53 These may have been the individuals who were sheltered from the imperial authorities by a *paterfamilias* or patron who had acted on behalf of all. They would have been pushing for the reconciliation of their benefactors. See *ep.* 55.13.2,15.1.

54 *Lap.* 28. No further decisions or actions regarding this class are recorded; they were ignored in the episcopal deliberations of 251 and 253 which formed policy for reconciliation of the certified and sacrificers.

55 *Lap.* 17–19.

56 *Lap.* 20, citing Mt. 10.32–3.

57 The martyrs in heaven who petitioned for vengeance in Rev. 6.9 were told to wait; the prophets often failed to influence God, *lap.* 18–20.

58 *Ep.* 55.13.2,15.1.

59 Thus the confessors presented themselves as coming to the assistance of the church by doing what the bishops lacked the authority to do, *lap.* 20.

60 *Epp.* 33.1.1–2, 43.5.2 provided the interpretative context for *unit.* 4, in which Cyprian spoke of Peter as the foundation of unity within the local church. Some years later he returned to this theme: no one could be in the communion of a church without being in union with its bishop, *ep.* 66.8.3. Similarly in *unit.* 13, he pointed out that no sacrifice could be offered in opposition to the priests.

61 *Ep.* 59.6.1,13.1–17.3.

62 *Ep.* 59.15.2–3.

63 *Ep.* 55.13.2,15.1.

64 *Lap.* 5–6 detailed the failures of all which had brought on the persecution.

65 See chapter 4.

66 *Vnit.* 1–3. On the dating of this treatise see Clarke, *Letters* 2:301–2, Bévenot in *CCL* 3:245–6, "Cyprian and his Recognition of Cornelius," *Journal of Theological Studies,* n.s. 28 (1977):346–59, esp. 357, n. 1. Clarke disputes Bévenot's grammatical argument and suggests that the treatise was originally written to deal with the laxist schism in Carthage and then applied to the rigorist schism in Rome, before a decision had been made between the contending candidates. The temptation to schism as a form of persecution had also been treated earlier in *ep.* 43.3.1,6.3–7.2.

67 *Vnit.* 12–13.

68 *Vnit.* 14–15. This argument was repeated in *ep.* 55.17.2,29.2.

69 *Vnit.* 20–4.

70 *Ep.* 26.1.2.

71 *Ep.* 55.6.1–2.

72 *Ep.* 55.7.2.

73 *Ep.* 59.14.2.

74 *Epp.* 45.4.1, 59.9.1,10.2–3,13.1.

75 *Ep.* 55.21.1–2.

76 *Ep.* 55.8.4,24.2.

77 *Ep.* 44.1.3–3.1.

78 Cornelius informed Cyprian of their departure; he indicated that Evaristus had been a bishop and supporter of Novatian, *ep.* 50.1.1–2. Cornelius and Cyprian spoke of Nicostratus as a deacon, *epp.* 50.1.2, 51.1.2. For discussion see Clarke, *Letters* 2:103.

79 Cyprian's *ep.* 55 responded to questions raised by one such letter.

80 *Ep.* 59.9.2.

81 *Ep.* 55.24.2.

82 Cyprian was contemptuous of them in *ep.* 59.9.3, in contrast to his shrill denunciation of the developing laxist hierarchy.

83 Cornelius had made such a concession to Trofimus, admitting him and his congregation to communion without penance. Trofimus, however, was admitted only as a layman. The rebel clergy in Carthage had promised their adherents that all would eventually be received into communion by the bishops as a group, *ep.* 59.15.1.

84 *Ep.* 59.10.2–11.1

85 *Ep.* 59.9.4, see Clarke, *Letters* 3:240–1, nn. 6–7.

86 *Ep.* 59.1.1–2.1. Cyprian was furious to hear that Cornelius had entertained the delegation. Cornelius may have been settling a score for the lengthy investigation of his own credentials a year earlier.

87 I am grateful to G.W. Clarke for this insight, communicated in conversation. The subordinationism of third-century African trinitarian theology assigned the unity of the divine rule to the Father, who delegated authority to the Son.

88 *Epp.* 44, 45, 48.

89 Eusebius, *h.e.* 6.43.16.

90 *Ep.* 49.2.4.

91 *Epp.* 55.24.2, 59.9.2.

92 The letters referenced in *ep.* 59 would have had to charge Cyprian with misconduct to justify his replacement; thus he defended his actions to Cornelius. Clarke, *Letters* 4:241, n. 7 builds the case for this interpretation.

93 *Ep.* 59.15.1.

94 A copy was sent to Rome for Cornelius' use, *ep.* 59.9.3.

95 *Epp.* 55.8.4, 59.6.1.

96 *Epp.* 55.11.1–3, 67.6.3, for Trofimus and the Spanish bishops.

97 *Epp.* 59.10.1–2, 65.3.2.

98 Eusebius, *h.e.* 6.43.10; *ep.* 52.1.2.

99 *Ep.* 59.10.1. There is no evidence that the council which deposed Privatus had been held in Carthage rather than Lambaesis. In either case, the weight of Donatus' endorsement, as presider or an additional signatory, was deemed necessary.

100 *Ep.* 68. The letter to Cyprian was written by Faustinus of Lyons.

101 *Ep.* 65.4.2.

102 *Ep.* 55.8.4 gave the *suffragium* to the people alone in electing Cornelius, while *ep.* 68.2.1 shared it between the clergy and the people in the same case. *Epp.* 59.5.2 and 67.4.2,5.1–2 specified the people's vote and the consent of the bishops.

103 *Ep.* 67.4.1–5.1.

104 *Ep.* 40.1.3. An identification of the Rogatianus to whom *epistula* 3 was addressed with the confessor and presbyter of Carthage, *epp.* 6, 40, 41, 43.1.1, would give a second instance of a presbyter of one church being chosen bishop in another. This elderly man's appeal to Cyprian for help in dealing with an insolent deacon might have betrayed an earlier supervisory role. *Ep.* 3 could be dated late enough for Cyprian's former presbyter to have been made a bishop. The constellation of texts (Deut. 17.12–13; 1 Sam. 8.5–18; Jn. 18.22–3; and Acts 23.4–5) justifying respect for the bishop occurred only in *epp.* 59.4 and 66.3, which are dated in 252 and 254 by G.W. Clarke,

Letters 3:235, 321–2. Num. 16.1–35 was otherwise used only in the baptismal controversy of 256, in *epp.* 67.3, 69.8, 73.8, and *unit.* 18.

105 *Ep.* 55.24.2.
106 Eusebius, *h.e.* 6.43.8–9.
107 *Ep.* 59.10.1–11.1, five of the twenty-five he claimed.
108 *Epp.* 44.3.2, 55.24.2, 69.3.2.
109 *Epp.* 45.3.1, 48.4.1.
110 *Ep.* 55.2.1,10.1–11.2,12.
111 *Ep.* 55.8.1–23.4.
112 *Ep.* 59.2.5,14.2.
113 *Epp.* 45.3.1, 48.3.2.
114 *Ep.* 45.2.1–3.
115 *Epp.* 44.1.2–3, 45.1.1,3,3.1, 48.2.1,3.2–4.1.
116 *Ep.* 45.1.2–3. The original letters and delegates were probably sent to Cyprian and were then received by the council which was actually meeting in Carthage at the time of their arrival. Cyprian later explained the problem he experienced in communicating to the church at Hadrumetum that letters were not to be directed to Cornelius until his claim had been verified, *ep.* 48.3.2. The communion letter originally addressed to Cornelius by Bishop Antoninus seems to have been sent to Cyprian for transmission, *ep.* 55.1.2.
117 *Ep.* 59.5.2.
118 *Ep.* 66.1.1–2,4.2,9.1.
119 *Epp.* 59.5.1, 66.5.1.
120 *Ep.* 43.1.2–3.
121 The divine approval of Cornelius was also confirmed in his public confession of faith while Novatian was ignored, *ep.* 60.3.2.
122 *Ep.* 55.24.2–4.
123 *Ep.* 60.3.2.
124 *Epp.* 67.4.1–5.1, 65.4.1. Thus the bishops gathered to install a new bishop must respect the decision of the laity who know the qualities of the candidates through regular contact.
125 *Ep.* 55.
126 *Ep.* 67.9.2.
127 Cyprian characterized the charge of the African episcopal delegation in *ep.* 45.1.1 as one of reconciliation, though he admitted its judicial function, *ep.* 45.1.1,3.1.
128 On the dating of this treatise see note 66 above. The role of the bishop in the local church had been treated before in letters during the persecution, especially *epp.* 33, 43.
129 *Ep.* 46.1.2. He may have sent copies of both *de lapsis* and *de unitate* at this time to the confessors, since in *ep.* 54.4, Cyprian reminded the confessors of the treatises which he had sent earlier. As he had to do earlier for the released confessors in Carthage, he reminded the Roman confessors that their salvation was not yet secure, that having stood firm once they were now being subjected to greater temptations, *unit.* 20–2.
130 *Ep.* 46.2.1, see also *ep.* 44.3.2.
131 *Ep.* 54.4, indicated that both treatises had been sent earlier, though no reference to them can be found in the surviving correspondence. It

will be recalled that *de lapsis* had been written and delivered prior to the relaxation of discipline in the episcopal conference in spring 251.

132 Reported by Cornelius in *ep.* 49.2.4. Clarke argues that Cornelius had approved and may even have dictated the formula of submission, *Letters* 2:273. For the parallel which might also have been the model, see *unit.* 23. This connection between the formula in Cyprian's treatise and the confessor's oath would bolster Clarke's argument for the treatise having been sent to Rome in spring 251.

133 *Ep.* 54.1.2.

134 Efforts have been made, principally by Maurice Bévenot, to link the shorter *Primacy Text* with the events of 251 and to identify the longer *Textus Receptus* as a revision prepared during the baptismal controversy, for the purpose of eliminating any basis for Stephen of Rome's claims to dictate policy and practice to his fellow bishops. See the introduction to the text in *CCL* 3:246

135 *Ep.* 54.4.

136 *TR* and *PT* differ only in chapters 4–5 and19. But the common text contains elements which could only have been written in 251 and other elements which must have been added in 256. The present analysis will concentrate on the former.

137 *Vnit.* 1–3,20–4. This repeated the admonition which had been given to the released Carthaginian confessors early in the persecution, *epp.* 13, 14, and reflected the argument which Cyprian was developing at the time of his return to Carthage: that schism was a second and more dangerous form of persecution, *ep.* 43.3.1,6.1–7.2; *lap.* 16. In *epp.* 46.2.1, 51.1.1, 54.1.2–3, he first chided the Roman confessors for failing to witness to the unity of the church and then congratulated them on having done so.

138 *Vnit.* 14,19 and *epp.* 52.1.2, 55.17.2,29.3, 60.4, as well as during the baptismal controversy, *ep.* 73.21.1.

139 All these text were cited in *de unitate* and in *ep.* 43, his last surviving letter from exile.

140 *Vnit.* 11 and *ep.* 43.5.1.

141 *Vnit.* 17 and *ep.* 43.5.2.

142 *Vnit.* 10; *lap.* 34, and *ep.* 43.5.2. It continued to be used to attack the schismatics, *epp.* 59.20.1,73.15.1.

143 *Vnit.* 6 and *ep.* 43.5.2; it recurred in the baptismal controversy, *epp.* 69.1.2, 70.3.2.

144 *Vnit.* 23 and *ep.* 43.5.2. In 256, he never passed up the opportunity to refer to baptism as well, *epp.* 70.1.2,3.1, 71.1.2, 73.4.2,13.3, 74.2.2,3.1,11.1. The full text is cited only in *unit.* 4 *TR* and in Firmilian's echoing it to Cyprian, *ep.* 75.24.3, with an additional reference in *ep.* 75.25.3.

145 *Ep.* 59.14.1, or the reference to Cornelius as the successor of Fabian and Peter, *ep.* 55.8.1. In spring 251, the laxist schism provided no context for interpreting the reference to the primacy of Peter and the equality of the other apostles which appeared in both *PT* and *TR* versions of *unit.* 4. The present hypothesis is that the *PT* version was introduced for transmission of the text to Rome and the *TR* version provided a necessary correction. The *TR* version of *unit.* 4 can be linked to the letters of the baptismal controversy.

146 *Vnit.* 4 *PT.*

147 The *TR* version of *unit.* 19, in which penitents were described as lapsed, fits the situation before Cyprian agreed to distinguish the certified and to reconcile them immediately, at the council in spring 251. Neither version described the situation during the baptismal controversy, since all the penitent lapsed had been reconciled three years earlier.

148 When the text was revised again in 256, none of the lapsed were still doing penance. Cyprian allowed the passage to stand as he had originally composed it in spring 251. Neither version of this part of chapter 19 can be identified with a revision belonging to the baptismal controversy.

149 See chapter 8, pp. 159–162.

150 *Vnit.* 7.

151 *Vnit.* 12.

152 *Vnit.* 8.

153 *Vnit.* 9. In *lap.* 33 and *ep.* 59.13.4 he characterized the leaders of the laxist schism in Carthage as blinded by God.

154 In *ep.* 54.3.1, Cyprian would object to the presumption of the Novatianists to pass a final judgment on the lapsed.

155 In *ep.* 54.3.1–2, he reminded the Novatianist confessors that no church leader was authorized to separate wheat from tares or to clear the threshing floor. In *ep.* 55.25.1–2, he leveled this charge of presumption at Novatian himself. Cyprian would later defend himself against the laxist charge of dividing the church by his rigorist stance toward the fallen, *ep.* 59.15.3–16.3.

156 *Epp.* 43.5.2, 59.7.3, 70.3.1, 73.11.1.

157 *Epp.* 59.4.1–3,5.1, 66.3.2,4.2. The first letter was written in defense against the laxist appeal to Rome, the second in response to a Novatianist in Africa.

158 *Epp.* 59.7.3, 66.8.3.

159 *Ep.* 66.8.2–3. The same point was made in *ep.* 59.7.2–3, though in *ep.* 65.5.1–2 Cyprian cautioned that the bishop must be sound and worthy.

160 He signaled particular difficulties with the sacrificers and adulterers who had refused to perform penance, *ep.* 59.15.2–3.

161 *Ep.* 59.17.1–20.2.

162 *Epp.* 65.4.1, 67.2.2.

163 *Ep.* 63.13.1–4.

164 *Ep.* 69.5.2.

165 *Ep.* 63.16.1.

166 See above, chapter 4, p. 63.

167 The plague appeared in Carthage during the summers. Cyprian's *de mortalitate* had addressed Christian concerns.

168 The problems caused by the survival of the apparently dying penitents were attested in *epp.* 55.13.1 and 56.2.1 where the bishops argued that those who fell under torture should not continue to be excluded.

169 *Ep.* 64.1.1. The case of Victor might indicate a level of impatience.

170 *Ep.* 56.1,2.1, see also *ep.* 55.13.1 where Cyprian answered a rigorist objection to the sacrificers remaining in communion.

171 *Ep.* 57.3.1–2,5.1.
172 *Ep.* 57.1.2,3.1.
173 *Vnit.* 4; *epp.* 33.1.1–2, 43.5.1–2.
174 *Ep.* 57.2.2.
175 *Epp.* 69.3.1–2, 70.2.1,3.1, 71.1.3,3.2, 73.25.2, 75.16.1–2,25.3 (assumed to reflect Cyprian's letter to Firmilian).

6 INITIATION INTO UNITY

1 *Ep.* 64.4.1–5.2 implied that infant baptism was normal; *lap.* 25 testified to the participation of infants in the eucharist, indicating their prior baptism.
2 The conciliar letter, *ep.* 70.2.3, referred to converts from idolatry.
3 Though with considerably less sympathy from the companions they had abandoned. Cyprian recounted the resentment his congregations showed toward them, *ep.* 59.15.1–4.
4 *Ep.* 59.10.1–11.3.
5 *Ep.* 50.1.2 recorded the first arrival of what might have been a rigorist bishop; *ep.* 59.9.2 indicates that a challenger to Cyprian might not have been in place until early 252.
6 *Ep.* 70 from the Numidian bishops to a council of Proconsular bishops meeting in Carthage. See Clarke, *Letters* 4:192–3 for dating.
7 Precise information on the length of catechumenate or penitence is not available, though the provision made for baptizing catechumens and reconciling penitents just prior to death indicated a specific period of time which was observed, *epp.* 18.1.1–2.2, 20.3.1. In *ep.* 56.1, reference was made to a three-year period of repentance as being adequate for lapsed who fell under torture.
8 Cyprian did not hesitate to appeal to the spiritual damage done to children in another circumstance, *lap.* 9,25. In this case, however, he regarded the schismatics either as sincere but deceived, *epp.* 70.2.3, 72.2.3, or responsible for accepting baptism in rebellion against the church, *epp.* 69.9.1–10.1, 73.21.2.
9 There was a plague in summer 252, and a looming renewal of persecution in spring 253.
10 Reference was made to Novatian's practice of rebaptizing all converts in *epp.* 73.2.1, 74.1.2, which are securely dated in summer 256. This communion, moreover, would have been concerned to establish the depth of the rejection of idolatry by its converts.
11 On his deposition and role in establishing the laxist hierarchy, see *ep.* 59.10.
12 On the status of the bishops in the new laxist communion, see *ep.* 59.10.1–3. Repostus' entire congregation had been guilty of following him into apostasy during the persecution.
13 *Ep.* 70.1.1, which is the earliest of the surviving documents of the controversy, was the response of a Proconsular synod to the inquiry of a Numidian synod on the question of receiving converts baptized in schism.
14 This hypothesis is different from that of my study of the rebaptism controversy in "On Rebaptism: Social Organization in the Third

Century Church," *Journal of Early Christian Studies*, 1 (1993):367–403.

15 Tertullian also cited Eph. 4.4–6 in *bapt.* 15. He referred to a more ample treatment in Greek which has not survived but which may have been known to Cyprian.

16 Clarke provides a summary of what may be known about this council, suggesting that it was held about 230, *Letters* 4:197–8.

17 The bishops in Numidia knew the policy adopted by Agrippinus' council but still raised questions of its application, *ep.* 70.1.2.

18 *Epp.* 70.1.2, 71.4.1.

19 *Ep.* 73.3.1.

20 *Ep.* 75.19.3–4.

21 Firmilian would have had his information not only from the dossier of letters Cyprian sent but from the messenger, the deacon Rogatianus, as well. He implied that a change in custom had been quite recent, though he might have been informed on Agrippinus' council. He asserted that his own church had never accepted heretical baptism and had, through a council, rejected schismatic baptism. See *ep.* 75.19.3–4.

22 The key point, the Proconsular synod replied, was that the baptism was performed outside the church, *ep.* 70.1.2.

23 Because the opponents did not really believe in the link between the church and the forgiveness of sins, *ep.* 70.2.1.

24 *Sent. episc.* 4,5,7,33. Only the latter two, of Lucius and Felix, presented distinct arguments against schismatics.

25 The prior instance would have been the Montanists, whose disciplinary dissent would have paralleled that of the Novatianists. The Cappadocian bishops had dealt with this as a distinct issue in their own council, *ep.* 75.19.4.

26 *Ep.* 73.24.1. He also asserted that Novatian was right to refuse to recognize the baptism of another church, since it would have undercut his own, *ep.* 73.2.1.

27 *Ep.* 70.1.1–2.

28 *Ep.* 71. Quintus was identified in *ep.* 72.1.3.

29 Cyprian referred twice to the enclosure of letters, *ep.* 71.1.1,4.2. The conciliar letter was clearly intended in the first instance; the second seems to be a private letter. Clarke surmises that the second reference was to *ep.* 69, addressed to Magnus. The next letter in sequence, addressed to Jubianus, however, referred only to the conciliar letter and that to Quintus, *ep.* 73.1.1–2. If a personal letter had preceded that to Quintus and was sent with it, Cyprian did not think to send it to Jubianus as well. A second letter enclosed with that to Quintus would have been either that to Magnus, *ep.* 69, or a different letter which has been lost. It is argued below that this letter to Magnus was composed later and thus could not have been the one intended in the closing paragraph of the letter to Quintus. See Clarke, *Letters* 4:211, n. 15, 221, nn. 2–3.

30 *Ep.* 72. The number of bishops was specified in *ep.* 73.1.2. All evidence of schismatic clergy recruited from among the African churches related to the laxists; the rigorist clergy seems to have been sent from Rome, see *epp.* 44.1.1,2.1,3.1, 50.1.1–2, 52.1.1–2.

31 *Ep.* 70 of the Proconsular bishops to the Numidians and *ep.* 71 of Cyprian to Quintus. This provided an indicator that all the relevant early correspondence has survived and that Cyprian's letter to Magnus (*ep.* 69) was written later.

32 *Ep.* 57.

33 *Ep.* 72.3.1–2.

34 Not only did the Africans seem to have been unconcerned about a different Roman tradition of reception by imposition of hands but they made no reference to what could have been a problem in Rome: the practice of Novatian, who did rebaptize converts. Had the Africans been concerned with the rigorists as well as the laxists, a fuller and more nuanced treatment of the issue might have been sent.

35 *Ep.* 73.2.1–3.

36 *Ep.* 73.14.3,20.2,25.1.

37 The three letters were read out at the beginning of the deliberations held on 1 September 256. See *sent. episc. proem.* This might have indicated that Jubianus was himself an African and known to the other bishops gathered at the meeting.

38 *Ep.* 74.4.1. If accurate, this report implied that Stephen did not regard Novatian as heretical. *Ep.* 73.2.1 provided the first evidence in the surviving correspondence of Novatian's practice of rebaptizing, from which Cyprian himself might have gained the knowledge.

39 Clarke tentatively identifies Pompeius as the bishop of Sabrata in Tripoli, who sent his proxy to the September meeting, *Letters* 4:236.

40 *Ep.* 75. Clarke argues that he must have been sent copies of *epp.* 69, 73, 74. This would indicate that the three letters shared a common purpose and were roughly contemporary. See *Letters* 4:248.

41 Magnus seems to have been an African, since he did not mention the Novatianist practice of rebaptizing, which a Roman would have known.

42 See pp. 110–12.

43 One of the bishops, Natalis, spoke as proxy for two of his colleagues, Pompeius and Dioga, who could not be present, so that eighty-seven *sententiae* were recorded. *Sent. episc.* 83–5.

44 *Sent. episc.* Only two bishops Lucius and Felix clearly distinguished between heresy and schism, *sent. episc.* 7,33.

45 *Epp.* 73, 74, as well as the response from Firmilian of Caesarea, *ep.* 75.

46 *Epp.* 50.1.2, 59.9.2.

47 See the correspondence between Cyprian and Cornelius on these events, esp. *ep.* 59.10.1–11.3.

48 *Ep.* 59.15.1–4.

49 *Ep.* 70.1.2.

50 The only reference to the baptismal interrogation focused on the link between the church and the forgiveness of sins, *ep.* 70.2.1. There was no question of difference in belief regarding God or Christ.

51 *Ep.* 62 was sent to eight of these bishops, who had requested financial assistance to ransom Christians taken captive in a raid. See Clarke, *Letters* 3:280–1 and 4:193–5 for the evidence and its limits. For Privatus, see *ep.* 59.10.1–11.3.

52 Lambaesis was more than 160 km from the sea by a fairly direct route. The quartering of *III Legio Augusta* at the site and the city's serving as

capital of Numidia would certainly have increased communication with Rome but would not necessarily have attracted the rigorists. The converts were likely to have come from a schismatic church established earlier under Privatus, who had been deposed perhaps a decade earlier (*ep.* 59.10.1–11.3). At the time of the inquiry, they would have been laxist communicants.

53 See Clarke, *Letters* 4:207.

54 See *epp.* 44.1.1,3.1, 45.1.2, 50, 52.1.2–2.2, 59.9.1–11.2 for the persons sent by Novatian.

55 Thus *ep.* 69, which fully discussed Novatian's rebellion, might not yet have been composed.

56 *Epp.* 70.3.1 (to Numidia) and 71.3.1 (to Quintus in Mauretania). In *ep.* 72.1.2 (to Stephen) Peter's ordering water baptism for Cornelius in Acts 10.44ff might have been particularly aimed at a Roman audience. For the parallel usage of Peter as a symbol of local unity in earlier letters, see *epp.* 33.1.1, 43.5.2, 59.7.3. Prior to the rebaptism controversy the much interpreted *ep.* 59.14.1 and *unit.* 4 *PT*, provided the only instances in which Cyprian seemed to assign Peter a role in the universal communion.

57 In the second stage of the controversy, Cyprian was more concerned to link the power to forgive sins in baptism to the gift of the Holy Spirit. There he linked Peter's privilege in Mt. 16.18–19 to the gift of the Holy Spirit in Jn. 20.22–3. The first instance of the change appeared in *ep.* 69.11.1. The letter of Jubianus referred to Peter as the basis for local unity but linked him to the other apostles, *ep.* 73.7.1–2,11.1. A similar approach was taken in *ep.* 75.16.1, where Firmilian was probably mirroring Cyprian's letters to Magnus and Jubianus. Cyprian's intention was clearest in the revision of *unit.* 4–5 *TR*.

58 *Epp.* 70.1.3,2.2–3, 71.1.3, 72.1.1,2.2. This second point was raised again in *ep.* 73.21.2 but without reference to the sinfulness of the ministers themselves.

59 See the letter on the laxist bishops sent to Cornelius, *ep.* 59.1.1–2,9.1,10.1–12.2.

60 Cornelius charged Novatian with cowardice during the persecution but not idolatry, see Eusebius, *h.e.* 6.43.16.

61 *Epp.* 70.2.2–3, 72.2.3.

62 Thus in *epp.* 69.4.2,9.1–2, 73.10.3. For the deception perpetrated by the laxists, see *ep.* 72.2.3.

63 The information about Novatian's practice was attributed to Jubianus' letter to Cyprian and might have been Cyprian's first information on the subject, *ep.* 73.2.1. Stephen asserted that the general practice of heretics was not to rebaptize, *ep.* 74.1.2,4.1.

64 *De rebaptismo* – which argued for reception by the imposition of hands alone – must have represented the practice of at least a segment of the African church.

65 The letter of the Proconsular bishops to their Numidian colleagues referred to just such converts, *ep.* 70.2.3.

66 *Ep.* 73.2.1 spoke of Jubianus' own observation. *Ep.* 73.4.1 referred to a letter which he included on the same subject. For the debate over the identity of this anonymous letter, see Clarke, *Letters* 4:223.

67 *Ep.* 73.1.2 referred to the meeting as recent; it betrayed no knowledge of Stephen's reply to the synod's letter.

68 *Ep.* 74.1.1 referred to Stephen's letter for the first time in the surviving correspondence.

69 See Clarke, *Letters* 4:248–9. It was not mentioned in the *acta* of the council of 1 September 256.

70 Jubianus observed that Cyprian was advocating Novatian's practice of rebaptism while Stephen asserted that the Africans were innovating and that no Christians, not even heretics, rebaptized – apparently either refusing to take notice of Novatian or classifying him as a heretic; *epp.* 73.2.1, 74.1.2.

71 *Epp.* 73.14.3,25.1–26.2, 74.2.2,4.1,8.2.

72 *Ep.* 69.1.1.

73 *Ep.* 69. Clarke discusses the chronology in *Letters* 4:173–4 and again in *CCL* 3D:702. He argues for an early dating from the calm and measured tone, without claims on previous tradition, the general rather than specific focus of the arguments, the absence of reference to the conciliar resolutions which are reported in *epp.* 70, 72, or to any other correspondence – despite the practice of including other letters in writing to Quintus, Jubianus, Pompeius and Firmilian. The letter to Magnus, moreover, was not listed among those sent to Jubianus, *ep.* 73.1.1–2, though it seems to have preceded it.

74 Clarke points out that Firmilian's arguments in *ep.* 75.10.5–11.1 seem to have been aimed at the objections raised by Magnus, which Cyprian had summarized and answered in *ep.* 69.7.1–8.1, see *Letters* 4:248. It may be presumed that Firmilian also received a copy of *ep.* 72, the African council's report to Stephen, which had provoked his harsh response. Firmilian's letter did not reference the items specific to the letters sent to the Numidian bishops and to Quintus in Mauretania, *epp.* 70, 71.

75 The letter sent by Jubianus provided the first information on Novatian's practice of rebaptizing converts, *ep.* 73.2.1, which Cyprian gave no indication of knowing in his reply to Magnus. Thus *epistula* 69 may be judged to precede *epistula* 73, and by implication, *epistula* 74.

76 *Epp.* 69.2.1, 74.11.2. *Epp.* 73.10.3, 74.11.2 added the paradise of fruit trees. These images were associated with Canticle of Canticles 6.8, 4.12. Cant. 6.8 was also found in *ep.* 69.2.1 and the revision of *unit.* 4 *TR*, though not elsewhere in the letters of this period.

77 *Epp.* 69.2.2, 74.11.3. Noah's ark appeared also in *unit.* 6, where it also referred to the impossibility of salvation outside the church.

78 *Ep.* 69.2.3, 74.6.2. Based on Eph. 5.25–6. The image was more elaborate in *ep.* 74, indicating that it might have been the later use.

79 *Epp.* 69.8.1, 73.8.1–2. Firmilian's response to Cyprian picked up the argument from the letter to Magnus, *ep.* 75.10.5–11.1. This incident was also mentioned in *unit.* 18, where it might have been part of the revision of the text. It appeared elsewhere only in *ep.* 3.1.2, which cannot be securely dated.

80 *Epp.* 69.11.1, 73.7.2; *unit.* 4 *TR*. It did not appear elsewhere in Cyprian's writings.

81 *Ep.* 73.24.3–25.1 appears to be a revision of *ep.* 69.11.1. It attributed the spirit of Elijah to John and explained that the apostles rebaptized

after him because John had not acted within the unity of the church. This shift seems to have been under the influence of Jn. 7.38–9, whose first verse was cited in *ep.* 73.11.1. If Cyprian was working from a written text rather than from memory, he would have noted that the next verse (Jn. 7.39) said that the Spirit was not given until Jesus was glorified. Thus he might have changed his interpretation of the giving of the Spirit to John the Baptist later in the letter. This might also indicate that the text was fresh in his mind, and that *epistula* 69 had, therefore, been written recently. The uncertainty in Cyprian's evaluation of John's baptism reflected Tertullian's treatment in *bapt.* 10.

82 *Epp.* 69.4.2,9.1–2, 73.10.3; contrast with *epp.* 70.2.3, 72.2.3.

83 *Ep.* 69.12.1–16.2.

84 Eusebius, *h.e.* 6.43.14.

85 *Ep.* 69.14.1–2. The link between the two questions was explicitly asserted in *ep.* 69.16.2.

86 *Ep.* 73.9.1–2. This followed the description of the effects of the different parts of the ritual in Tertullian's *bapt.* 6.

87 The precise point made in *ep.* 73.9.1,24.3–25.1 regarding the baptism performed by Philip in contrast to that performed by John the Baptist.

88 In addition it might be noted that the first three letters are of similar, short length (97, 86 and 79 lines in *CCL* edition) while the latter three are significantly longer (380, 473, and 250 lines in the same edition), *CCL* 3C.

89 Clarke observes that *epistula* 69 did not share the acerbic tone of the later letters and made no reference to the decisions of the councils of 254–5 and spring 256. The issue in this letter to Magnus was Novatian's power to baptize, and not his practice of rebaptizing, of which Cyprian learned only later from Jubianus, *ep.* 73.2.1. Reference to the two councils dealing with just this problem (apparently among the laxists) would not necessarily have been expected. The silence and failure to include prior letters, were any relevant, would count as an argument against the dating proposed here.

90 *Epp.* 70, 71, 72.

91 *Epp.* 69, 73, 74, 75.

92 *Ep.* 71.1.2.

93 *Ep.* 70.3.1, parallel to *unit.* 4 *PT*.

94 *Ep.* 70.3.2, quoting Lk. 11.23 and 1 Jn. 2.18–19. The charge was repeated by Cyprian in his own *ep.* 71.1.2,3.2, without giving the texts themselves, which were quoted in the accompanying *ep.* 70.

95 *Ep.* 71.1.3.

96 *Ep.* 70.1.3. *Ep.* 72.2.2 used Lev. 21.17 and Ex. 19.22, 30.20–1 which had been used earlier in *ep.* 67.1.2 to urge the deposition of the Spanish bishops who were guilty of idolatry and blasphemy.

97 *Ep.* 70.2.1.

98 *Ep.* 70.3.3 and repeated by Cyprian in *ep.* 71.2.3.

99 *Ep.* 70.1.3–2.3.

100 *Ep.* 70.3.1

101 *Ep.* 72.1.2.

102 Cyprian nowhere explicitly stated such an argument but always interpreted the imposition of hands as the second part of the baptismal ritual rather than the reconciliation of a penitent, *epp.* 70.3.1, 72.1.1–2, 69.11.3, 73.6.2, 74.5.1,7.1–2, though he recognized the contrary view, *epp.* 71.2.2, 74.1.2.

103 *Ep.* 71.2.1–3.

104 *Epp.* 70.1.3–2.3, 72.1.1. He was more circumspect in speaking of the effects of rituals performed within the Catholic communion by unworthy ministers. See chapter 7.

105 *Ep.* 70.3.2–3, 72.1.3–2.2. The characterization was applied to the laxist clergy who had originally opposed Cyprian's election and administration in *lap.* 33 and *ep.* 59.13.4. It did not fit Novatian as well, from whom he received crucial support during the persecution.

106 *Ep.* 70.2.2–3,3.3.

107 *Ep.* 72.2.3. Thus even those clerics who repented of their rebellion and were admitted to the Catholic church as laymen faced a terrifying judgment.

108 *Ep.* 69.1.1–4. "Whoever is not with me is against me; and whoever does not gather with me scatters" (Lk. 11.23); "As you have heard that antichrist is coming, so now many antichrists have come. From that we know that it is the last hour. They went out from us, but they did not belong to us; for if they had belonged to us, they would have remained with us" (1 Jn. 2.18–19); "If the offender refuses to listen even to the church, let such a one be to you as a Gentile and a tax collector" (Mt. 18.17).

109 *Ep.* 69.2.1–3.

110 *Ep.* 69.4.1–2.

111 *Ep.* 69.5.1. The text of Jn 10.30, "I and the Father are one," was interpreted by Tertullian in *Prax.* 22.10–11 as establishing the unity of will and disposition between the Father and Son. This seems to be Cyprian's meaning, since he implied a subordinatist Christology, as in *ep.* 73.18.2–3. Interestingly, Novatian referred the text to the common deity, *de trinitate* 13.6 and 15.10 but to the concord of two individuals in 27.2–3, *CCL* 4:33,38–9,63–4.

112 *Ep.* 69.5.2.

113 *Ep.* 69.3.1–2.

114 *Ep.* 69.7.2. In *ep.* 70.2.1, the bishops addressed this argument to their colleagues who wished to accept the opponent's baptism, asserting that such Catholics must either change their own baptismal interrogation or concede the church itself to the opposition. In *ep.* 69.7.2, Cyprian's point was that Novatian himself should not use such an interrogation because he did not have the church.

115 *Ep.* 69.8.1.

116 *Ep.* 69.11.3.

117 *Ep.* 69.10.2–11.3.

118 "Receive the Holy Spirit. If you forgive the sins of any, they are forgiven them; if you retain the sins of any, they are retained."

119 *Vnit.* 4–5 *TR.*

120 *Ep.* 69.11.2. Later, Cyprian would have to revise his estimation of John, whose baptism was repeated by the apostles. See *ep.* 73.25.1, and the explanation in note 81 above.

121 *Ep.* 69.14.1–16.1.
122 *Ep.* 69.16.2.
123 *Ep.* 69.6.1–3.
124 *Ep.* 69.8.1–9.2. The citation of the rebellion of Core, Dathan and Abiron served the purpose of undercutting the argument from the unity of faith, which could be raised in cases of schism but not heresy.
125 *Ep.* 69.10.2.
126 *Ep.* 69.4.2. Cyprian remained sensitive to the charges of cruelty which had been leveled against him earlier, see *ep.* 59.15.1–16.3. The distinction between those forced out and those who left voluntarily fits the laxists and rigorists adherents. He regarded the laxist leaders as objects of divine wrath, *lap.* 33; *ep.* 59.13.4.
127 *Ep.* 69.9.1.
128 *Ep.* 69.9.2.
129 The language, however, remained that of ritual contamination: they were defiled by sharing the sacrilegious sacrifices, *ep.* 69.9.2.
130 *Ep.* 73.16.1–17.2.
131 *Ep.* 73.18.1.
132 *Ep.* 73.18.2–19.2.
133 *Ep.* 73.4.1–6.2.
134 *Ep.* 73.21.1.
135 *Ep.* 73.13.3.
136 *Ep.* 73.14.1–2; see Phil. 1.18.
137 *Ep.* 73.9.1–2; see Acts 8.14–17.
138 *Ep.* 73.24.1–25.2, referring to Acts 19.1–7. Cyprian refused to recognize that John had received the Holy Spirit – as he had argued in *ep.* 69.11.2 – and attributed to him the spirit of Elijah instead. The two arguments are compatible, but Cyprian was hardly candid in making both. See note 81 above, where the change is offered as an argument that *epistulae* 69 and 73 were contemporary but that *epistula* 69 preceded.
139 *Ep.* 74.2.2–3.2. The response of Firmilian indicated that the argument came from Stephen, *ep.* 75.5.2.
140 *Ep.* 73.2.1–3,25.2.
141 *Ep.* 73.20.2.
142 *Ep.* 73.22.1–23.1.
143 *Epp.* 73.10.3,11.1, 74.11.2–3.
144 *Ep.* 74.6.1–2,7.2,8.2.
145 *Ep.* 74.4.2.
146 *Ep.* 73.11.2–3.
147 *Ep.* 73.7.1–8.2. The same point was made in *unit.* 7.
148 *Ep.* 73.6.1,10.1,21.2.
149 *Ep.* 73.20.1–2,22.3.
150 *Ep.* 73.24.1–3.
151 *Epp.* 73.13.1–2, 74.10.1–3.
152 *Epp.* 73.18.3,19.3, 74.2.1.
153 *Epp.* 73.10.2,11.2, 74.8.4–9.1.
154 *Ep.* 73.26.2.
155 *Ep.* 73.26.1.
156 *Ep.* 75.1.1 refers to Cyprian's letter and to Rogatianus.
157 *Ep.* 75.4.1–2.

158 *Ep.* 75.15.2. Cyprian's own letter to Firmilian, which was not preserved, may have presented these developments.

159 *Ep.* 75.14.1.

160 Using 1 Cor. 11.27; *ep.* 75.21.3. Cyprian had made a similar point about the lapsed, with examples, in *lap.* 24–5. In the letter to Pompeius he spoke about the communication of sin through the eucharist, *ep.* 74.18.3,19.3 a point which Firmilian picked up in *ep.* 75.23.1.

161 *Ep.* 75.5.2–3.

162 *Ep.* 75.6.1.

163 *Ep.* 75.7.3–4,19.3–4. The change is presumed to have been made in Agrippinus' council.

164 *Ep.* 75.10.1–5. This seems to show an awareness of the argument made by Magnus and answered by Cyprian in *ep.* 69.7.1–2.

165 Cyprian noted and responded to the objection in *ep.* 73.23.1. Firmilian took it up in *ep.* 75.21.1–3.

166 *Ep.* 75.21.1–2.

167 Thus in *ep.* 69.13.3–14.1 and in *ep.* 74.7.1, dealing with the attempt to separate baptism from the imposition of hands.

168 *Ep.* 75.23.2.

169 *Ep.* 73.23.1, though he dealt with only those catechumens who died as martyrs. During the persecution, it will be recalled, he was especially concerned that any catechumen in danger of death from illness should receive baptism, *ep.* 18.2.2.

170 The main argument was that there was only one baptism in the one church: *sent. episc.* 1,2,14,17,21,23,24,33,34,36,44,45,46,50,55,58, 66,67,68,72,75,77,79,80.

171 *Sent. episc.* 3,22,33,34,42,44.

172 There heretics did not have the Father, Son or Spirit, hence not baptism: *sent. episc.* 10,16,47,67,73.

173 *Sent. episc.* 9,40,48.

174 *Sent. episc.* 1,12,15,20,40,41,53,81; see *epp.* 73.18.3,19.3, 74.10.1–3.

175 *Sent. episc.* 5,18. See also *sent. episc.* 80, which argued that the heretics will blame the bishops because they were not baptized when they came to the church and thus did not get remission of sins and consequently were damned. The position paralleled that of Firmilian in *ep.* 75.21.1–2,23.2.

176 Only four of the *sententiae* even indicated a distinction between heresy and schism. Most of the others referred to the opponents as heretics. *Sent. episc.* 4,5,7,33.

177 The treatise engaged a particular but unnamed opponent. On a number of issues, however, the author seems not to have known the surviving writings of Cyprian. Cyprian had, for example, responded to the concern for the baptism of the sick (*rebap.* 5; *ep.* 69.12.1–16.2) and the martyrdom of catechumens (*rebap.* 12; *ep.* 73.23.1). In addition, the treatise ignored Cyprian's major point in *ep.* 69.7.1–8.3, that the church itself was part of the Christian confession of faith (*rebap.* 12–14).

178 "On that day many will say to me, 'Lord, Lord, did we not prophesy in your name, and cast out demons in your name, and do many deeds

of power in your name?' Then I will declare to them, 'I never knew you; go away from me, you evildoers.'" Cited in *rebap.* 7.

179 "Then if anyone says to you, 'Look! Here is the Messiah!' or 'There he is!' – do not believe it. For false messiahs and false prophets will appear and produce great signs and omens, to lead astray, if possible, even the elect." Cited in *rebap.* 12.

180 *Rebap.* 7,12.

181 *Rebap.* 10.

182 *Rebap.* 6 said that it would not save but did help a person when supplemented by spirit baptism; *rebap.* 12 said that it would be a burden to those who subsequently failed to seek Christ.

183 *Rebap.* 10.

184 *Rebap.* 4–6. Thus the baptism of Cornelius in the Spirit preceded the water baptism; the spirit baptism of the disciples at Pentecost forgave the sins they had committed in denying Jesus after their water baptism.

185 *Rebap.* 3–5. In response to the standard examples of the Samaritans baptized by Philip, the treatise cited the separation of the water and spirit baptisms of the apostles themselves. The author rejected the notion that someone other than the bishop could confer the Holy Spirit.

186 *Rebap.* 10. Spirit baptism was being substituted for water baptism as the saving ritual; the author, therefore, had to provide for its conferral, even in heaven.

187 *Rebap.* 10.

188 *Rebap.* 6–7 used Mt. 7.22–3 to condemn the outsider as an evil doer. *Rebap.* 11 condemned heretics because, even as martyrs, they did not confess Christ himself but only his name. *Rebap.* 12 condemned surviving heretics for failing to seek the Lord himself after his name was invoked upon them.

189 *Rebap.* 10.

190 *Rebap.* 4, a point which Cyprian explicitly rejected, *ep.* 69.12–14.

191 As Cyprian insisted it could in *ep.* 69.12.1–14.2.

192 *Bapt.* 6.

193 *Rebap.* 13.

194 *Ep.* 71.2.1–3.2.

195 See above, chapters 3, 4.

7 PURITY OF THE CHURCH

1 *Ep.* 8.3.1.

2 *Ep.* 20.3.2.

3 In *ep.* 55.13.1, Cyprian dealt with the problem of penitents who recovered from the illness during which they had been reconciled, arguing that they did not constitute a threat to the church.

4 *Ep.* 1 refused prayers for a bishop who involved a presbyter in secular work; *ep.* 3 instructed an episcopal colleague to remove an insubordinate deacon; *ep.* 52.3 reported the financial and family crimes of the presbyter Novatus, who was facing excommunication at the time the persecution broke out.

5 Cornelius admitted the apostate Trofimus only as a layperson, *ep.* 55.11.1–3; he made an exception in allowing the presbyter Maximus to return to his office after going into schism, *ep.* 49. The case of the apostate bishops in Spain was discussed in *ep.* 67.

6 *Ep.* 59.10.1.

7 Cornelius admitted Trofimus as a layman, *ep.* 55.11.1–3. In Africa, the ordinary practice seems to have been excommunication, *epp.* 1.2.1, 4.4.1, 34.3.2, 52.2.5, 59.10.2–3, 65, 64.1.1–2. The exception involved a deacon guilty of insubordination, *ep.* 3.3.3, where Cyprian indicated that the punishment of demotion was within the discretion of the bishop. Such persons could be reconciled and readmitted only as laymen, see *ep.* 72.2.1. The clergy of the church of Carthage who withdrew during the persecution were temporarily demoted upon their return; the disposition of their case was not recorded, *ep.* 34.4.1–2.

8 *Ep.* 11.1.2,2.1–5.3.

9 *Epp.* 13.5.1, 14.1.1.

10 *Ep.* 11.1.3.

11 *Ep.* 11.6.1.

12 *Ep.* 11.7–8.

13 *Epp.* 15, 16 and 17.

14 *Ep.* 15.1.2–2.1.

15 *Ep.* 16.1.2–2.2.

16 *Ep.* 17.1.2–2.2.

17 *Ep.* 20.2.1.

18 *Ep.* 15.1.2, to the confessors,"Whoever, therefore, eats the bread or drinks the cup of the Lord in an unworthy manner, will be answerable for the body and the blood of the Lord." *Ep.* 16.2.2, to the clergy, "You cannot drink the cup of the Lord and the cup of demons. You cannot partake of the table of the Lord and the table of demons."

19 *Ep.* 20.2.2.

20 Item cum conperissem eos qui sacrilegis contactibus manus suas atque ora maculassent uel nefandis libellis nihilominus conscientiam poluissent exambire ad martyras passim, confessores quoque inportuna et gratiosa deprecatione corrumpere sine ullo discrimine atque examine singulorum darentur cotidie libellorum milia contra euangelii legem, litteras feci quibus martyras et confessors consilio meo quantum possem ad dominica praecepta reuocarem.

(ep. 20.2.2; CCL 3B:107.25–108.32.)

21 *Ep.* 20.2.3–3.1, see also *ep.* 16.1.1–2,4.1–2 for the continued divine warnings.

22 *Lap.* 5–12.

23 *Lap.* 18.

24 *Lap.* 20.

25 *Lap.* 33. This was repeated in *ep.* 59.13.4.

26 *Ep.* 65.4.1.

27 *Ep.* 58.2.2. He had suggested this as an appropriate form of repentance in *ep.* 19.2.3 and *lap.* 36.

28 *Ep.* 61.3.1.

29 *Ep.* 16.2.2.

30 *Ep.* 15.1.2.

31 *Ep.* 20.2.2. The Roman confessors picked up this theme, declaring that

the presbyters who administered the eucharist to the fallen were throwing pearls to swine, *ep.* 31.6.2, and added the pollution of the eyes which had looked upon the idols, *ep.* 31.7.1.

32 *Omnis mundus manducabit carnem; et anima quaecumque manducauerit ex carne sacrificii salutaris, quod est Domini, et inmunditia ipsius super ipsum est, peribit anima illa de populo suo.*

(lap. 15; CCL 3:229.302–5.)

33 *Lap.* 15–16.
34 *Lap.* 22.
35 *Lap.* 24–26.
36 *Lap.* 25–26.
37 *Ep.* 24.1.1.
38 *Ep.* 25.
39 "Qui sacrilegis contractibus manus suas atque ora maculassent uel nefandis libellis nihilominus conscientiam polluissent." *ep.* 20.2.2; *CCL* 3B:107.25–108.27, writing to the Roman clergy.
40 *Epp.* 30.3.2, 31.7.2.
41 *Ep.* 55.13.2,6.2,17.3.
42 *Ep.* 55.14.1–2.
43 As shall be seen below, Cyprian would make the same argument for converts who came into voluntary but erroneous contact with schismatic rituals.
44 *Ep.* 59.12.2,14.1,15.3. Novatian had accused Cornelius of soiling himself by communion with sacrificers, *ep.* 55.2.2,10.2.
45 See below, pp. 145–7. He apparently considered the ceremonies of the schismatics as demonic, like those of the idolaters.
46 It should be recalled that unworthy clerics were excluded from office by well established practice. See *epp.* 1.2.1, 4.4.1, 52.2.5, 64.1.1–2, 65.
47 *Ep.* 54.3.1.
48 *Ep.* 55.27.1–3; he noted the scriptural practice of linking adultery to idolatry.
49 *Ep.* 54.3.1.
50 *Ep.* 55.20.1–2.
51 *Ep.* 59.12.2,14.1,15.3.
52 *Lap.* 6.
53 *Ep.* 55.10.12.
54 *Ep.* 55.11.3.
55 *Ep.* 65.2.1. The three texts are: "No one ... who has a blemish may approach to offer the food of his God," "The priests who approach the Lord must consecrate themselves or the Lord will break out against them," and "or when they come near the altar to minister in the holy place; or they will bring guilt on themselves and die."
56 *Ep.* 65.2.2,4.1, "God hears not the sinner, ... "
57 *Ep.* 65.1.2,4.1–2,5.1–2.
58 *Ep.* 65.3.1–2.
59 Quod ne tales ad altaris inpiamenta et contagia fratrum denuo redeant omnibus uiribus excubandum est, omni uigore nitendum ut quantum possumus ab hac eos sui sceleris audacia retundamus, ne adhuc agere pro sacerdote conentur qui ad mortis extrema deiecti ultra lapsos laicos ruinae maioris pondere proruerunt.

(*Ep.* 65.3.3; *CCL* 3C:430.62–7.)

60 *Ep.* 65.4.1–2.
61 The bishop had been unworthy even before the persecution exposed him; the danger arose only afterward.
62 *Ep.* 59.10.1–3.
63 *Ep.* 59.20.1.
64 *Ep.* 67.2.2. Similarly, Is. 29.13, "This people honor me with their lips but their heart is far removed from me," itself cited in Mt. 15.8–9 and Mk. 7.6–7, was used to warn of the danger of despising the divine mandates, *ep.* 64.2.1.
65 Nec sibi plebs blandiatur quasi inmunis esse a contagio delicti possit cum sacerdote peccatore communicans et ad iniustum atque inlicitum praepositi sui episcopatum consensum suum commodans, quando per Ose prophetam comminetur et dicat censura diuina: *sacrifica eorum tamquam panis luctus, omnes qui manducant ea contaminabuntur,* docens scilicet et ostendens omnes omnino ad peccatum constringi quique fuerint profani et iniusti sacerdotis sacrificio contaminati.
(*Ep.* 67.3.1; *CCL* 3C:450.53–451.60.)
66 *Ep.* 67.3.2.
67 *Ep.* 67.9.1–2,5.3–4 made clear that Stephen was deceived but negligent.
68 *Ep.* 59.10.1–3.
69 The charges themselves were not specified in Cyprian's response, *ep.* 66. G.W. Clarke reconstructs them: the irregularity of Cyprian's election (1.2), flight during persecution (4.1–2), authoritarian style of governance (3.1), responsibility for the laxist schism (8.1), and reliance on private revelations (9.1–10.2). See Clarke, *Letters* 3:322.
70 *Ep.* 66.5.2.
71 *Ep.* 66.7.4.
72 After demonstrating the absurd consequences of Puppianus' charge that Cyprian was an unworthy bishop, he mockingly begged his adversary to restore and rescue all by reversing his private judgment of Cyprian, *ep.* 66.5.2.
73 *Ep.* 67.4.1–5.2.
74 *Ep.* 67.5.3–4,9.1–3.
75 It has been argued above, pp. 106–12, that *epp.* 70, 71, and 72 were composed first and dealt with the problem of laxist baptism in Africa. *Epp.* 73, 74 and 75 are explicitly concerned with Novatian. In its arguments and use of scriptural precedents, *ep.* 69, which also deals with Novatian, seems to belong with the latter rather than the former group and thus should be dated somewhat later than is now customary.
76 *Ep.* 59.10.1–3.
77 Cyprian rehearsed this argument for Cornelius in *ep.* 59.10.1–3,12.1–2,18.1.
78 *Ep.* 43.3.1.
79 *Ep.* 60.3.2.
80 Thus in *ep.* 43.3.2,5.2; *lap.* 17, he charged them with sacrilege for setting up a second altar and human institutions to rival those established by God.
81 *Ep.* 70.1.3,2.2–3.
82 *Ep.* 70.1.3,2.2.
83 *Ep.* 72.1.1.

84 *Ep.* 70.2.3. The possibility of error had been recognized during the persecution itself, when Cyprian indicated some understanding and appreciation of the desire of the lapsed to regain access to the communion of the church and exhorted the clergy and confessors to restrain and educate them, *epp.* 15.2.1–2, 17.3.1. The Roman confessors were excused by Cornelius, and by Cyprian, because they had been deceived by Novatian, *epp.* 49.2.4, 51.1.2. Cyprian made a similar excuse for African Christians who erred in following the confessors, *ep.* 51.2.2. The hardening of attitudes through the bitter schism seems to have eradicated the tolerance of error.

85 *Ep.* 65.2.2,3.3,4.1, for Fortunatianus and *ep.* 67.3.1–2, for the bishops in Spain, which may have come from the same synod.

86 *Ep.* 72.2.2. What may have been the same synod cited the same texts of Ex. 19.12, 28.43 and Lev. 21.17,21 in *ep.* 67.1.2 to deal with the apostate bishops in Spain. See Clarke, *Letters* 4:139–42 for the dating.

87 *Ep.* 72.2.1–2.

88 *Epp.* 68.2.1, 69.1.4.

89 *Ep.* 73.11.2,21.2.

90 *Ep.* 67.3.1–2.

91 *Epp.* 69.8.1,9.1–2, 73.8.1.

92 *Ep.* 69.9.2.

93 *Ep.* 73.8.1.

94 The two, distinct charges were clearly articulated in the first council to deal with the problem of rebaptism, *ep.* 70.2.3.

8 UNITY OF THE EPISCOPATE

1 *Epp.* 45, 48. See chapter 5 for a discussion of the process of selection, installation and deposition of bishops.

2 *Epp.* 59.10.1–3, 65.4.2, 68. The people could object to or even desert their bishop but they could not themselves replace him without the collaboration of other bishops.

3 *Ep.* 67.

4 Thus each case was to be judged where the crime had been committed, *ep.* 59.14.2.

5 *Epp.* 8.3.1, 20.3.2.

6 *Ep.* 21.3.2.

7 *Epp.* 23, 26.1.1–2.

8 *Epp.* 55.6.1–2, 57, 72.

9 *Epp,* 59.10.2–3, 65.1.1.

10 *Ep.* 45.4.1.

11 *Epp.* 69–74 and *sent. episc.*

12 *Epp.* 45.3.1, 55.10.2.

13 *Ep.* 45.4.1.

14 *Epp.* 65, 68.

15 *Ep.* 55.6.1,11.1–3 for the decisions made in Carthage and Rome regarding the lapsed, which drew upon scripture and pastoral necessity. *Ep.* 57.1.2 indicated that signs and warnings were used for deciding whether to reconcile the sacrificers.

16 This matter has been treated more fully in chapters 3–4. Consider, briefly, the characterization of the loosening in heaven as a possibility

rather than a certainty in *ep*. 57.1.1, the letter of the council which granted reconciliation to the sacrificers, and the limitation of Peter's authority to loosening on earth in *ep*. 73.7.1.

17 *Epp*. 71.3.2, 73.13.1–2.

18 *Epp*. 73.13.3, 74.2.4–3.1. Cyprian seems to have been aware that the decision made under his predecessor Agrippinus was a change in policy, even before Firmilian of Caesarea pointed this out to him, *ep*. 75.19.3. He argued that the apostles did not have to face the heresies which he and his colleagues did, *ep*. 74.2.4–3.1.

19 *Ep*. 59.

20 *Epp*. 67, 68.

21 *Sent. episc.*

22 Cyprian wrote at least to Firmilian of Caesarea.

23 *Ep*. 55.21.1–2.

24 The exclusion of the clergy who had granted reconciliation without penance was confirmed by the synod in spring 251, *ep*. 45.4.1–2.

25 *Ep*. 64.

26 *Ep*. 56.3.

27 *Ep*. 57.5.1–2. The application of pressure may have been associated with the danger of giving support to the Novatianists, whose stance was not a factor in the deliberations in the council of 251.

28 *Ep*. 55.21.1.

29 *Ep*. 68.4.3–5.2.

30 *Ep*. 72.3.1–2, on the number of bishops, see *ep*. 73.1.2. This freedom was reasserted in *epp*. 69.17 and 73.26.1–2 after sustained arguments in favor of the African practice. In *ep*. 74.8.2, Cyprian objected to Stephen's threat of excommunication of dissenters from his own policy.

31 *Ep*. 55.6.1. The debate, it must be recalled, resulted in a change in Cyprian's own views of the church's power to forgive the sin of apostasy and to distinguish the certified from the sacrificers.

32 *Ep*. 55.3.1–7.3.

33 *Epp*. 69, 70, 71, 73, 74; *sent. episc.* Bishops who continued to dissent might also have absented themselves.

34 *Epp*. 55.22.1–23.2, 57.5.2, 71.2.3,3.2, 74.11.1.

35 Firmilian of Caesarea evinced a similar attitude. Regional variations in the date of celebrating Easter could be tolerated, but within a province the bishops had to take the same stance on the validity of heretical baptism, *ep*. 75.6.1,19.4.

36 *Ep*. 2.2.3.

37 *Ep*. 62.

38 *Epp*. 77.3.2, 78.3.1, 79.1.1.

39 *Ep*. 56.

40 *Ep*. 70.

41 *Epp*. 57, 72.

42 *Sent. episc.*

43 See Eusebius, *h.e.* 7.4–9.

44 The council which condemned Privatus had ninety participants, *ep*. 59.10.1; that of September 256 counted eighty-five, *sent. episc.*

45 *Epp*. 1–4, 25, 56, 65, 69, 70, 71, , 73, 74.

46 *Ep*. 48.3.1.

47 *Epp*. 57, 72, 75.

48 *Epp.* 67, 68.
49 His very insistence upon the independence of each of the individual bishops belies the influence which he must have exercised, *sent. episc. proem.* He introduced the question but was the last to offer his *sententia*, *sent. episc.* 87.
50 *Ep.* 48.2.2, in which he recounted a visit to Hadrumetum and *ep.* 58.1.1, where he apologized for his inability to make a planned trip to Tribaris. G.W. Clarke is the source of this suggestion, in conversation.
51 The status of Lambaesis as a legionary base would have given a similar role to its bishop, who could also facilitate communications among his colleagues, as well as with Carthage and Rome.
52 *Epp.* 45.3.1–2, 55.24.2; *unit.* 5.
53 *Vnit.* 5; *epp.* 55.6.1–7.3, 57.
54 The point is made in both versions of *unit.* 4, and in *epp.* 59.7.3, 66.8.3, 70.3.1, 71.3.1.
55 *Vnit.* 4 *PT* may have been modified when the original text was sent to Rome, either as part of the episcopal commission's mission of repairing the schism or in the attempt to convince the Novatianist confessors to return to Cornelius. See above, chapter 5, p. 94.
56 *Ep.* 59.14.1.
57 *Ep.* 73.11.1,7.1–2 and *unit.* 4 *TR.*
58 *Vnit.* 5; *epp.* 57.5.2, 59.14.2, 69.17.
59 This was particularly practiced in removing bishops who prevented repentance by granting peace to the fallen, *epp.* 59.10.2–3, 65.1.2.
60 *Ep.* 68.3.2–4.2, arguing that Stephen must intervene to remove Marcianus of Arles.
61 The equality of the other apostles to Peter was common to both versions of *unit.* 4.
62 *Vnit.* 4 *PT.*
63 *Vnit.* 4 *PT* and 4–5 *TR.*
64 *Vnit.* 8. In a contemporary letter to the Novatianist confessors, he warned that they had separated themselves from the peace and harmony of the flock of Christ, *ep.* 46.2.1.
65 The image was used in *unit.* 20–4, a section whose appeal to the confessors indicated that it formed part of the original version, written in summer 251.
66 *Epp.* 66.8.3, 68.3.2, 73.26.2. The image may have been drawn from Tertullian, *pud.* 5.9.
67 In *unit.* 8 and *ep.* 55.24.4, Cyprian linked the unity of the Spirit and the bond of peace of Eph. 4.2–3, hinting at a later idea of the common holding of the gift of the Spirit by all the bishops.
68 In *lap.* 17–18 he had argued that only Christ could forgive the sin of apostasy. The agreement of many bishops was used as an argument to defend Cornelius' allowing Trofimus to return to communion, *ep.* 55.11.3. When Marcianus dissented, he was said to have lost the common Spirit of the episcopate, *ep.* 68.5.2.
69 *Epp.* 64, 68.
70 *Ep.* 59.14.2.
71 *Epp.* 67.6.3, 68.5.1.
72 Thus Novatian's appeal to the Africans, *epp.* 44.1.1, 45.2.2; Privatus' appeals for reinstatement, *epp.* 36.4.1, 59.10.1; Fortunatus' appeal to

Cornelius, *ep.* 59.2.1,9.1. Novatian and Privatus both proceeded to establish their own networks of bishops, *epp.* 55.24.2, 59.10.1–11.1.

73 *Vnit.* 4. Both *PT* and *TR* reject the notion that Peter held some authority over his fellow apostles, though *TR* provided a fuller foundation by adapting Jn. 20.22–3 to the purpose.

74 *Ep.* 65.6.1.

75 *Epp.* 74.8.2, 75.24.1. The extraordinary African rejection of the practice which Stephen made the basis of his action clearly demonstrates that they could not conceive of such an authority of one bishop over many, much less outside his own province.

76 Thus the attempt to interpret Cyprian's use of the term *primatus Petri* in that sense which would begin to emerge only in the fourth century appears anachronistic.

77 *Ep.* 69.11.1–2.

78 *Ep.* 73.7.1–2.

79 *Ep.* 73.9.1–2. The same practice was still observed, he remarked, with the newly baptized being presented to the bishop to receive the Holy Spirit through his prayer and imposition of hands.

80 Acts 19.1–7.

81 *Ep.* 73.25.1.

82 In chapter 6, note 81, pp. 218–19, it is suggested that Cyprian may have been influenced as well by Jn. 7.38–9 which asserted that the Holy Spirit was not poured out until Jesus was glorified. Allusion was made to this text in *ep.* 73.11.1.

83 *Vnit.* 4 *TR* and *ep.* 73.7.1–2. The texts were together cited back to Cyprian by Firmilian of Caesarea in *ep.* 75.16.1, probably on the basis of *ep.* 73.7.1–2. Earlier emphases on Peter's role appeared in *epp.* 70.3.1, 71.3.1.

84 Thus in *unit.* 23 and in the citation in *unit.* 8 of the prior verses, as well as in *ep.* 43.5.2. In none of these instances was any reference to baptism included.

85 *Epp.* 70.1.2, 71.1.2, 73.2.2,3.1,13.3.

86 *Epp.* 70.3.1, 73.4.2,11.1. The text was quoted in full in *unit.* 4 *TR*. The entire text was also cited back to Cyprian by Firmilian, *ep.* 75.24.3.

87 *Epp.* 70.3.1, 73.11.1.

88 The incident recorded in Num. 16.1–40 was used in this way in *ep.* 69.8.1. In *ep.* 73.8.1 and its reflection in 75.16.2, it was linked to Mt. 16.18–19 and Jn. 20.22–3. The text was used in the same way in *unit.* 18. In the contemporary, *ep.* 67.3.2, it was used for unworthy bishops and in the undatable *ep.* 3.1 for a rebellious deacon.

89 The incident was recorded in Lev. 10.1–2 and used in *ep.* 73.8.2 and *unit.* 18.

90 *Vnit.* 18, from 2 Chr. 26.16–20.

91 Ex. 12.46 and Jos. 2.18–19, were cited in *ep.* 69.4.1.

92 *Vnit.* 8. The prior version of the text would have moved smoothly from the quotations of 1 Cor. 1.10 and Eph. 4.2–3 to the reflection on the dove as the sign of the Holy Spirit in *unit.* 9.

93 Canticle of Canticles 6.9; *Vnit.* 4 *TR*, and *ep.* 69.2.1.

94 Canticle of Canticles 4.12,15, appearing in *ep.* 69.2.1 but not in *de unitate*.

95 Canticle of Canticles 4.13; *epp.* 73.10.3–11.1, 74.11.2.
96 *Epp.* 69.2.2, 74.11.3. The text of Canticle of Canticles 4.13 was cited by Firmilian with and without the link to the ark of Noah, indicating the presence of these texts in the documents sent to him by Cyprian, *ep.* 75.14.1,15.1–2,23.1. Reference to Noah's ark appears only in *unit.* 6.
97 See above, chapter 5, p. 94.
98 *Ep.* 69.2.1.
99 *Epp.* 69.2.1, 73.10.3–11.1, 74.11.2.
100 D. Van den Eynde's "La double édition du De unitate de S. Cyprien," *Revue d'histoire ecclésiastique*, 29 (1933): 5–24, is useful for dealing with the texts which appear in the *TR* version of chapter 5. It does not consider the other texts of parallel usage which are listed here. The debate over versions of *de unitate* has been unfortunately restricted by the manuscript tradition.
101 *Vnit.* 18; *epp.* 67.3.2, 69.8.1, 73.8.1–2 and 75.16.2. Only *unit.* 18 adds the punishment of Uzziah.
102 *Vnit.* 8 and *ep.* 69.4.1.
103 *Vnit.* 11 and *epp.* 70.1.2, 72.1.1, 73.21.1.
104 *Vnit.* 5 and *epp.* 45.3.2, 57.5.2, 59.14.2, 68.3.2–4.2, 69.17.

9 CYPRIAN'S AFRICAN HERITAGE

1 This might have been justified by appeal to Cornelius' practice with Maximus, the confessor-presbyter who had supported Novatian's schism. While Cyprian defended this action, he had not made such allowance in Africa. On the conflict see Yves Congar's note in Augustine, *Traités Anti-Donatistes*, *Bibliothèque Augustinienne*, Paris, Desclée, 1963, vol. 29, pp. 724–5.
2 As has been seen, Cyprian actually found a means of asserting the efficacy of the ritual of reconciliation, though he did limit it. Placing a repentant sinner in a leadership role incurred problems of the community's approval of the sin as well as that of impurity.
3 Thus the historical evidence which Augustine introduced at the Conference of Carthage, which convinced the imperial commissioner that Caecilian and Felix were innocent, could not be accepted by the Donatists.
4 This may have been the position taken by the Roman bishop regarding the Novatianists, see J. Patout Burns, "On Rebaptism: Social Organization in the Third Century Church," *Journal of Early Christian Studies*, 1 (1993):367–403.
5 As Magnus had suggested to Cyprian in the case of sick-bed baptism by infusion, *ep.* 69.12.1–16.2.
6 As Cyprian himself allowed had happened in the past and might continue to happen when a bishop decided not to rebaptize a schismatic convert, *ep.* 73.23.1.
7 Augustine, *ep.* 153.3.6–8.
8 Augustine also described the bishops as the agents of Christ. The coherence of the two explanations was maintained by the identification of the society of saints as the body of Christ.
9 1 Pet. 4.8.

10 *Ep.* 71.3.1.
11 *Lap.* 18. He found the answer in the suffering of the lapsed who
     approached the eucharist under the patronage of the martyrs and in the
     witness to Christ of those who had undertaken penance.

BIBLIOGRAPHY

Benson, E.W. *Cyprian: His Life, His Times, His Work*, London, Macmillan, 1897.

Bévenot, Maurice "Hi qui sacrificaverunt," *Journal of Theological Studies* 5 (1954):68–72.

—— "The Sacrament of Penance and St. Cyprian's *De Lapsis*," *Theological Studies* 16 (1955):175–213.

—— *The Tradition of Manuscripts: A Study in the Transmission of St. Cyprian's Treatises*, Oxford, Clarendon Press, 1961.

—— "Cyprian and his Recognition of Cornelius, *Journal of Theological Studies*, n.s. 28 (1977):346–59

Burns, J. Patout "On Rebaptism: Social Organization in the Third Century Church," *Journal of Early Christian Studies*, 1 (1993):367–403.

—— "Confessing the Church: Cyprian on Penance," *Studia Patristica*, ed., Edward Yarnold, S.J. and Maurice Wiles, Leuven, Peeters, 2001, 36:338–48.

Clarke, G.W. "Some Observations on the Persecution of Decius," *Antichthon* 3 (1969):63–76.

—— *The Letters of St. Cyprian of Carthage*, translated and annotated, 4 vols, *Ancient Christian Writers*, vols 43–4,46–7, New York, Paulist Press, 1984–9.

Congar, Yves M.-J., OP, Introduction and Notes, in Augustine, *Traités Anti-Donatistes*, *Bibliothèque Augustinienne*, Paris, Desclée, 1963.

Countryman, L. William *The Rich Christian in the Church of the Early Empire*, Toronto, Edward Mellen Press, 1980.

Douglas, Mary "Cultural Bias," in *The Active Voice*, Boston, Routledge & Kegan Paul, 1982, pp. 183–254.

—— *Natural Symbols*, 2nd edn, Barrie and Jenkins, 1973, and with a new introduction, London, Routledge, 1996.

Fahey, Michael A., SJ *Cyprian and the Bible: a Study of Third-Century Exegisis*, Tübingen, J.C.B. Mohr, 1971.

Frend, W.H.C. *The Donatist Church*, Oxford, Oxford University Press, 1952.

233

Knipfing, J.R. "The Libelli of the Decian Persecution," *Harvard Theological Review*, 16 (1923):345–90.

Quasten, J. *Patrology*, Westminster, MD, Christian Classics, 1986–8.

Sage, Michael M. *Cyprian*, Cambridge, MA., Philadelphia Patristic Foundation, 1975.

Van den Eynde, D. "La double édition du De unitate de S. Cyprien," *Revue d'histoire ecclésiastique* 29 (1933):5–24.

INDEX

Aaron 111, 143, 147, 161, 162, 221n

Abiron 111, 143, 147, 161

Agrippinus: council of 103, 104, 109, 183n, 184n, 215n, 222n, 228n

Antonianus 141

Antoninus 211n

apostles: baptism 119, 122; original episcopal college 156; power of forgiveness 120

Augustine 231n

Augustine of Hippo 167; and the Donatists 171; position on reconciliation and unity 172–4

Aurelius 166, 181n, 187n, 208n

baptism 16; African understanding of 128–9; apostolic tradition 119, 122; of Christ 160; cleanses idolatry 68; common policy of bishops 152; cosmic efficacy of 44–5; Cyprian on 105, 159–62; divided Church 100; established practice 119; first stage of controversy 112–14; forgiveness of sins 64, 118; the Holy Spirit 113–14, 125, 129, 150, 160, 171, 173; imagery of 115–16; imposition of hands alternative 169; name of Jesus 118, 124; the opposing bishops 106–12; post-Constantine position 169–74; rigorists' views 73–4;

schismatics 9–10, 103, 104, 149–50; scripture 159–62; second stage of controversy 115–24; vote by bishops 123–4

Basilides 93, 143, 144, 152, 204n, 227n

Benson, Archbishop G. W. viii

Bévenot, Maurice viii

bishops: African independent judgements 152–6; apostolic heritage 156–8; appointment of 93–9; authority of 49–50, 96–7, 98–9, 120–1; the Donatists 167–9; lapsed 141–4; meeting (251) 38, 60; meeting (252) 101; meeting (253) 39–41, 62, 97–8; meeting (256) 123–4; necessary for unity of church 162–5; removal from office 133, 141–4; role of 15, 113, 129; structures of collaboration 152–6; tradition of Peter 156; unity of 151–2, 156–9; *see also* Peter

Búvenot 196, 205, 209

Caecilian 166, 167, 169, 171

Caldonius 138, 180–1n, 191n, 194n, 201–2n, 208n

Canticle of Canticles 161, 162

Carthaginian church: appoints Cyprian bishop 1; attempts at reconciliation 97–8; authority of clergy and members 49–50; cosmic consequences of the